Supplying the British Army in the First World War

Supplying the British Army in the First World War

Janet Macdonald

Pen & Sword
MILITARY

First published in Great Britain in 2019 by
PEN & SWORD MILITARY
An imprint of Pen & Sword Books Ltd
Yorkshire – Philadelphia

Copyright © Janet Macdonald, 2019

ISBN 978-1-52672-537-0

Typeset by Concept, Huddersfield, West Yorkshire.
Printed and bound in England by TJ International Ltd, Padstow, Cornwall.

Pen & Sword Books Ltd incorporates the Imprints of Aviation, Atlas, Family
History, Fiction, Maritime, Military, Discovery, Politics, History, Archaeology,
Select, Wharncliffe Local History, Wharncliffe True Crime, Military Classics,
Wharncliffe Transport, Leo Cooper, The Praetorian Press, Remember When,
White Owl, Seaforth Publishing and Frontline Publishing.

For a complete list of Pen & Sword titles please contact
PEN & SWORD BOOKS LTD
47 Church Street, Barnsley, South Yorkshire, S70 2AS, England
E-mail: enquiries@pen-and-sword.co.uk
Website: www.pen-and-sword.co.uk
or
PEN & SWORD BOOKS
1950 Lawrence Rd, Havertown, PA 19083, USA
E-mail: uspen-and-sword@casematepublishers.com
Website: www.penandswordbooks.com

Dedication

This one is for Mick Crumplin, who provided most of the illustrations from his personal collection.

'When Honour is divided, and victory is won,
Don't think the only hero is the man behind the gun, ...'
(Start of a poem written by a local baker working with the ASC,
Holmforth Express, 1916)

Contents

List of Plates

Unloading supplies at a railhead.

A troop convoy.

Women mechanics at a Women's Volunteer Reserve garage.

Wounded men waiting for transport.

Loading a hospital barge.

Camels carrying wounded men in cacolets.

Dead men's effects.

A refreshment stall near Bazentin on the Somme.

Sand mats being used to extract a lorry from the mud.

A food convoy in Mesopotamia.

Donkey transport in the Middle East.

A Rolls Royce converted to an armoured gun carrier.

A supply dump.

A train-load of British Army barbed wire.

Author's Note

The terms 'wagon', 'truck' and 'lorry' tend to be used indiscriminately throughout the sources. To avoid confusion, I have used 'wagon' to mean a horse-drawn vehicle, 'truck' to mean a railway vehicle, and 'lorry' to mean a mechanical road vehicle.

Acknowledgements

My thanks for assistance to: Ian Radford, Neil Llewellyn, Aubrey Bowden, Charles Webb, Charles Griffen, John and Joyce Dudeney, Andy Spatcher, John Norris, Paul Strong, Mick Crumplin, and the staff at the National Archives, the Prince Consort's Library, the Royal Army Medical Corps Museum, the Royal Logistics Corps Museum, and the library at the Royal Military Academy at Sandhurst. And, as always, my husband Ken Maxwell-Jones for driving, photography, proof-reading and making the excellent coffee that keeps me going.

Glossary

Buffers – devices at the end of a railway line, or part of the recoil mechanism of a gun, used to soften the impact.

Case goods – small items of groceries packed in cases.

Combing – of wool, separating the fibres into straight lines, using a comb.

Creosol – disinfectant liquid.

Fascine – a brushwood bundle used to fill ditches or shore up the sides of a trench.

Gabion – a wickerwork or wire cage, filled with stones, used to build temporary fortifications.

Governor – a device used to limit the speed of vehicles.

Jib – of a horse, to balk or shy.

Kip – leather made from the skin of a young animal, and thus soft.

Lumber – felled trees.

Maltese cart – basically just a flat platform between two large wheels.

Rocade – a railway line which connects two other parallel lines.

Sponsons – side pieces of early tanks.

Tack – equine equipment such as saddles and bridles.

Timber – standing trees.

Travois – a primitive weight carrier. Dragged by a horse, it consisted of two poles, one each side of the horse, connected at the far end, with the package on top.

Tumplines – lines from a backpack that cross the forehead.

PART I

THE WESTERN FRONT

The area known as the Western Front covered Northern France and Flanders, and was the location where much of the action during the First World War took place, and where the greatest number of British troops were situated.

Of the total of 8,700,000 men who served at some time during the war, 5,400,000 (62 per cent) served on the Western Front.

Introduction

No matter how brave the soldier, he cannot win a war on courage alone. He needs weapons, clothing and food, and leadership that understands the importance of these things. In the First World War, this leadership was not always available. Apart from a conviction that 'It'll all be over by Christmas', which reached from the government all the way down to the man in the street, the administration of supply had never had a high priority in the military, and it was not until well into the war that this attitude changed.

Not expecting the conflict to be prolonged or widespread, the government had paid insufficient attention to forward planning and it took numerous complaints of shortages from the field to rectify this omission. The first step towards doing this was to appoint an Inspector General of Communications, with the responsibility for keeping track of the day-to-day location of supplies, and ensuring that once they had arrived at the main bases, they were speedily shipped up the line to the front. But this was a little late in the chain.

To a large extent the problem started at home. The sequence of events was this: the manufacturers of the desired items of *materiel* produced and delivered to the orders of the Ordnance Department and the Quartermaster General. The goods then moved to the ports and across the Channel to the bases in France and Belgium and then on to the front. Although this seems straightforward, problems occurred at every stage. Since the UK relies on imports for most of its raw materials, a war inevitably meant shortages of the materials needed to manufacture supplies for the army, not least of those required for the production of explosives.

There was a shortage of TNT, and almost as soon as the war started the War Office took steps to restrict exports of its British-produced constituents: benzol, nitro-toluene, phenol and coat-tar toluol. This did not solve the problem and the government imposed a licensing scheme to restrict consumption of these materials to what it considered essential users (i.e. the munitions industry). It moved on to organise central purchasing for certain items such as acetone, passing this control to the Ministry of Munitions.

Once the necessary materials were available, the manufacturers ran into the second problem: a shortage of skilled labour. Prompted largely by patriotism, but also by a prediction that a short war would disrupt trade to a point of mass unemployment, many skilled men had joined up to fight. Board of Trade figures issued in May 1915 showed that recruitment averaged 20 per cent in mining, iron and steel working, engineering and electrical engineering, ship building, small arms manufacture, and chemicals and explosives, the latter standing at 23.8 per cent.

This was not helped by a general assumption that men in civilian clothes were too cowardly to enlist. Super-patriotic bands of women thrust white feathers (a symbol of cowardice) at men in civilian clothing, without enquiring about their occupation. Worse than this were over-keen recruiting sergeants who pounced on these uniformless men. The firm of Vickers came up with a simple answer: a 'war service' badge to show that the wearer was engaged in what later became known as 'works of national importance'. The first of these badges were issued to dockyard workers, and the practice then spread to workers at the royal arsenals and other important factories. However, this badge scheme did little to alleviate the shortage of skilled labour.

After much pressure, the War Office issued 'A Circular Memorandum to all Recruiting Officers and Secretaries of Territorial Associations' listing skilled tradesmen who should not be recruited. However, this list was somewhat restricted and missed many tradesmen such as those in steel works, and like the response to the badge scheme many recruiters just ignored the lists. At the same time, the Board of Trade approached the trades union and asked them to relax traditional work rules which tended to lower production. A conference was held and a form of what came to be known as Dilution was agreed. This covered the use of non-union workers and women as well as fully automatic machines.

The pressure from all sides – trades unions, manufacturers and recruiters – continued and eventually the newly created Ministry of Munitions pressed for, and obtained, a Munitions of War Act which was passed in January 1917. This effectively required each skilled man to work at full capacity unhindered by the varied restrictive practices espoused by the trades unions, including strikes.

The attempts to produce sufficient skilled workers continued, including one plan to import these men from abroad. Belgian workers were favoured at one point, but it proved difficult to integrate Belgians or other foreigners into British workshops. One solution was to create separate Belgian-staffed departments in the factories; another was to create a completely Belgian-staffed factory in County Durham.

In addition to this and many other schemes, two new ones were started: the Volunteer Munitions Brigade and the Women Munitions workers. Overall, these schemes helped tremendously in maintaining the skilled workforce, but that only addressed half of the problem.

Inside the army, there was a lack of sufficient trained staff officers to handle the administration of supply. Certainly before, and at the beginning of the war, the training of staff officers was not considered a matter of importance, not least by young officers. At a time when most promotions came through patronage, these young men were understandably reluctant to remove themselves from under the eyes of their patrons for two years at staff college. Once at staff college they found the syllabus was based on command rather than logistics, a situation paralled by the Field Service Regulations, in which the emphasis was on command matters.

Part I of the Field Service Regulations dealt with command matters. The duties of the Commander-in-Chief, who was theoretically in overall charge in the theatre, did not require him to oversee the activities of administration officers except in an emergency. Even then, fearing the blame for the emergency would fall on them, command officers tended to let the administration officers sort it out on their own. Unlike those of the general staff, the branches of the Adjutant General and the Quartermaster General were not considered part of the main chain of command and did not fit in either of the two usual ways of obtaining supplies: 'pull' or 'push'. Pull is the situation where the commanding officers of a fighting unit order what is needed as supplies are getting low; push is where the administrative commanders behind the lines observe what is being used on a regular basis and send it at regular intervals. Items which did not fit into this scenario would still have to be pulled when needed.

Once out in the field, officers trained under this curriculum soon found that while it had worked well enough in small colonial wars (although there was much criticism of the administration in the second Boer War), it was not good enough for the larger conflict on the Western Front. By December 1915, although the administrators in London were usually able to obtain the necessary supplies, they could not guarantee their arrival at the front; even this situation began to deteriorate as production failed to keep up with demand.

Part II of the Regulations, which dealt with administrative matters, was much smaller than Part I. It had four basic principles:

- Firstly, the Commander-in-Chief was to be the supreme authority in the field.
- Secondly, the administration organisation should be sub-divided but still under central control, i.e. one senior administrative officer managing subordinates who managed various departments. At the beginning of the war, this meant that all the administrative directorates reported to the Quartermaster General. When the post of Inspector General of Communications (IGC) was created, the directorates of railways, remounts, works, veterinary services, postmaster general and ordnance services were moved to report to him, but he reported to the

Quartermaster General. It was not until later that the IGC reported directly to the Commander-in-Chief and became a member of the general staff. The other members of this general staff were the Chief of the General Staff in charge of actual operations, the Quartermaster General in charge of army signals, medical services, supplies and transportation, as well as those listed above, and the Adjutant General, in charge of the paymaster's department, and other finances, until 1916 when discipline, military law, personnel, casualties and medical and sanitary services were added.

- Thirdly, the objective (as in Clausewitzian doctrine) was to defeat the enemy's field armies, so the administrative structure was to provide the fighting force with what it needed to achieve this objective.
- Fourthly, the 'general concept of a hierarchical command and control structure' was described. Unfortunately this led to a splitting of duties so that command and administration rarely interacted. Another problem was with the creation of the post of IGC, whose responsibilities included control and coordination of all traffic on the line of communication up to and including the rendezvous points with fighting formations beyond the railheads.

The general staff in theatre controlled the pull of demanding supplies, while the Quartermaster General's staff pushed them from behind. With his department's priority being that of commanding movements on the Line of Communication, they were neither push nor pull.

At the beginning of the war, the supply system was run by only a few organisations, but as the scale of the conflict grew, and the locations of action spread, other organisations were added or split off from the originals. The main organisations at that time were the Army Ordnance Corps (AOC) and the Army Service Corps (ASC). In simple terms, the AOC acquired and stored all the army's needs, and passed it to the ASC for local delivery to the fighting units. The Army Ordnance Corps was made 'Royal' late in 1918, as was the Army Service Corps.

At its high point point in 1918, the AOC had 2,133 officers and 37,342 other ranks, split 33,906 in the store section, 2,075 armourers and 1,361 artificers. There were also numerous civilians working in ordnance departments, numbering 23,287 men and 6,385 women in 1917, and 4,386 men and 3,644 women in the army clothing department.

Chapter 1

Money, Contracts and Control

The normal (peacetime) method for financing military stores in Britain was for the various departments to work out what they would need in the coming year, price it all, and submit these estimates to the Treasury, which then took them to Parliament, where, after some debate, a vote agreed the amount to be spent after which the Treasury retained control of the actual expenditure. The process required time, but there was normally no great hurry. The speed with which the First World War started and developed threw this orderly process into chaos, with two interlinked problems: the magnitude of what was required, and the urgency with which it was needed.

Once military activity expanded as rapidly as it did, the various departments could no longer make accurate estimates of how much they would need. As the author of the *Official History of the Ministry of Munitions* remarked, 'In the emergency of a great war, contingencies which defy all forecast make it impossible for the War departments to frame any reasonably close estimates of their probable expenditure.' Instead of voting in advance of specific spending amounts, parliament could only vote to accept what had actually been contracted for, under what was known as a 'vote of credit'. The first of these votes of credit, for £100,000,000, was granted by the House of Commons on 6 August 1914. These continued throughout the war, several times each year, and seven times in the fiscal year 1916/1917. The amounts of each vote rose, until the last two votes, in August and November 1918, were each for £700,000,000, making a grand total for the period from August 1914 to November 1918 of £8,742,000,000.

This money could not be obtained by the usual methods of taxation and excise duties, and so it had to be borrowed, increasing the National Debt from £650,000,000 in 1914 to £7,400,000,000 in 1919.

This did not mean there was no Treasury control over department spending. It did exercise close scrutiny after the event, and in several cases was able to press for changes in procedures and standard contract terms. Amongst these changes were that departmental personnel could be appointed on a temporary and non-pensionable basis, with the levels of salaries being fixed. In January 1916 a major qualification was imposed on contracts with suppliers in America and Canada; if these were likely to require payments in those countries in excess of £50,000 it should be reported to the Treasury at an early stage in the negotiations. This was due to the difficulties of American exchange, which eventually became so extreme that in January 1917 the limit was reduced to £5,000.

The first task when ordering supplies is to decide which firms should be given contracts. In peacetime this was comparatively simple: the firms which were known to be capable of providing what was needed were circulated and invited to tender. Those with the best prices were usually chosen; this process was called competitive tendering. The comparatively small amounts required were usually well within the reach of the usual suppliers, who were in whatever trade was involved, but even though some of these suppliers were quite large, they were not ready to supply in tens of thousands items which they were accustomed to supply in hundreds. Some were in a position to expand, but asked for assistance in the form of capital payments or payment in advance to allow them to enlarge their premises and purchase new machinery. This was known as 'assisted purchase'. The government had little other option but to accede to these requests. This even extended to purchasing, or at least leasing, land to build on. The numbers of such payments grew, until in October 1917 the Treasury requested that any new spending over £50,000 was approved by its officials before any payment was committed.

The only alternative was to offer contracts to numbers of smaller firms. Depending on the items required, this could be easy enough: for instance, any firm making clothing for civilians could easily adapt to making military clothing, any firm making wooden handles for garden tools could easily make them for entrenching tools, and any firm working on simple metal items could soon learn to make shell cases. For all of these, and the larger firms, detailed specifications had to be provided, and there had to be a formal inspection system set up to ensure that the specifications were met. An eighth of an inch one way or the other on a pair of trousers would not be a problem, but that eighth of an inch, or even less, on a shell case or bullet would mean it would not fit the weapon and thus would be useless.

However, with almost all these suppliers, producing the finished item would require several other parts which the manufacturer had to buy in (e.g. buttons for jackets) and these also had to be precisely specified and purchased from a reliable supplier who would produce them when they were wanted. In modern terms this is known as 'Just in Time' supply, and means the user neither has to keep a large stock nor has to wait for items to arrive. For this reason the government would want to oversee the manufacturer's choice of sub-contractor.

A larger problem was the availability of essential raw materials. Although many of the trades involved in production of war *materiel* tended to be in certain geographical areas, even the wholesalers in those areas were not in a position to maintain or obtain stocks of these raw materials in sufficient quantities. The government could, and duly set up what were called 'stores' to hold what was needed, and issue it under a system of vouchers so the eventual payment to the manufacturers could be adjusted. We would call this 'stock-holding' today. Only the government could arrange to buy the whole year's wool clip from Australia to make the serge for uniforms, or the shiploads of the various metals and chemicals needed to produce small arms cartridges. These included zinc or spelter with copper to make the brass for the case, copper and nickel to make cupro-nickel, which with lead formed the bullet, and a combination of cotton waste, pyrites, nitrates, fats and oils and wood distillation to make the cordite.

The first of these purchases was made in July 1915, when several thousand tons of the impure zinc known as spelter were bought and distributed. One or two situations were discovered where the main supplier had charged a sub-contractor a greater price for raw materials than he had been charged by the government stockholder.

A Select Committee on National Expenditure was formed and amongst other things suggested that the Treasury should recuit the help of some experienced men from industry and finance to investigate the profit ratios and other conditions in contracts. The second report of this committee stated that it believed the degree of Treasury control was inadequate and again stated its opinion that Treasury staff should include 'the addition of men of ability and administrative experience from outside'. This recommendation did not go down well with Treasury staff, who jealously guarded the traditions by which they worked.

However, such men were brought in and soon proved invaluable in advising on the true costs of manufacturing various items. It is often asserted that people or firms who supply war *materiel* can become rich from 'profiteering', but in the First World War attempts at this were soon nipped in the bud. Once there were people available who knew the true cost of efficient production, their expertise could be utilised when negotiating contract prices. However, this did not take place for some time and it is probable that until then advantage was taken, but as Churchill said of the Ministry of Munitions in a speech in the House of Commons in 1918:

It must never be forgotten that the Ministry of Munitions was called into being by the convulsions of war; the one overpowering need of the moment was to supply the troops with weapons and munitions which were required. What else mattered? What else compared for a second with that? An extraordinary improvisation without parallel in any country in the world took place in our industrial system. Thousands of people who knew nothing at all about public business or public departments, thousands of firms which had never been used for warlike manufacture, were amalgamated together, brought hastily together, and out of this ever-growing and enormous organisation that great flow of material of all kinds which raised our Army to the very forefront of the combatant armies was immediately produced. If at that time you had enforced strict and circumspect financial control and procedure, with every kind of check and countercheck operative both before and after the event, you might indeed have saved several millions – I dare say that is a modest figure – but you would have cramped and paralysed the whole of the organisation, and by doing so would have run grave risk of causing military injury which would manifest itself in the loss literally of scores of thousands of lives.

Within each department there was an accounting officer, who was appointed by the Treasury. This meant that he was effectively part of the Treasury and answerable to it for spending. He had no responsibility for policy, nor for contract prices; these came under the aegis of the Director of Contracts. The accounting officer was considered to be the watchdog of the Treasury, but his presence was often the cause of friction.

In the Ministry of Munitions, a chartered accountant, Mr H. Lever, was appointed, with several tasks to perform, the first of which was to install cost accounting systems in the National Factories. The results of this were used to reduce some contractors' prices in the winter of 1915/1916. Lever's other tasks were to devise and install a general system of store accounting, to use engineers and other qualified persons to examine proposed capital expenditure on new munitions factories, and keep a check on what are now called term payments (i.e. those which fall due on completion of parts of the building work), to examine all contracts, both existing and future, which involved such capital expenditure, and to ascertain that they were properly carried out.

From various comments in *The Official History of the Ministry of Munitions*, one gathers that Lever either had a bee in his bonnet about cost accounting or thought it was more important than his other tasks: 'From the first [he] threw himself with great energy into the inauguration of cost accounting ... The routine work was in fact to some extent sacrificed to the urgent need for this novel development', and 'the inevitable consequence that Mr Lever could not give his full powers to the superintendence of [the accounts department]'.

Lever also seems to have caused a major problem with Cammell Laird, stating that he had forced them to lower their prices by invoking the inspection powers under the Munitions Act. Cammell Laird stated that this public statement was misleading, and wanted it to be retracted or at least altered.

Lever left the Ministry of Munitions in December 1916 to become Finance Secretary to the Treasury; he had only been at the Ministry of Munitions for fourteen months, which does not seem like sufficient time to effect any lasting adequate changes.

Contracts

A contract is, in the simplest of definitions, an agreement between two parties, for each to do something to which they are bound by law. Contracts can be verbal, but in most business situations, and certainly those which involve the government, they are on paper, signed by both parties. They consist of the terms by which the supplier agrees to provide the buyer with certain goods or services, and the buyer agrees to pay for them.

There were two basic types of contract: the simple form where a price is agreed for a specified item or number of items to be delivered at a specified time and location. This was the situation before the war, when quantities and timing were known, but in wartime, when the need was likely to be extended over a long time, the price and delivery timing were another matter. The other type was known as 'running contracts' and, given the likelihood of financial conditions changing, they were often done on a 'cost-plus' basis, where the price was recalculated at intervals. The cost side of this would seem to be simple, i.e. that the buyer could inspect the seller's books. This tended to be unpopular with many sellers, and it was necessary for the government to have statutory powers to do this. Theoretically it should have been possible for the government to say 'no inspection, no more orders' but this was not feasible when demand was constantly higher than supply and alternative suppliers were not easy to find. The relevant powers of audit were covered by Acts of Parliament, with the added inducements that the government could take control of the supplier's workshops. This power rarely had to be used, but its existence did make recalcitrant suppliers more amenable.

Another way of calculating reasonable costs came when the government began to operate National Factories. At first these were just for munitions (especially for filling shells) but later they were extended to other items, such as gas masks. Having arrived at acceptable economical costs, the 'plus' aspect had to be considered. A simple addition of a percentage of costs could be used, or the supplier could be awarded a 'reasonable' profit of a specified sum. Not surprisingly, suppliers did not always accept what the government considered a reasonable profit, but eventually the concept was accepted to everybody's satisfaction.

All contracts required a precise definition, or specification, of what was wanted. With multiple suppliers, precision was essential. Obviously this would vary according to the type of goods, and might have included a sample of what was wanted. Where a service was involved, there might be industry norms which could be referred to, for instance 'standard gauge' railways, which means 4ft 8in wide. For uniform jackets, the specification would include the shape and location of pockets and the number, location and spacing of buttons.

Contracts also needed to include:

- The quantity of goods or other definition of the size of the order. This might require the work to be done and the goods delivered in batches at specified intervals, which avoided storage problems, noting the location to which the goods/services must be delivered, and who had to pay for this. At first this was Woolwich, but later other stores were opened as more capacity was needed.
- If appropriate, how the goods should be packed and how they should be marked: this marking always included the broad arrow but might also specify the wording to be used, if the cargo was going through, or to, countries where English might not be understood. The contract might also specify the sizes of the packing cases, whether they should be padded, and how they were to be made up. This type of clause became more prevalent once the army became more salvage or re-use conscious. Certain items had to be made up in sets, for instance horse-shoes (two front and two back) with the correct number of nails.
- To whom any correspondence should be addressed, and what references should be used.

The final clause would determine the end of the contract, and whether compensation was to be paid if this was not met. A top limit of £1,000 was fixed for compensation payments if the requirements were changed by the buyer.

Break Clauses

However, there might be difficulty over the ending of the contract, especially at the end of the war. At the beginning of the war the standard form of contract in use did not include any wording on how the contract would be dealt with at the end of the war. These were known as 'break clauses' and they were particularly relevant to contracts for the supply of munitions. Most of these were 'running' contracts, where production was not intended to stop at a specified time or after delivery of a stated number of items. They were usually brought to an end by notice of termination being given. The notice was never less than fourteen days, or sometimes more (e.g. in the case of heavy guns which took considerable time to make), the purpose being to protect the supplier who would have money and a workforce committed to this production.

The Contracts Department then proposed in May 1916 that all contracts with delivery dates after September of that year should include a clause allowing the buyer to stop the supplier's work without penalty. There were usually two time factors built in, the first being as brief as possible a period for the supplier to continue work at full capacity, and the second at sufficient production to finish any work in progress. The purpose of this was to allow the supplier to change over to peace-time working with little or no dislocation. Sometimes the buyer would take over the supplier's stock of components, work in progress and workers' wages.

While the notice given for munitions was usually three months, for motor cars and lorries it varied from six weeks to three months. There were twenty-five suppliers of motor vehicles, twenty-one supplying lorries and the rest cars. These firms employed some 3,700 sub-contractors, and since they were likely to be able to turn their production to civilian vehicles almost immediately, there was felt no need to employ break clauses in their case.

The phrase used was usually on the lines of 'if the present war shall terminate or if the Minister is of the opinion that the war is likely to terminate shortly', which immediately begs the question of the definition of 'termination of war'. After much deliberation, and after seeking a legal opinion, the following definition was achieved:

> The war cannot be said to end until peace is finally and irrevocably obtained, and that point of time cannot be earlier than the time when the treaty of peace is finally binding on the respective belligerent parties, and that is the date when ratifications are exchanged.

For the First World War, this meant the Treaty of Paris on 28 June 1919, not the Armistice of November 1918.

This is not the place to discuss the competence or otherwise of the accounting functions of the various departments and the Treasury, nor the ongoing friction between the supply and contracts departments, but the repeated reorganisations of the accounting systems and the instigation of internal audit procedures suggests that at the very least the accounting departments were out of their depth; the ever-increasing volume of complex work once the government realised that the war was not going to be all over by Christmas, and the lack of experienced staff and the necessary recruitment of new personnel led to serious confusion. There were 600 clerks and accountants in June 1916, about 1,200 in December 1916 and about 3,500 in November 1918.

Chapter 2

Supply Depots

In 1913 a five-day exercise was held at Aldershot. Major J.M. Young of the Army Service Corps (ASC) reported on their activities during the exercise and the valuable lessons learned in the process. The main supply depot was located at Aldershot, and maintained a force of about 37,000 men and 12,000 horses in the field. The depot had the use of the bakery and other buildings in the Aldershot supply depot; apart from this, everything was done on 'active service conditions'. They had a central office with a commandant, assistant commandant, officer in charge of waybills and accounts, depot superintendant and clerical personnel, plus six departments covering issues to depot personnel, a petrol department, a butchery department and a preserved meat department, an oats and hay department, a grocery department and a bakery department.

On completion of loading for each formation, details of what had been loaded were sent to the central office, which used them to complete waybills that were then passed to the railway transport office. They made out detailed carriers' notes which went to railheads. One important lesson learned was that the load in wagons should be distributed evenly across the floor of the wagon: if all the heavy items were at one end it could flatten the springs, leading to the wheels rubbing and starting fires. As an experiment, one train was sent to a regulating station with the trucks in mixed order. This took thirty shunts to sort out at the regulating station and Major Young remarked dryly that 'the experiment was not repeated'.

Until the system changed to one where basic supplies in France were sent automatically to fighting units on a daily basis, all requirement requests had to be sent to the War Office; they were then passed to the main ordnance depot at Woolwich, from where the items required were sent for despatch from the relevant port. At first all supplies for France went from Southampton, Newhaven, Woolwich and the Albert Docks in London, then in 1915 Littlehampton was added.

Originally, all types of stores went first to the main base at Woolwich from the manufacturers, but its capacity was soon overwhelmed, so more warehouses in the docks were hired or built and certain types of goods went direct to these. The main exceptions were small arms, which were handled at Weedon in Buckinghamshire, and ammunition, which was run by the new Ministry of Munitions. Other premises were used at main manufacturing and railway centres, including Didcot near Swindon, where 600 acres were acquired and numerous corrugated iron sheds erected. This base was served by 30 miles of track and workshops. It could handle 2,000 truckloads per month. There was some initial difficulty in obtaining sufficient labour, but this was resolved by volunteers and then two labour companies were moved in, each of 500 men, and some 1,560 male and 756 female civilians joined.

In the first year of the war supplies were despatched via specially designated wharves at Southampton and Newhaven; in 1915 Littlehampton and the Albert Docks in London were added. By February 1918 train ferries, where the train itself was driven onto the ferry, sailed from Richborough to Calais, and later from Southampton to Dieppe. Richborough was also used to load barges which were towed across the Channel.

There was an inspection branch which rose from 347 to 5,700 men. Prewar procedure had been for deliveries at Woolwich to be inspected and delivered to storehouses if they passed the inspection, but this was too cumbersome for the enormous quantities of goods needed in wartime, so further inspection teams were located at large industrial centres, most importantly at Birmingham. Finally inspectors were posted to contractors' works to view goods during and after manufacture. This saved much delay, but had to be closely supervised, since many 'mushroom' firms had sprung up; where these were unconcerned about their long-term reputation there was a possibility of collusion and bribery. A nucleus of experienced staff helped train the new personnel, toured the manufacturers and moved the junior inspectors frequently to prevent a build-up of collusion.

The work of the ordnance depots in the UK fell into four phases: the first was the mobilisation of the British Expeditionary Force (BEF), who were all regular soldiers and thus already had much of their equipment and clothing. They did, however, take almost all of the available stocks. The second phase lasted until the end of 1915, when the territorial army was mobilised and recruiting for Kitchener's new armies started. Nineteen new territorial and army divisions were set up over the next few months; during this period when demand was high but stocks were still low and time was needed to build them up, the ability to improvise was a valuable skill for Army Ordnance Corps (AOC) staff.

In the third phase order was restored and work in the depots became more routine. There were some difficulties in Ireland from the Fenian rebellion, and depots holding arms and ammunition had to be well guarded. A barrack store at Dublin, with all its contents, was burnt down and an attempt was made to do the same at Phoenix Park. The fourth phase was demobilisation.

In France the bases were mostly located in or just outside large modern towns with well equipped ports or railway stations able to deal with bulk supplies. The lines of communication between these towns and the fighting

SUPPLY AND TRANSPORT DIRECTORATE
WAR OFFICE

Chart showing system of Supply to the various Expeditionary Forces and the Troops in the United Kingdom, exclusive of Fortresses and other Garrisons abroad

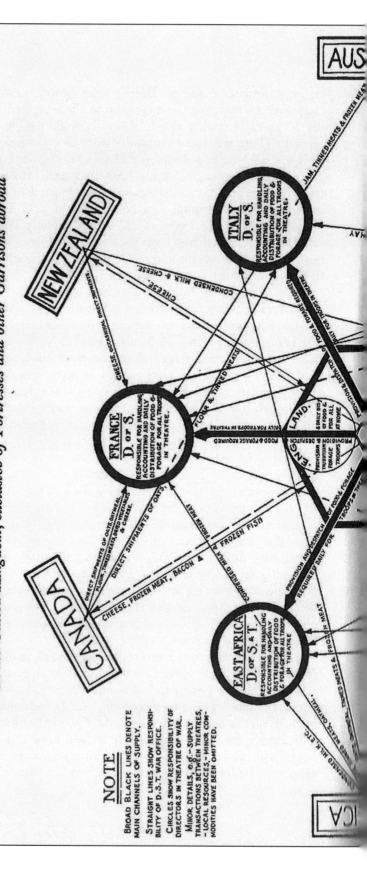

NOTE

BROAD BLACK LINES DENOTE MAIN CHANNELS OF SUPPLY.

STRAIGHT LINES SHOW RESPONSIBILITY OF D.S.T. WAR OFFICE.

CIRCLES SHOW RESPONSIBILITY OF DIRECTORS IN THEATRE OF WAR.

MINOR DETAILS, e.g.:— SUPPLY TRANSACTIONS BETWEEN THEATRES, — LOCAL RESOURCES:— MINOR COMMODITIES HAVE BEEN OMITTED.

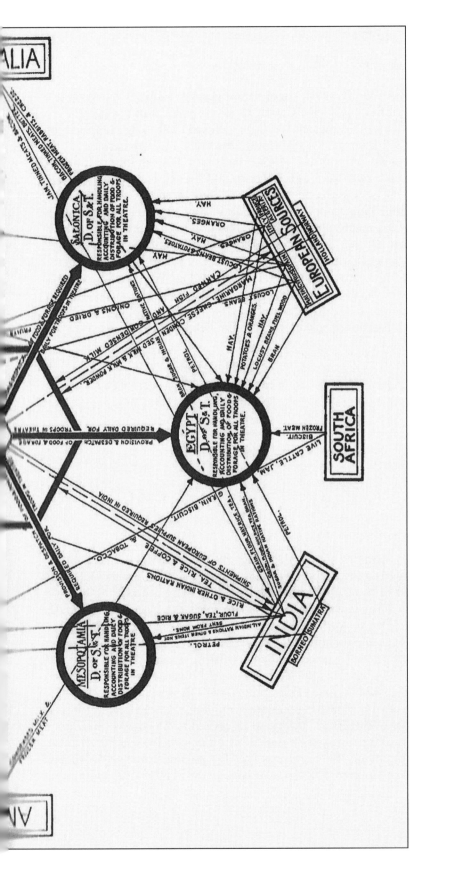

front were comparatively short, there were extensive railway systems and a good network of durable roads. Obstacles to the passage of transport were mostly in the forward areas which had been wrecked by shelling. Supply ships in the English Channel were not seriously threatened by submarines.

The arrangements for port use were worked out well in advance of the start of the war. In each port were found British and French commissioners, the French members having charge of the entry and berthing of vessels, the British of disembarking troops and unloading cargo. For the cargo work a certain number of French stevedores would be supplied to work under British orders. Cranes and other appliances would also be supplied. Storage space for depots would be allocated at each port, with an advanced depot at Amiens, but the British would provide the labour at these. The designated base ports would be Havre, Boulogne and Rouen, with Calais as an alternative to Boulogne if this was found to be necessary.

In the event, dock tonnage (shown here for February 1917) was:

	Quay	*Barge*
Dunkerque	17,750	4,000
Calais	16,200	7,414
Boulogne	36,036	
Dieppe	13,877	
Rouen	42,588	
Havre	22,198	2,800
Etaples	0	0
St Valery	1,940	
Treport	135	
Fecamp	1,000	
Cross-Channel Barge Services		2,661

There were two sorts of supply depot on the Western Front. Base Store Depots were located at the ports, where goods arrived from the UK and elsewhere; most of these goods at these depots passed on down the lines of communication but a few were dispersed to local users such as hospitals. Advanced Store Depots were a little way inland and were the first stop after the base store depots; many of these also passed some supplies to local users. In addition, there were what were called regulating stations, which were the places where trains carrying bulk goods were broken down into smaller quantities which could then be made up into trains for specific units. When a bulk train arrived at a regulating station, a number-taker went along it and took the number of each truck and listed its contents. He entered this into a book and sent it to the supply train regulating officer who was responsible for distributing the contents. Some were assigned to go into store and the rest to sections, and this information was passed back to the number-taker who went

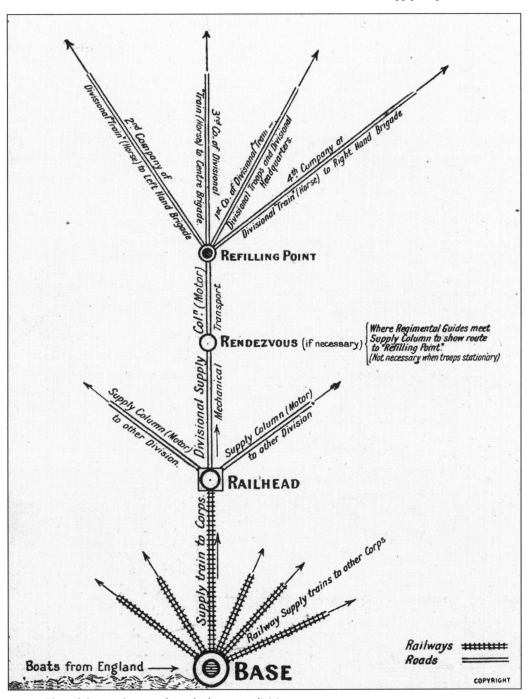

Plan of the supply route from the base to a division.

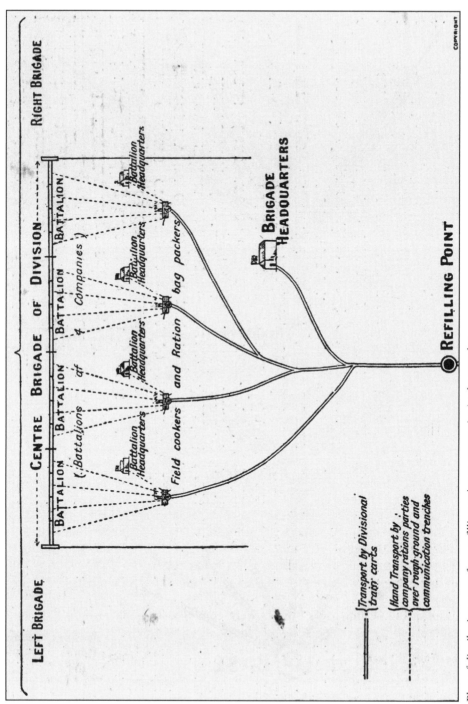

Plan of distribution route from refilling point to companies in the trenches.

back to the train and marked each truck accordingly. The trucks could then be marshalled for onward transmission.

The base store depot at Havre (now known as Le Havre) was in the middle of the dock at the Hangar Aux-Coton, and a vast tented city sprang up close by. This port could take all sizes of ships and all overseas cargoes could come alongside the quay at Hangar Aux-Coton; this vast shed covered 9 acres. There were three railway lines inside the hangar and one immediately outside. All unloading had to be done onto the quays; barges were not allowed to receive cargo from the other side of the ship.

The arrangements at the base supply depot at Calais were much like those of Havre but ships were discharged on both sides into barges. The depot handled case goods (small bottles and tins packed in cases) and forage on the sides of the canal which was in two branches emanating from a Y junction. In each hangar the medical comforts group had concrete floors; elsewhere there were only concrete walkways between the stacking areas. This arrangement unfortunately allowed access to numerous vermin.

At the highest point of activity, the supply depots at Havre, Rouen and Calais provided food for over 3,000,000 men. They also provided a total of over 27,000,000 gallons of petrol, more than half of this from Calais. By the beginning of 1918 the monthly usage of petrol in France had risen to some 8,000,000 gallons.

The work of the offices at the base store depot consisted of five sections: indents, regimental duties, returned stores, workshops and the group which dealt with issues, accounts, transit, yards and labour, and any other group ordnance officers. At the main depots anything up to 2,000 indents could be received each day and the clerks prided themselves on passing these forward on the day they arrived. The first task was to sort through each batch for guns or other urgent items for immediate issue, having first checked that no movement order had been made for the unit since the indent had been sent. Copies of all movement orders were sent to the base depot by telegraph. Then the rest of the indents were checked and separate orders were made for each type of item and sent to the stores which kept those items. There the orders were assembled and packed with address labels attached before being loaded onto the appropriate railway truck for delivery. The paperwork accumulating for all these activities was entered into ledgers, which were checked in the quieter hours of the night.

Six of the headquarters officers were employed on train loading, one in charge and five assistants who with their staff obtained, loaded, labelled and despatched their trucks and checked their contents. Each of the lines held seventy-two trucks. The inside lines were used for bulk loads and the outside line for section trains. The main factor was the number of trucks available; if this was insufficient, the demand was reduced. If there was a surplus, all were loaded with various useful items and sent to the advanced supply depots. Each bay had an assortment of stacks to avoid unnecessary shunting.

On average about 110 men were required as labour every day for loading and unloading at the stacks. Divided into gangs, the labour was distributed among the different commodities: preserved meat, bread, and as sweepers. A forty-two truck train of mixed forage needed 120 men, or 160 men for boxed goods, while a boxed goods train of thirty-six trucks required 140 men. Frozen meat needed 100 men, each working on this task for no more than one hour at a time. As far as possible, all the labour was contracted out.

The general duties of each base depot needed an average of twenty-five motor vehicles and twenty-eight horse transport vehicles. Lorries took an average of seven loads per day, each of 14 tons. The horse transport carried 1 ton per load, with each vehicle doing six or seven loads. The train loading officer had twelve horse transport vehicles and the rest were on general duties.

The base supply depots packed bread and meat, and labelled them by sections, while case goods were sent to the advanced supply depot for storage. Forage and coal were sent to regulating stations in bulk. The stocks at advanced supply depots were mainly case goods to supply the trucks of groceries and other case goods per section. These stocks were stored close to the hangar doors so they would be readily to hand when a lorry came for them.

For case goods, the railway transport officer loaded and unloaded all trucks, made out waybills and handed them over to the rail traffic officer. Outside the depot at Fontinettes was a twenty-nine line regulating station. Despite the care taken over checking, labelling and sealing trucks discrepancies occurred at railheads 'for which no adequate explanation could be given'.

The base supply depot at Boulogne was situated in the dock area known as the Bassin Loubert; this was divided into the transit hangars and the base supply depot. The docks discharged all ships into trucks or over the side into barges, thus emptying ships more quickly. The routines were much like those at Havre, except that there was no forage space in the depot, so forage had to be discharged into trucks for the advanced supply depots. If there were not enough lorries, it sometimes had to be stored outside, as was some biscuit.

There were two coal yards at Boulogne capable of holding 9,000 tons of coal, 3,500 tons of coke and 2,000 tons of fuel wood. The limited space did not permit standard stacks, but each shipment was kept separate. All the labour in those yards was provided by prisoners of war, who were found to be superior to the Chinese coolies who provided the rest of the labour.

After the retreat from the Marne, the contents of the depot at Boulogne were temporarily moved to Havre by sea. The advance depot at Amiens had little stock and a few lorries which, being fit only for the scrap heap, were just abandoned. The personnel from there went to Rouen. Havre supplied temporary depots at Le Mans and Nantes. Although Nantes had a deep-water port, it was a long way from the main action in Flanders and it was closed quite quickly. Rouen developed into the main base for mechanical transport, where a small separate depot was established and a workshop set up.

Oil was stored for fourteen days' worth of local issues. Although situated in the middle of the depot, the storage tank was surrounded by raised earth banks for fire prevention. Fire precautions elsewhere in the depot were fully developed, with hoses stored under the railway lines and brought out onto the platforms at night.

Oil ships unloaded at Bassin Ouest, using a series of tank farms, each consisting of four smaller tanks with a total filling capacity of 4,200,000 gallons. In addition to supplying the British, French and Belgian armies, this depot also supplied the American army and some civilian requirements.

There were floating suction and elevator plants which were placed between the ship and the quay. Bulk cargoes of oats were bagged at this point. The cargoes were often damaged and there was much pilfering. However, this method emptied the ships and freed the quay quickly. It was an overall policy of the docks to unload ships and send them on their way quickly.

Two lines of communication started at Boulogne and Calais, with advanced bases at Havre, Rouen, Dieppe and St Valery for the northern line, and an advanced base at Abancourt and regulating stations at Romescamp and Mautort. More berths for forage were needed at Havre, so additional facilities were used at St Valery for lines of communication requirements and at Dieppe for the front. Later Fecamp was added.

Each of the lines of communication had its own deputy director of supplies, and subordinate to him were some assistant directors. They dealt with provisions, which in this case did not mean food and drink but all the other items provided from the depots.

A base depot for the northern line of communication opened in June 1915 at Calais, in a former timber yard still full of timber. This was purchased from its owners, the firm of Valdelievre; subsequent price rises gave a profit of £10,000.

On the northern line of communication forage was landed at Dunkirk, Dieppe and St Valery, case goods at Calais and Boulogne, and coal at Calais and Dunkirk; all meat was supplied from Boulogne; Boulogne and Calais had bakeries. On the southern line of communication forage was landed at Havre, Dieppe and St Valery; bread was baked at Rouen, Havre and Dieppe; coal and charcoal went from Dieppe; and oil from Rouen. Coal dust was supposed to be made into briquettes with the addition of tar and sawdust but this was not always done.

There had been three months between the acquisition and opening of this new depot at Rouen and it had been able to accumulate all the stock it needed except guns and components for heavy artillery. Given that the concentration of use of this armament was closer to Calais than Havre, it was eventually decided that Calais should handle all of it, and it was duly transferred in June 1917.

A report on base supply depots remarked that at some depots mechanical goods handling aids were used on platforms (e.g. mechanical conveyers and gravity rollers), and it was felt that more of these were needed.

Store base depots were set up early in 1916, at Les Attaques and Abancourt. Havre and Rouen became subsidiary store depots. The depot at Les Attaques received its stores from Calais, Dunkirk and Boulogne. It supplied the three northern armies and lines of communication. It was situated between the Calais–St Omer canal and the railway. Branches of the railway were extended into the depot and wharves were constructed along the canal for items brought in by barge. The depot was originally 50 acres, but soon enlarged to 65 acres as the quantity of stores built up. A large timber depot of 150 acres was created on the other side of the railway.

At Abancourt there was no canal, but the depot was located at a junction of railways from Havre, Rouen and Dieppe. It received its stores from Havre, Rouen, Dieppe and Fecamp, and supplied the two southern armies and lines of communication. It soon grew from the original 32½ acres to 163 acres. A further wharf was acquired at Rouen, where most of the timber from overseas arrived.

Each station had a number of rail lines, arranged on each side of a central line where the bulk trains came in; there could be as many as fourteen of these side lines, and trucks were shunted on to these lines and on to trains going out to fighting units.

The advanced supply depot at Mautort separated supplies into three groups, A, B and C. Group A (eight blocks) and B (six blocks) were for groceries and other case goods, with another for medical comforts. Group C was for forage. Each group was completed with all supplies and stocked and each block, which was standardised into twenty days' supplies for two sections, was finally complete with everything required daily for the section pack trains.

A book was kept for each block, listing the items by cases, not by weight. This went to the group office each evening where they were all consolidated into a block state, which indicated the distribution of stores arriving. The practice was to unload from alternate blocks, leaving the others for receiving. A loading table was made out and sent to each blockman. At the end of each day the group state and the block state were compared and had to agree.

Details of trains arriving from the base supply depot went to the depot superintendant's office. A shunt list was made out in triplicate, one copy for the rail transport officer to show him where to place trucks, one to the officer in charge of receipts and one to the receiving group. The officer in charge of receipts requested labour and checkers and sent a debit note to the receiving group and the accountants. The waybills went straight to the accountants who checked them against the debit notes. If a train was discharged into more than one group, each used the same procedure.

Forage was stacked at the advanced supply depot. To avoid a build-up of old forage it was only issued from stock, to turn over the reserve. It was stacked on raised platforms 120ft wide and the stack beds were fixed to 90ft by 30ft, which gave stacks of approximately 300 tons of hay and 600 tons of oats. Labour was contracted out as much as possible. Trains of forty trucks came into a siding on one side of the stack platforms and section trains were loaded from the other side. This allowed simultaneous use of the stack area.

At Calais an average of three forage ships arrived each day from England, and there were usually five or six ships in the port. Handling this quantity of forage required four officers and eighty-eight other ranks. The daily output to sections was approximately 1,100 tons of oats and 500–600 tons of hay. In addition, altogether the French received up to 400 tons of oats per day and the Belgians 274 tons per day. A conveyor for lifting hay from barges to shore was being erected at the time of the report.

At the advanced supply depot and regulating station at Outreau the normal stock held was twenty-one days' worth of rations for 500,000 men and twenty days' forage for 120,000 horses. It was divided into four groups under cover and two groups outside. The four groups inside the hangar were separated by fire-proof concrete walls and fire-proof double doors for communication.

The northern petrol stores were held at Fonbriettes, Beaurainville and Vron; this separation was a precaution against air raids. Beaurainville held 500,000 gallons of motor spirit and 250,000 gallons of petrol. Vron consisted of two depots, each with the same capacity as Beaurainville. At Fonbriettes there were four separate depots a mile apart and there was an additional storage depot with 5,000,000 gallons capacity if needed.

Until mechanical transport was accepted as reliable, it was thought desirable to keep two days' worth of grain and preserved food in horse transport. The supply of food was based on daily issues of fresh meat and bread; the individual soldier carried a day's reserve ration.

'Weekly states' reports included all stocks landed and cargoes broached. Groceries and case goods were sent in bulk from base supply depots to advanced supply depots where they were packed by sections for the front. Bread, frozen meat and oils were loaded by sections at the base. Other base supply depots were in use at the time of the report for special purposes.

There was a standard form for demanding hospital supplies, rations and forage. Royal Engineers required a different form. Each divisional unit sent this form to the brigade supply officer who compiled them all and put the total requirements on another form. This one went to the senior supply officer of the division who consolidated it with demands from each of the brigades. This went overnight to the supply officer for each supply column who worked out load tables for his lorries. The next morning these were given to the railhead supply officer who made the necessary issues from the supply train coming to his railhead for the section to which that division belonged. Any surplus items from the train went into store to make good future deficiencies. The strength of the sections were passed to the base supply depot each day.

The battle state gave the grouping and distribution along the front, showing where each should be supplied and where their needs should be packed. Each section had a unique number which it retained if it moved. No unit could move from the southern to northern line of communication or vice versa without notification from the director of supplies.

There was further specialisation: sandbags, picks, shovels and barbed wire were held at Blargies Sud and Les Attaques, winter clothing and blankets at Paris, and other clothing at Rouen. There were also numerous other small depots for short-term storage at the various railheads. By the summer of 1916 one ordnance officer per corps was stationed at these railheads. As well as checking and handing over what had arrived, they dealt with unused items returned from the front. If in suitable condition these could be reissued, otherwise they went back to the base depot.

Demands were received daily from the armies by telegram and entered into a train regulating book. As the demands constantly changed, all entries were made in pencil but not erased when changed, just struck through with the new amount entered alongside. The most frequent corrections were of strengths and quantities. The officer commanding this regulating section had a colour coding system, using different colours for different sections.

The original method of delivering supplies from trains was to take it to dumps, from where it was collected for onward delivery. Then the system changed to what was called 'tailboard to tailboard': lorries or wagons backed up to each other and items were transferred between them without being dumped on the ground.

Much of the store issuing was done with a system of indents, as many as 2,000 of these arriving daily at each depot. Guns and other urgent items were dealt with first, other items as swiftly as possible. The issue sections were divided into bays, some for each formation and one for local units; these were filled from stock by men known as 'layers out' and then packaged and labelled before being loaded onto trucks and despatched to the appropriate railhead, while clerks entered the details in ledgers.

The function of the dock at Havre was mainly gross intake from overseas and output to regulating stations. The overseas intake included all transatlantic shipments of frozen meat, preserved meat, pork and beans (presumably in tins), oats, flour and oatmeal, cheese and milk. Any remaining shipments went to the home supply base at Newhaven. Some coals, oils and medicinal comforts were held in stock for local use.

There was a fire piquet of two NCOs and nine men, the sergeant of which should have previously worked in a fire brigade. The piquet was permanent and the members had to sleep in the depot. One NCO and two men were allowed out each day. There was a practice fire drill every Sunday morning. All permanent staff in the hangar had a fire post; others fell in on the fire alarm. They had a fire pump made by Merryweather & Sons stabled nearby. There were also two chemical fire engines in the hangar with a 60 gallon capacity, which would throw a jet about 20ft from the nozzle of a 20in pipe. There were numerous fire hydrants on the quay sides, chemical extinguishers and plentiful sand and fire buckets, but there were no fireproof partitions or screens.

This advanced supply depot had a sheep farm, capable of holding 400 to 800 animals. These were a North African type of sheep. The ground was low and wet, which might be expected to lead to foot rot but there was actually very little of this. However, a very high proportion were found to be afflicted with liver fluke.

There were cross lines between the main supply depots, with two shunting engines constantly working between the depots (except for the depot at Outreau which had no shunting engine, instead using horses to move trucks); they could turn out six forty-truck trains per day. There was also equipment for steam cleaning empty oil drums and washing them out with warm water and caustic soda. They were then tested for leaks with air pressure of 3.5 kilos per cubic inch. All this produced about 150 gallons of mixed heavy oils per day; this was converted into lubricants for heavy vehicles, and some into grease for heavy machinery.

Surplus Stores

Inevitably, given the vast amounts ordered and the shifting nature of combat, a substantial quantity of the *materiel* purchased and sent to stores ended up as surplus. Colonel W.N. Nicholson, a staff officer who wrote of his experiences during the war, reported that his last task in France was the disposal of surplus stores. These included large items such as vehicles, light railways and timber, a collection assessed as being worth some £700,000,000. These items were at various dumps, 'looked after' by troops anxious to be demobbed so they could go home. On the other side of the picture was the local population, hoping to acquire stores to rebuild their wrecked homes. The first step was to let divisions sell batches of stores to a value of £200. There turned out to be over a million different items, many duplicated throughout departments; for instance, cranes were owned by the Director General of Transport as well as the Director of Docks. A further complication came in the form of French customs officers, who delayed sales and auctions by declaring that since all the stores had entered the country duty free, import duty must be paid if they were to remain there after being sold. However, they would not set a specific rate, and it was suspected that there was collusion at work; sufficient delay would reduce the price, perhaps to a 'giveaway' level.

Over time, the returned stores departments dealt with more salvaged items than those which were sent back unused. No matter how dirty or damaged salvaged items were, they could be used in some way, even if it was only to be sold as scrap.

Salvage

Salvage operations were considered so important that a new department was set up at GHQ, with a Controller of Salvage who worked with a similar official at home to set up policy; he had a small crew to supervise salvage collection.

There was a large salvage department which collected empties returned from the front, rebaled hay and rebagged grains which had burst their bags. Empty returned sacks were sorted into two types: Class 1 sacks were refilled, Class 2 sacks were used for bagging charcoal. Charcoal required 40,000 sacks each month. Any sacks which were too bad for either class went to England for pulping. Flour sacks were also sent to England, while bread sacks went to the bakeries. Cardboard was packed and sent to England. Oats were screened, winnowed and sacked, the plant providing up to 20 tons per day. All hay that was suitable was rebaled, while short hay and hay seed went to the veterinary hospitals.

A Salvage Section, including men from the employment companies made up of those unfit for trench duty, was attached to each formation. The first collection of salvage material was in September 1914 after the retreat from the Marne; this included 500 greatcoats and other equipment found in a church at Coulommiers. After the Second Battle of Ypres in May 1915 the 4th Division sent out a party every morning. Records of what each company found were issued and it became quite a competition; one company found an abandoned brewery which contained numerous copper pots and pans.

As well as the salvage departments, two main depots for returned stores were established near Havre and Calais, 'manned' largely by local women, who performed what was thought at the time to be ordinary women's work such as washing and sewing. They also cleaned wagons and unloaded barges carrying barbed wire. Much of this material was reissued after cleaning and mending.

Scrap metal had to be sorted into different categories, including items that could be melted down in foundries (rails, iron pickets, horseshoes, etc.), metal castings (fire-bars, stoves, agricultural machinery), and iron or steel wire for re-melting. Other non-ferrous metals, including lead and nickel from firing ranges, should be packed separately, ideally in sacks, and labelled to show their contents. Anything containing explosives ('dud' shells, grenades, etc.) should not be included with other scrap metal.

Armourers could repair much of the metal salvage, made up rifles from cannibalised parts and replaced rivets in steel helmets.

Even battle wreckage was collected, and was sent with other items to the division repair centres on empty supply wagons. There it was sorted, repaired if possible, or cannibalised for other repairs, or sent for scrap if too bad for anything else. Ammunition boxes and shell cases were returned to Britain by ship from Havre, loaded on board by German prisoners.

There was a great deal of German ammunition. This had to be handled with extreme care, partly because it had different fuse mechanisms, and partly from a fear that it might have been booby-trapped. In the worst weather of the year, it seemed unfair to make British troops to do this work, so German prisoners of war and Chinese coolies were employed instead.

Waste paper and cardboard were urgently required in the UK. It should be baled for collection, but first sorted into types: white, no printed matter; coloured; brown; printed matter including newspapers and magazines; and sundry, including cardboard. Separate sacks should be used for each type and clearly labelled. If it was impossible to separate the paper at the point of origin, it should be labelled 'Waste Paper, not sorted'. Secret and confidential documents should not be included. The sacks should be kept under cover.

The solder from bully beef tins could be re-used after recovery. The tins were often placed in kilns for this process, but instructions were that they should not be cleaned of fat before being placed in the kilns, as the fat served as fuel. Using blow lamps to melt solder was found to be uneconomical and was not recommended. Other tins, such as those for tea and biscuits, were to be cut into flat plates and the solder-bearing edges removed.

Before the value of rags was realised, many items of dirty (and bloody) clothing and blankets were just burned; later they were cleaned and used to make sacks, mess-tin covers, haversacks, belts and even water bottles. Canvas material, such as tents and trench covers, was to be returned for repair and overhaul before being reissued.

Jam cases (presumably wooden) were to be collapsed after removing the wire, tied together and handled with care so they could be re-used immediately on return to UK. Pickle jars were urgently required for bottling the pickles made in Egypt.

Meat or bacon condemned as unfit for human consumption should have the fat extracted before the residue was destroyed. The fat was to be put into tins in the usual way but marked 'U'. For collection of other fat, presses were available.

Stock sheets were compiled regularly and sent to the War Office, which decided what should be sent home. The rest was disposed of in France by a Disposals Board which had been specially set up to handle this task. Large quantities were taken by the French government to rebuild areas that had been wrecked in the war, much of the clothing went to prisoners of war, and some went to Russia. The rest was sold in batches at dispersal camps.

At the end of the war the French authorities were pushing for the release of premises rented 'for the duration', especially at Havre, one of the main commercial ports. So a new depot was opened at Dunkirk for items which would otherwise have gone to Havre. The contents of inland depots were transferred to base ports and they were cleared, starting with those on the Seine. By April 1919 enough had been cleared at Havre to allow release of the big hangars.

Camps were formed at various ports from Antwerp to Havre, each able to house 100,000 soldiers while their kit was refurbished, old boots and uniforms replaced by new ones, and clean underwear issued; they had to hand in their arms and military accoutrements. The supply departments had just as much, if not more, to do in providing these items. They also had to inventory their remaining stock, and sell it off, at the same time dealing with returned stock and salvage. The work on salvaged items continued, as the British had left much stuff behind during their advance and the Germans even more as they retreated. At Namur 1,200 barges were found containing German war stores, including thousands of machine guns. And, of course, much of this had to be sold, either where it was or after being returned home. In general there was a demand on the spot, especially for such items as building materials, lorries and cars, and even horses, particularly heavy horses for farm work.

At the end of the war the British government was anxious to restore the British economy and to find employment for as many men as possible. It was decided that the first men to be released from military service were those termed 'pivotal men', that is those who were necessary to set essential industries going again. The classic example was coal workers, whose product was needed to fuel almost all other industries, including the railways and shipping. These men were the first to be provided with demobilisation clothing. The rest of the men were demobilised in batches, precedence being given to those who had a guaranteed job to go to, and to others with certain qualifications, formal or vocational. This scheme proved so unpopular that after what was effectively a strike at Calais in January 1919 it had to be abandoned in favour of a new scheme based on length of service.

Returned equipment was collected, checked over and stored. Civilian suits, in brown, blue or grey, with a cap, collar and tie, had to be available to those demobilised men who were prepared to accept them in lieu of a special bonus of 52s 6d. A special Discharged Soldier's Suit section was formed in Battersea Park; operating from December 1918 to August 1920, it despatched 1,500,000 suits by post.

There were soon fewer men to look after the remaining stores at regimental level so the burden of this fell on the Army Ordnance Corps. There were still some 4,000 AOC personnel in France two months later. These were mainly clerks and storemen, as the artificers from the workshops, being no longer required, had been on the preferential list for early release. There was a big demand for all types of tented accommodation, partly because it was thought important to keep those compelled to stay as happy as possible. Mobile workshops were turned into classrooms for rusty artisan soldiers to catch up on their trades and tool use, and at bases classes were held on mechanical crafts, draughtsmanship, mathematics, and general subjects such as literature, history and languages.

Chapter 3

Horses

In a world where there were few mechanical vehicles, an army going to war needed horses in vast numbers. Many people think that horses plus army equals cavalry, but this is not so. For the First World War we have good figures: at the end of August 1918, when the total number of horses and mules was 828,360, the number designated as riding horses was 193,747, or 23.4 per cent. And that is riding horses, not cavalry horses. We don't have a number that separates cavalry horses from the other riding horses, but one estimate for the 1880s, for a force of eight infantry regiments, three cavalry regiments, two artillery batteries, officers for all these and a general and his staff, gives 1,200 cavalry horses and 363 other riding horses. These figures are just for a fighting force; add officers and NCOs for all the other non-combatant units and the percentage of cavalry horses drops still further.

Horses used by the British Army were of three sorts. The tall (over 15 hands high), fast animals for the cavalry were, and still are, known as 'hunter' type, which come in three sizes: lightweight, medium weight and heavyweight. These 'weights' refer to the substance of the horse itself, and the size and weight of the rider it is intended for, being able to carry these riders at speed across country and over fences and other obstacles. Smaller animals, known as cobs, were preferred for the dragoons and mounted infantry, and as 'ride and drive' gun horses for the artillery. Finally, draught horses, either heavy or light, were used for various types of supply wagons and to pull heavier guns.

A London traffic census conducted in 1913 found that only 6 per cent of all passenger vehicles (buses, trams and cabs) were horse-drawn, but 89 per cent of goods vans were still using horses. A General Horse Census made in 1912–1913 showed just under 900,000 horses suitable for the Regular and Territorial armies: more than sufficient for the army's immediate needs. A Horse Registration Scheme had already been set up, where the army paid owners of suitable horses an annual fee to keep them available if called upon.

Several years before war was actually declared in August 1914 it was becoming obvious that conflict could not be avoided, and schemes for rapid mobilisation were set up. This meant obtaining a large number of horses at short notice, bringing the peacetime establishment of 25,000 animals up to 165,000. When the time came, this was achieved in twelve days, the animals being purchased from the lists of the Registration Scheme. The horses called in were taken to collection stations in each district, then moved on by train to remount depots. After this episode of urgent buying, few horses were taken from the lists of the Registration Scheme, the rest coming through the work of the Remount Service. This organisation purchased and trained all horses and mules; it was part of the Quartermaster General's department until 1941, when it became part of the Royal Army Veterinary Corps.

As the numbers of equines used in the war increased, so did the staff of the Remount Service, from 121 officers and 230 men in 1914 to 423 and 20,560 respectively in 1917; numbers then reduced in 1919 to 258 and 6,731 respectively. To avoid withdrawing army officers from their normal duties, many of the Remount Service officers were drawn from the landed gentry, Masters of Foxhounds and others with experience of horses, including several renowned artists.

The Remount Service had other responsibilities at home: the Board of Agriculture started a Food Production Department and needed 10,000 draught horses to work on farms; the Remount Service bought 6,800 for them and transferred 3,200 army horses which were no longer suited for military service. They also lent unfit horses to the Department of Draught Horses, which got them fit by ploughing at prisoner of war camps, whereupon they were returned and exchanged by the Remount Service for another lot of unfit ones.

An equine's ability to work properly over many years arises from his shape and what is known as good conformation. This basically means that he is put together in a way that enables him to do his job without unnecessary wear and tear on his joints, heart and lungs. His condition is also important; horses are considered to be in good condition when they feel firm when stroked and are neither thin nor over-fat and flabby. Unfit horses tire quickly and then move unevenly in walk and trot, or sweat and have difficulty breathing properly. They often stumble and may fall and damage their knees. If pushed to make an extra effort, they may sprain a tendon.

A fit horse should be able to cover 20 to 25 miles in a day. Most of this would be done at a walk, at an average pace of about 4mph. A forced march of 40–45 miles a day might have to be done at 5–6mph, necessitating the occasional use of the trot, a pace averaging 8mph. Royal Horse Artillery (RHA) harness horses could do about the same, when pulling guns and their wagons to keep up with cavalry. Draught horses pulling heavy loads would be much slower. However, this level of work could not be sustained every day and the horses needed at least rest one day each week.

As far as the army was concerned, the term horse included mules, and it was only in specific situations where instructions differentiated.

Mules proved to be far more resistant to adverse circumstances than horses: mule deaths from disease or during transportation on land and sea were less than half of those among horses, and they could be kept in good condition on 75 per cent of the food ration allotted to horses. They were less liable to disease (including mange) so formed a smaller proportion of the patients in veterinary hospitals. Their skin is harder and less sensitive to rain and sun, and their hooves are harder than horses' hooves; for this reason they are better able to tolerate going unshod. The mule is more capable of bearing fatigue than the horse, and is less restive under heavy loads. Males (horse mule or john mule) can carry larger loads than females (hinnies).

The reputation of mules for being stubborn is more a myth than reality. They can dig their heels in and refuse to move, but this is usually in a situation where the mule believes danger is waiting. In such a situation they can neither be forced nor frightened into moving. Those mules bought by the army were usually already broken-in, but when they had to be broken-in from scratch, this needed to be done gently and calmly, taking care to establish confidence.

Almost 470,000 equines were bought in Great Britain, and some from India, Australia and South America, but the greatest number came from North America. Once it had become apparent that sufficient numbers of animals could not be obtained in Britain, a new Remount Commission was formed to buy in the United States and Canada. During the course of the four-and-a-half years that the Remount Commission operated in North America, 484,636 horses and 287,564 mules were purchased, giving a grand total of 772,375 animals. Of the horses purchased, less than 30 per cent were for riding. The rest, and all the mules, were for draught purposes.

Newly purchased animals were branded. This was done at the centres where the animals were brought for pre-purchase inspection. Each of the purchasing officers had his own personal brand, which was added below the usual broad arrow; these personal brands consisted of one or two letters. The brands were applied to the near-side quarter of the animal, 4in below and 4in to the right of the point of the hip. Mules were marked on the hoof until it was realised that this would not be permanent as the hoof would be pared away as it grew; it was also difficult to see in muddy conditions.

The Remount Department ran four types of depot in America: purchasing, collecting, off-loading and embarkation; where these were adjacent to train stations, they often used the existing stock yards, adding their own corrals, additional buildings and veterinary hospitals.

Personnel at the depots in the UK where animals were assembled included farriers and shoeing smiths, saddlers, and numerous grooms and horse-trainers. At its highest point, personnel at these depots numbered 423 officers and 6,731 men. These depots were originally manned by civilian grooms and stable lads, with military officers in charge, but many of these civilians were drafted for military service and had to be replaced by inexperienced men who had to be trained in horse care. Another solution to this problem was to use experienced horsewomen. There was an all-female remount depot at Russley Park near Baydon in Wiltshire.

Horse Care

Many of the veterinary problems which arise with horses come about from a lack of proper care and housing. As one head of veterinary services remarked, 'Freedom from disease is in direct relation to the degree of care bestowed on an animal, and the spread of mange or contagious disease is a certain indication of neglect in management and supervisory care.' For this reason manuals on horse and stable management emphasised the necessity for good but draught-free ventilation, cleanliness and a regular stable routine.

The individual accommodation in stables could either be loose-boxes or stalls. Loose-boxes are literally that: the horse is not tied and can move around freely so the box must be big enough to allow this. Each box has its own double door, with the top door left open except in extreme bad weather. Stalls – narrow sections of a large building – are usually divided by stout timbers, and each horse is tethered on a rope which goes through a ring to a wooden ball too large to go through the ring. This allows the horse some freedom of movement and enough space to turn round to be tethered again facing outwards.

When on a long-distance march, horses might be billeted at town stops, often in cab or omnibus stables, in mews or inns. These billets would have been listed well ahead of time by a billet master, but they were also checked again the day before the unit was expected by a billeting party which went ahead of the rest of the unit. The stables had to be secure, but if lockable more than one key should be available in case the horses had to be evacuated in a hurry. The tack room should certainly be lockable, as should be the feed store if the unit was carrying its own supplies.

In all stables, and any other places where straw and hay were kept in bulk, there was a strict 'No Smoking' rule.

In less permanent situations, such as base camps in the field, tented stabling might be used. If no overhead cover could be provided, wind screens would be erected to help prevent chills. Ideally the horses should be on hard standing to avoid problems from wet and muddy feet. This standing should be raised above the surrounding ground and drainage had to be attended to regularly, without waiting for bad weather.

Within these tents, or outside with no cover, the horses would be picketed (tied to a horizontal rope). The picket rope could be at ground level, but it was preferable for it to be breast high to prevent horses getting a foot over it, and horses were tied to it on both sides. The rope should always be firmly secured and kept taut. The horses on the line should have at least 5ft space between them, or they would not lie down to rest.

It was possible to attach a single horse straight to a picketing peg, but this meant the head-rope should be short and a heel rope used. This was the preferred method of picketing kickers. Alternatively one foreleg could be tied to the peg with a rope 12–18in long. Kickers could also be restrained by hindleg hobbles, fitted above the hocks, with an 8in rope between them.

Picket line guards had to be posted at night and when no other attendants were present. They checked head and heel ropes and adjusted them if necessary; shortened nosebags if the horses were tossing them up to get at the feed at the bottom, and removed them when the horses had finished eating; ensured haynets were in a position that allowed the horse to eat comfortably, removed droppings and kept the lines clean; talked to the horses to help them feel secure; and at the slightest sign of a stampede, called for help.

The picket site should be chosen to keep the horses out of wind, rain and mud. It was recommended that anti-bomb traverses should be erected: these should be 6ft high, 3ft thick at the top and 7½ft thick at the bottom. They should leave a passage behind the horses 8ft wide. They could be made of plain earth covered with sods, or alternate layers of earth and dung, the final layer being earth. If it was all pressed down well, and covered with sods, flies were unlikely to breed in it.

Although the horse is a large animal, he does not have a large stomach capacity, and the best rule to observe on feeding is 'little and often'. In military situations this usually means three corn feeds and two or three issues of hay per day, and some grazing whenever possible. The day's ration should not be given in equal parts. The morning corn feed should be the smallest, the midday feed a little more, and the evening feed the largest as the horses will have plenty of time to digest it overnight. The usual corn was (and still is) oats, which are relatively soft and easy to digest. Barley could also be given, and was the usual choice in India (and was taken to the Western Front by Indian troops fighting there); in America maize (also known as Indian Corn) was often used. All these grains should ideally be crushed for easier digestion. Draught horses might also be fed dried split beans or peas, 'opened up' by mixing them well with chaff (chopped hay or straw). In the stable, this feed would be put in a manger; elsewhere nosebags were used. Whenever possible, hay should be given in nets, since if just put on the ground it can be trodden in or blown away. Nets were the only way to be sure each horse received his proper ration. The standard army daily ration per horse was 12lbs hay, 10lbs oats and 8lbs straw, with an additional 2lbs of oats for draught horses.

Hay is made of dried grasses, cut when the grass is tall and flowering. A small amount of any of the clovers or lucerne is good in hay, but hay which contains buttercups should be rejected as buttercups are a blistering agent. Newly made hay is not as good for horses as older hay, the general rule being that it needs a minimum of four months to mature. However, hay (or corn) which smells or looks mouldy should never be fed as it will do more harm than good. Good hay smells sweet and grassy.

By the start of the First World War, hydraulic presses were in use; these could reduce loose hay into bales; this was the only practical way to transport hay any distance, either by land or sea. Other feed items such as linseed were sold in compressed cakes, as was a form of 'compressed forage' consisting of chopped hay and oats, sometimes with the addition of peas, beans or maize. This was issued on field service, but had to be broken up and dampened well before feeding.

Some of the straw ration could be exchanged for other items of feed: bran, linseed, roots (carrots or turnips but not raw potatoes) or green food. The latter, and the roots, should be chopped or sliced small and mixed with the feed. Carrots are particularly popular and will often encourage a sick horse to eat. A mash of bran or bran and linseed mixed with hot water and left to cool before feeding was given once a week, usually on the evening before a day off. Bran is a mild laxative when given wet, as is linseed: both were soaked in hot water and left to stand until cool enough to eat.

At home, a lump of rock salt would be placed in the manger for the horses to lick at, otherwise they would have a little salt mixed in with their feed. Other than this lump of salt, the manger had to be kept clean and any crumbs of grain that were left, especially from a bran mash, were removed as they might go sour and taint the next feed.

In November 1918 the shipping programme allowed the importation of 93,100 tons of oats per month for use in the UK, France and Italy. By 10 March 1919 supplies had been reduced as necessary, until at that date shipments to France and Italy had reduced to 25,000 tons and 900 tons respectively; supplies to the UK had ceased in January. Sufficient stocks were then held in the UK to last until September 1920, when more as needed would be bought from home supplies.

Oats were originally supplied through arrangements made by the Director of Contracts with a firm of brokers, and by an arrangement with Canada which agreed to supply some amounts. Eventually, the UK's requirements, which were about 85,000 tons per month, came from Canada, the USA, Central America and the River Plate area. Only the Canadian supplies were bagged; the rest came in bulk. Floating pneumatic suction plants to deal with bulk oats were installed at each of the base ports in France; this saved about £10,000 per day in freight and stowage and reduced labour time.

As the requirements increased, forage committees were set up to encourage farmers to grow hay. With the shipping difficulties, the whole of the 1916 hay crop was taken into possession by the War Department. A little more than a million tons of this was actually needed by the army, and the rest was released for the use of farmers and the public. The same was done in 1917 and 1918, but the control was lifted for the 1919 crop. In other theatres, hay was obtained from India and Egypt.

Horses need up to 10 gallons of water a day. In stables, they usually take 3–4 gallons at a time, except in the early morning when they take about half this amount. They usually take about five minutes to drink. In permanent stables, water would be available from a tap or hose, and could be given to horses individually in their stable.

Watering should always be done before feeding, never immediately after. On long marches, frequent small quantities of water should be given, but never from public water troughs as these may have been used by horses with contagious diseases. The horses should not be allowed to drink their fill on the march, unless they were restricted to a walk for 30–45 minutes afterwards.

If using a stream for drinking, the place chosen for the horses should be downstream of that for the men's drinking water but upstream of that for their washing. Watering should commence at the lowest part of the stream, with successive parties working their way back, so the water was not fouled. Where the bottom was muddy and there was sufficient gravel available, some should be thrown in to prevent the horses stirring up the mud. Steep banks should be ramped in two places, one for access and the other for departing, the latter being downstream from the other.

It was always preferable to water from troughs, if necessary filled by pumping from streams. A makeshift trough could be created using a sheet of canvas stretched between four posts.

All the manuals on horse care emphasised the importance of daily grooming. It is important for the horse's health that his pores are cleaned of dirt and scurf; this helps prevent skin diseases and galls from saddlery rubbing on dirty patches. Each horse should have his own grooming kit, consisting of a dandy brush for removing mud and brushing out the mane and tail, a body brush to clean out scurf and dried sweat from the coat, a curry comb to clean the body brush, a wisp made of twisted straw, a sponge to wipe the eyes and ears and under the tail, and inside the sheath of male horses, and finally a hoofpick to clean out the hooves. Picking out the hooves also allowed incipient problems with shoes could be detected.

Horses change their coats twice a year, in the spring and in autumn, when they grow a thick winter coat. With that thick coat, they sweat if worked hard and it is difficult to get them dry, leaving them at risk of a chill. They also take longer to groom and the long coat may harbour lice, mange or other skin diseases. The practical answer to this was to clip them and give them a rug when they were not working. Horses which were transported from a cold climate in the winter to a location south of the equator needed to have their thick coats removed, and many of the transport ships carried clippers for this purpose.

Until the winter of 1917, British horses on the Western Front were normally clipped right out (the 'full' clip – i.e. all the hair cut very short), which may have been the cause of the heavy mortality rates the following spring. Riding horses continued to be clipped right out, but for animals which were only worked at the walk and thus did not sweat so much, the half-clip or 'trace' clip was used. This left a portion like a rug, with the head, neck and belly clipped clean, and the hair on the legs left long.

Clipping was done once in late autumn and again in late January/early February. After some experimentation, it was concluded that if the clipping was done once only, between mid-September and the end of November, the winter coat would continue to grow, but it would be short and thick, providing protection from the cold but still easy to keep clean.

In its natural state of carrying no weight, the horse does not need shoes, nor does it need to have the growth of its hooves pared away. But in a domestic situation, where the horse is carrying or hauling weight and needs extra traction to do so, or spends much of its working life on metalled roads or on rough mountain tracks, it does need shoes to protect its feet and gain extra grip.

The area through which the nail is passed is comparatively narrow, and a badly applied nail will soon cause lameness or a serious infection deep in the foot. At the very least, the shoe will not stay on. For this reason, and also because horses' feet are not all exactly the same, making and fitting horse shoes (farriery) is a very skilled job. Before the profession of veterinary surgeon came into being in the mid-eighteenth century, it was farriers who were the skilled horse 'doctors'.

Shoes were usually replaced at monthly intervals. With much roadwork, or on hard rocky ground, they would be worn down, and the horny exterior of the hoof would have grown enough to prevent the frog touching the ground, so even if the shoe was not worn, it would still have to be removed and the horn trimmed. The frog is a V-shaped spongy tissue on the underside of the foot which serves as a form of shock absorber, and it is important that it should touch the ground.

The shoes themselves have a central groove on the underside (for grip) in which nail holes were punched. There are three to five nail holes on each side, the farrier choosing how many to use. Usually six nails were used on the fore feet and seven on the hind. Fore and hind shoes were different shapes, as were the hooves, the front feet being almost circular, the hind feet narrower but still rounded at the front. Either could have a short section of the shoe at its rear, known as a calkin, turned down for additional grip on slippery surfaces, and one or two clips (one at the front for fore feet and two at the quarters for hind feet) which gripped the hoof horn. Additional studs could be added to prevent slipping in icy conditions.

Most regiments of ridden horses would use just one size of shoe, and many troopers carried spare shoes for replacement on the march.

The health of horses was dealt with by the Army Veterinary Corps. This organisation was formed in 1796, and received royal approval in November 1918.

At a time when most army transport, as well as offensive actions (cavalry), involved horses or mules, it was necessary to employ numerous veterinary officers as well as farriers, grooms, saddlers, etc., to maintain the animals' health and ability to work. Rather like the arrangements made for human sick/casualties, hospitals and organised evacuations for sick animals removed them from danger zones to rehabilitation centres.

It had long been obvious to the veterinary profession that good animal management was effectively good preventative 'medicine'. The ignorance of soldiers and officers about horses caused so much wastage in France in the First World War that it was decided to provide classes at veterinary hospitals on the lines of communication, in addition to those given at the Army Veterinary School at Aldershot. Each course took ten days and taught ten officers and fifty NCOs, with lectures and demonstrations on the basics of recognising the signs of disease, good horse care, proper fitting of saddles and harness to avoid sore backs and galls, the correct use of picket lines, and farriery. There were other topics but these were the most important.

Horses, like humans, suffer from numerous complaints. Some were incurable or sufficiently contagious to require the animals to be destroyed; some could be quickly cured so that the animal could get back to work, others could be cured but it took some time for this to happen and thus the animal could not return to work quickly.

Animals in barracks or semi-permanent camps could be treated in situ unless their problem was one which required hospitalisation for special treatment. For problems encountered on the march or in temporary camps, it was better to move the animal to an evacuation centre or hospital. This decision was made by the veterinary officer attached to the unit.

The commonest diseases included Glanders and/or Farcy, both caused by the same bacterium. Glanders is manifested by discharge from the nose, ulcerated mucous membranes inside the nostrils and swelling of the lymph glands beneath the lower jaw. Farcy is seated in the tissues beneath the skin, breaking out in open sores. Both diseases can pass to other animals. Equine influenza, like the human sort, is caused by a virus and is highly infectious. It can take up to six weeks for recovery, but there is little to be done except keep the victim warm and hydrated.

There are many skin diseases which can affect horses and mules. Mange is caused by a parasitic mite which burrows under the skin, and sweet itch is caused by bites from midges which are most active in the early morning or late evening. It is actually an allergic reaction to the anti-coagulant which the insect injects as it bites. Both these conditions are extremely itchy and affected animals may rub themselves raw against any convenient surface. Mud fever and rainscald are bacterial skin conditions most commonly found during long periods of wet weather. Rainscald is found on the back, mud fever on the lower legs. Oozing sores break out and serious swelling may occur. Treatment is to remove the crust of the sores and apply soothing creams.

Lameness has numerous causes. When it comes on suddenly, it is usually as a result of an injury, either that of striking the inside of one foot with the other, or by piercing the sole of the foot by treading on something sharp. One common cause was treading on discarded nails around camps, where wooden packing cases had been pulled open. Having removed the offending object (if it was still present), the usual treatment was poulticing to draw out infection. Other causes, where the lameness builds up over time, are more likely to be the result of strains or overwork, and can be cured by rest.

Saddle or harness galls are caused by ill-fitting equipment which rubs against the skin. Treatment consists of rest, and sometimes by using a different type of harness which does not touch the injured area.

Hospitals/Evacuation Centres

Evacuation of sick and wounded animals from their unit was considered essential, as keeping them with their unit impeded that unit's mobility and used personnel who should be combative. Evacuation stations were usually situated close to railheads. There were also convalescent depots which were not just for horses fresh out of hospital and those needing an extended rest. These convalescent depots grew out of the situation at the beginning of the war when hostilities on the Marne and the Aisne produced numerous debilitated horses. Some 3,000 of these were turned out to grass; in two weeks they were transformed and the idea of dedicated convalescent depots was born.

At the beginning of this war there were six veterinary hospitals for 250 animals each, eleven mobile sections, and two base store depôts, manned by 122 officers and 797 other ranks. By the end of 1917 this had increased to eight hospitals, four convalescent depots, seventeen veterinary evacuation centres, sixty-six mobile units, five base store depots, a bacteriological laboratory, and seven carcase economisers, manned by 651 officers and 15,200 other ranks.

Transporting Horses

While men could jump up onto or down from a train anywhere it chose to stop, horses required a platform to entrain and detrain. All stations used for horses had to be provided with ramps, and troughs and buckets should be available at all stops, even if the horses were to stay in their trucks. Ideally, larger stations should be chosen for loading and unloading horses, these being equipped with long platforms, sidings, and storehouses for feed. Gangs of porters had to be available to assist in unloading equipment. Where large trains were involved, a couple of days should be allowed between trains to allow for restocking feed and other stores.

The trucks were inspected to ensure that the flooring was strong enough to hold the horses and to withstand their pawing. Cross-battens were used to give good holding for the horses' feet; straw or a layer of earth would help in this, and also deaden the hollow sound which might frighten the horses. The trucks should be wide enough for the attendants to move in front of the horses to give them feed and water; there should be at least one attendant in each truck. Each railway truck could hold up to eight medium-sized horses with all their saddlery and feed for the journey, but only six draught horses.

The horses could be arranged either parallel to the rails, or transversely. The latter arrangement usually meant fewer horses could be carried in each wagon, in order to leave room for the grooms. It did, however, make for a more comfortable ride for the horses, and the noise of trains passing in the other direction was less likely to frighten them. For this reason it was recommended that horses travelling transversely should face away from the other track.

The Remount Manual stated that 'as a rough guide, stock should be detrained for five hours after every journey of twenty-eight hours'. At this time they could be fed and watered, walked around and allowed to roll.

Although the horses might walk up a gangplank onto the deck of a sailing ship alongside a quay, they could not walk down to the hold and the usual method was to hoist them up (and then down) in slings. Many horses did not take kindly to being hoisted in a sling, kicking and heaving, and, in one reported case, a horse kicked a member of the ship's crew over the side of the ship, injuring him so badly that he was unable to sail with the ship.

Although horses could be loaded onto ships quite quickly (as many as forty per hour in the right location and with practice), each ship had to wait until the whole fleet was ready to go. There could be long delays, which were not good for the horses, especially in the matter of ventilation into the hold, until such time as electricity allowed fans to be used. When the ships were moving, carefully angled wind-sails or rotating cowls were placed to direct air down the hatches, but this did not work while at anchor. For this reason, it was recommended that horses should be the last thing loaded, just before the ship sailed.

As well as organising the fitting of horse transports, the hiring authority required the owner to provide slings, ship halters, implements for mucking-out and general stall cleaning such as brooms and shovels, pumps and buckets for drawing water and serving it to the horses, and other hardware needed for feeding the horses. A supply of empty sacks should be carried, that could be filled with straw and used as padding for injured or exhausted animals.

There was a ban on smoking anywhere except the top deck, and often some 'guards' would patrol to enforce this rule, and also to ensure that the stalls were kept clean.

Training Horses

Although most of the horses purchased for the army were already 'broken' (i.e. trained to carry a rider or pull a vehicle), they still needed more training to make them ready for their job. This was done at the remount depots in the UK before they were sent on elsewhere. All this training, for riding and driving, is done in small increments, as the object is not just to accustom the horse to the idea of carrying or pulling loads, but also to develop his muscles in the process. He may happily accept the mental parts of his job, but if he is rushed into full work before his muscles are built up, he will soon 'break down' and be useless for a long time, if not permanently.

To a predator, horses represent mobile meat; being instinctively aware of that, they are always ready to take flight when alarmed. Young equines who have not grown accustomed to new surroundings and the objects and noises they meet are more likely to shy or try to run away when they encounter something new, or to misbehave on a windy day when moving vegetation or flags might conceal a lion or a dragon. The simple answer to this is to make sure that youngsters are accompanied by an older steady horse until they have accepted that the world is not going to bite them. However, even mature horses can take fright and bolt.

Modern police horses and ceremonial military horses are given 'nuisance' training so they become used to sudden and potentially frightening events: children's balloons, umbrellas opening, crowds cheering and even gunshots and artillery fire. As with all things equine, a wiser older horse who takes such things in his stride will help youngsters learn to tolerate all sort of 'dragons', even skateboards!

Getting horses accustomed to all the things they might encounter in the field of war was necessary. This included burning objects, the frightening sight of a mass of shining arms, regimental colours and standards, the sound of swords being drawn and returned to the scabbard, and dead horses, which are naturally frightening to a horse and a common sight (and smell) on the battlefield. In addition, they had to be taught to stand quietly when the rider used a firearm. They should not move after the weapon was fired until told to. Ideally they should be turned away from the direction of fire, so the bang was not directly over their ears.

By the start of the First World War, it was by no means certain that new army officers would be able to ride; this was an increasing problem as more and more young gentlemen grew up in towns rather than in the countryside. As a result, most regiments insisted that officers new to the regiment should attend a riding school for as long as the commanding officer thought necessary. It was essential that they could stay in the saddle at all times, especially at the end of a charge.

Saddlery, Accoutrements and Horse Clothing

The back of the horse is a convenient shape for riders, with a dip behind the wither to sit in. However, although a skilled rider can do everything bareback that the less skilled rider can only do with a saddle, in general a saddle with stirrups is needed, especially for military purposes. The mounted swordsman or lancer needs the security of seat which a properly shaped saddle gives, and being able to push down onto the stirrups allows extra security and a solid base from which to wield a weapon. Stirrups also allow a rider to stand up, giving him better reach in battle.

Saddles consist of a leather cover stretched over a wooden frame held together by steel arches at back and front called a 'tree'. This will be padded in such a way that it sits level on the horse's back, but clear of his spine. Some were fitted on top of a folded blanket or a felt pad called a numnah. The advantage of the blanket was that it could be folded more thickly as horses lost weight on long campaigns. The saddle is kept in place by a girth; this has a buckle at each end, which attaches to plain straps on the saddle.

Saddles have a stirrup on each side, consisting of two parts: the stirrup iron, a tall D-shaped piece with a flat base on which the foot rests, and the leather: a plain strap with a buckle at one end and holes near the other, so the length can be adjusted. The leather slides over a bar, the end of which can be turned up to keep the leather in place; this is not usually done as it is safer for a rider who falls off backwards for the stirrup to come off the saddle so he is not dragged.

By 1912, a new type of Universal Pattern saddle had been adopted, but in the early part of the First World War there was a serious shortage of horse equipment, exacerbated by the need to supply the initial mobilisation of the BEF. This shortage became so severe that the War Office appealed for civilian owners of spare hunter-size saddlery to donate it, complete with girths and stirrups; bridles were also required. Although such items could not be used by the BEF itself, they could be used for training.

The problem was caused partly by the small number of British saddleries that could make military saddles and harness, and partly by a shortage of the right sort of leather to make these items. However, both the leather and the necessary expertise were available in America and Canada, and by February 1915 these countries were providing large quantities of tack.

Bridles are the main method of controlling a horse, by the use of reins which go from the horse's mouth to the rider's (or driver's) hand. Just as the horse's back is conveniently shaped for a saddle, so the horse's mouth is conveniently shaped to take a bit, having a gap between the incisors at the front and the molars at the back; the bit sits in this gap, over the tongue, with the ends of the bit in the corners of the mouth. Control is gained either by pulling the bit straight back against the corners of the mouth, using reins attached to a bridoon bit (now commonly known as the snaffle), or by applying pressure to the bars of the bottom jaw with a curb bit. This pressure is greater or lesser, depending on the length of the side bars of the bit and the point at which the reins are attached.

From 1902 the preferred military bit was the Universal Pattern Reversable or 'elbow' bit, which is a single bit incorporating the action of both. This bit has two sets of reins. In the civilian world this is known as a Pelham bit, and since there are two places where the curb rein can be attached to the bit, the severity of the bit can be modified.

The bit is attached to the bridle with a strap called a cheek-piece, which passes from one side of the bit up through the loop of the browband, over the horse's head behind the ears, and down through the loop on the other side of the brow band and then buckles to a shorter cheek-piece from the other side of the bit. This strap incorporates a further strap which goes from below the brow band under the horse's throat, known as the throat-lash.

The bridle is held together by the browband, a leather strap long enough to fit across the horse's face just below the ears. It has a loop at each end, through which the other leather parts of the bridle pass, continuing up behind the ears. These consist of the strap of the noseband, and the cheek-pieces which hold the bit in place. The main cheek-piece incorporates the throat-lash which goes, as its name implies, under the throat; this prevents the bridle slipping forward. For added security, the cheek-pieces may be sewn together rather than buckled.

To put on the bridle, the reins are put over the head and laid on the neck, the headpiece of the bridle is then presented to the top of the face, with the bit/s in front of the teeth. Many horses will open their mouth to receive the bit, and some horses will even reach down to take it. For those which do not, the thumb of the left hand is slipped into the mouth in the gap between the two sets of teeth and pressed down to open it. In very cold weather a kind person warms the bit/s in his hand first.

The first winter of the First World War was particularly hard. Fortunately, the Director of Remounts had asked the Ordnance Department for more rugs and blankets at the end of 1914. Although saddle blankets could be used to keep equines warm at night in the winter, it was better to use shaped horse rugs which would stay in place. These covered the back and were cut to meet across the breast where they were buckled. These fitted rugs allowed the animal to lie down and move about without dislodging the rug. A padded surcingle passed over the back just behind the withers to buckle on one side. For use where the animal was under cover, or in dry climates, rugs were usually made of jute, bound with leather, but where they were outside and it was wet they needed to be waterproof and were made of canvas (at least until lighter waterproof materials had been invented).

The official instructions were that all tack should be handled with care, not dropped or thrown, which could damage the interior of the saddle, or laid down where a horse might step on it. When not in use, bridles should be hung up as though on a horse's head, and saddles placed on a rack or saddle horse with the cantle outwards. In the field where these items were not available, tack should be kept under cover with the saddle placed upright. Wet blankets should be spread out to dry. Wet leather should not be left near a fire as this would dry it out too much and render it vulnerable to cracking. All parts of the tack were to be checked at least once a week and repaired immediately if worn or stretching.

Surfaces which come into direct contact with the horse tend to get built-up accretions of sweat; this should be brushed off pads and washed off leather. This should be done gently with a sponge, warm (never hot) water and soap. The instructions do not define this soap, but it would have been a form of soft soap. Once washed, the leather should be dried with a soft cloth. A knife should not be used to scrape built-up sweat from leather or other materials. The Army Service Corps instructions for 1917 say that leather girths should be treated with grease to keep them supple, but the type of grease is not specified. Bits or other metal items, if made of iron or steel, should be wiped over with water, then with an oily rag, to prevent rust forming.

Cavalry

Cavalry is a generic word used to mean mounted troops. In the British Army these were dragoons, who were a sort of mounted infantry who rode to the battlefield and then fought dismounted; lancers, who were mounted troops armed with lances; and hussars, who were basically what is now known as light cavalry; later, heavy cavalry was introduced, used for massed shock tactics. There are many incorrect concepts about the cavalry, notably that their work consisted entirely of charges. It did, when necessary, but there were other duties which were just as important, so charging was not as important a part of their role as has come to be thought.

There are two principal requirements for a major cavalry charge. The first is that the terrain should be suitable: more or less flat, solid enough to allow the horses free movement at speed, and unencumbered with rocks or debris that might trip the horses, or other hazards. The second is that the enemy against whom the charge is aimed should first have been 'softened up' (i.e. their formation broken) by infantry or artillery. Horses are liable to pull up or jib when faced with a square bristling with sharp weapons, but are happy to pursue a running mass of men who can then be despatched with sabre or lance. There are psychological and practical issues here: firstly, it is easier for the attacker to kill a man when he doesn't have to see his face and look into his eyes. This effectively turns the opponent from a fighter to prey which can be hunted down. Secondly, since the fleeing enemy carries his weapon in his right hand, he can be attacked on his left side and is unable to parry. Most of the killing done by cavalry took place during such pursuits.

The work of the cavalry was more likely to involve reconnaisance, patrols, protecting the rearguard of a marching army or other escort duties, piquet duty, outpost duties and skirmishing. Reconnaisance was carried out by a small group of men, acting as 'the eyes and ears of the army'. When on the march, columns were preceded, flanked and followed by small cavalry patrols. Two men rode well in front, or 'at point', and small groups rode at the other positions. When in camp, piquets or vedettes rode around as an early warning system, piquets close in and vedettes further out, but still close enough to gallop back and give warning of approaching enemies. They often acted as a screen against incoming enemy, frequently placed in a curved line. Skirmishers moved about 200 yards in front of their lines and mounted snap attacks on the enemy.

There are several myths about the cavalry in the First World War. The first is that the army's high command was dominated by cavalry officers with ingrained ideas; the second that machine guns would always win over horses (sometimes they did, sometimes not, and the cavalry actually had some good successes against them); and the third that feeding cavalry horses was a waste of resources, especially shipping, that could have been better used elsewhere. This particular myth becomes obvious for what it is when it is remembered that cavalry horses formed only a small proportion of all the horses in that war.

All the draught horses except those used by the artillery were controlled by the Horse Transport section of the ASC. By the Armistice, this section consisted of 51,501 men, of whom 37,172 were in France and the rest in other theatres. There were also 1,755 farriers, 1,153 saddlers and 1,481 wheelwrights in France, with others in other theatres.

Medical officers were provided with a horse, and carried their equipment on mules or in a horse-drawn cart. Ambulances were made from four-wheeled wagons with high sides, a frame for a waterproof cover, and suspension points for stretchers. These could accommodate up to six stretchers or twelve seated patients, or a mixture of the two, with room for the attendants to move in the middle. They would be drawn by at least two horses.

Mobile field hospitals were necessary for active campaigns, to move forward or back with the troops, but stationed at a safe distance from the fighting.

These mobile hospitals required numerous wagons for stores, rations, surgeons' equipment, drugs and dressings, and even a basic operating room for bone-setting or amputations. Surgeons or assistants working among the troops giving first aid would also need horses to keep up with the fighting troops.

Disposal

After the war ended, there was the question of what to do with the horses in foreign theatres. At the beginning of the First World War, it was policy to allow contractors to remove carcases for free, although some would pay a small amount for them. Otherwise they were buried by AVC personnel. Towards the end of the war special buildings were erected for the disposal of carcases, allowing substantial amounts of money to be obtained for them. The French were experiencing a civilian horse shortage after their requisitioning programme, and asked if animals no longer suitable for military use by the British Army could be made available. This was agreed, and unwanted horses were branded with an inverted broad arrow before being sold at auction. Most of these were older horses, but were still useful for civilian work.

In France, over 28,000 equines were sent from hospitals and evacuation centres to a central abattoir in Paris where they were slaughtered and dressed for human food. Others went to local butchers in towns near veterinary hospitals. Those which were unfit for human food, and the by-products of most of the others, were sold to various trades. Seven installations known as 'Horse Carcase Economisers' were set up on lines of communication. Each of these had fourteen workers who dealt with up to thirty carcases per day. Hides were cured, and the flesh was dried and went into pig, poultry and dog food. Bones were crushed and degreased and ground into bone-meal. Oil from carcases (up to 5 gallons per animal) went to soap manufacturers, and the hooves became glue. Many of these products were sent to England.

The official statistics give some figures on these disposals and also of numbers of equines in the army at various times. By October 1917 a total of 225,856 horses and mules had been killed, died, destroyed or went missing, and 30,348 were cast in France and England. Losses were particularly high in June 1917, due to a very cold spring and the offensive on the Somme. At the end of the war 499,161 equines were sold for work.

Chapter 4

Animal Transport

Army Service Corps

The Army Service Corps (ASC) provided transport, both horse-drawn and mechanical, to the army. Its duties were defined in King's Regulations as 'furnishing transport, provisions, fuel, light and supplies, for the use of all branches of the army, and with the allotment of barracks and quarters and their equipment, as laid down in the Regulations for Supply, Transport and Barracks Services'.

There were several of these essential units. The largest, in terms of numbers of horse-drawn vehicles employed, was the Army Service Corps, which started its life as the Royal Corps of Waggoners in the Peninsular War. It became known as the Royal Army Service Corps on 27 November 1916 and later still as the Royal Logistics Corps. This corps dealt with most of the supplies needed, from the general to the more specific, such as clothing. With the exception of the artillery and a few cavalry units, all horse-drawn transport belonged to and was manned by the ASC. This included pack animals.

Prior to 1911, the ASC consisted of three types of road transport to carry ammunition, food and other stores. It was then reorganised in 1914 and numerous depots were set up; as there was a shortage of serving ASC officers, a number of retired officers were recalled to run these depots. On the declaration of war, the plans worked perfectly. The first soldier to land in France was Captain C.E. Terry of the ASC, to command the supply depot for the first overseas base. The first supply ships were being unloaded before any troops arrived.

The advantages of reorganising the transport and supply services were claimed to include the increased mobility of the expeditionary force; that there would no longer be a need for transport officers and baggage masters on the strengths of fighting units; that the roads in the rear of fighting troops would be clearer; that there would be a reduction in the time taken for refilling transport by trained ASC transport officers controlling supply trains; that there would be proper organisation for exploiting local supplies; that fewer horses would be needed in the field; that there would be better arrangements for evacuating the sick and wounded; and that the accompanying cattle and their slaughter would be kept well away from the fighting units.

Contrary to the popular belief that this organisation was a safe place for men at war, there were numerous casualties in the ASC:

- Killed in action: 79 officers and 1,507 other ranks
- Died of wounds: 42 officers and 967 other ranks
- Died of other causes (disease, etc.): 159 officers and 5,713 other ranks
- Wounded: 384 officers and 7,262 other ranks
- Captured: 22 officers and 98 other ranks

In addition, two ASC men were awarded the Victoria Cross.

*   *   *

By 1912, the administrative control of the corps was via the War Office. It was thought that the space at Woolwich being used at that time would prove inadequate in war-time, and a better site was chosen at the former Deptford foreign cattle market. It had a 1,000ft river frontage, covered storage of 32 acres, and was also close to the Royal Navy's principal victualling yard at Victoria Dock. The War Office took over this site seven weeks after the outbreak of war, and finally purchased it after the war.

On mobilisation in 1914, this site was staffed by three ASC officers and thirty-five civilians, and employed about eighty casual labourers each day. This was not enough, and to make up the shortfall retired officers were recalled. By 1 December 1918 the horse transport section alone consisted of 51,501 men, of whom 37,072 were in France, the rest in other theatres:

- On 1 August 1914 the ASC comprised 498 officers and 5,933 other ranks;
- by 1 August 1915 there were 5,224 officers and 156,190 other ranks;
- by 1 August 1916 there were 6,144 officers and 236,585 other ranks;
- by 1 August 1917 there were 9,195 officers and 314,552 other ranks;
- by 1 August 1918 there were 10,477 officers and 314,693 other ranks; and
- by 1 August 1919 the figures had been reduced to 5,937 officers and 109,849 other ranks.

However, the available statistics do not separate these numbers into those working with horse-drawn transport and others.

Carts and Wagons

Numerous and varied horse-drawn wheeled vehicles were used by the British Army. Many of these were used at home, carrying supplies to barracks and encampments, while numerous others were needed on campaign.

The smallest and lightest load carrier is called a cart, drawn by a single horse harnessed between two long (usually wooden) shafts. With a light load and good roads, the cart can achieve good speeds; the driver sits at the front of the cart and uses long reins. For a heavier load, the 'driver' walks leading the horse, with the reins hooked up out of the way. Such loads must be carefully balanced, with as much weight as possible at the front of the vehicle, as otherwise it may lift the shafts, and sometimes even the horse.

Two-wheeled carts, although obviously not capable of carrying such heavy loads as the four-wheeled wagons, did have some advantages. They could go on secondary roads which were not suitable for the heavier wagons, and if they should get into difficulties in mud, were more easily extracted with the help of a few men. Whatever the road, carts can move more speedily than fully loaded wagons, and can carry urgently needed stores from the larger wagons at the back of the column to the front. They are best when used on level ground, as an improperly balanced load makes it difficult for the horse to get traction on steep uphill slopes and it is more difficult to slow the cart when going downhill.

For heavy loads the army used four-wheeled wagons drawn by at least one pair of horses harnessed to a single shaft called a pole, extending from the centre of the wagon. Wagons could be driven by one man on a seat on the wagon, or, since they rarely moved at more than a walking pace, he might walk at the front with the horses. Where two horses were used, the 'driver' might ride one of the horses, sitting on the nearside animal of each pair. Saddles for this purpose had low cantles and very short fans, if any, and lacked the usual attachments to carry the driver's accoutrements; instead his baggage was carried on a small saddle or blanket pad on the off-side horse.

The best type of vehicle to use in the field really depends on the country involved. Although it is tempting to think that a General Service Pattern wagon could be used everywhere, it was usually better to employ the types of transport in common use in each location, as these will have evolved over the years to best suit the terrain. They also have the advantage of being available, rather than having to be transported from home to the theatre of war. Although heavy wagons are useful for carrying heavy bulk loads from ports or railheads to centralised stores, lighter and more speedy wagons or pack animals were better for supplies which have to keep up with moving troops.

General supply wagons were open-topped and their loads were kept dry (and secure from sticky fingers) with a tarpaulin. These wagons would carry all the necessities for living and fighting, including food and drink, tents, firewood, clothing and ammunition for both artillery and small arms.

The main Horse Transport vehicle on the Western Front was the standard four-wheeled General Service Wagon, which could be used where decent roads were available. The commonest version was the Pole Draught General Service (PDGS) wagon. There was a lighter version (LGS) which was better in hilly or roadless country, as it had a lower centre of gravity, four large wheels and a greater angle of lock on the front wheels. It required only two men and four horses, compared with the GS wagon with three men and six horses. LGS wagons could be either open or fitted with ribs to support a canvas cover (called a tilt). Other horse-drawn vehicles in use were lighter limbered wagons, water carts and mobile kitchens, but all these required a reasonably levelled and surfaced road. Elsewhere pack animals were used. On the Western Front, these were horses and mules, with a few donkeys, although the latter could carry only small loads compared with the others.

There are some statistics available on the numbers of wagons sent to the Western Front between August 1914 and the beginning of March 1919. The figures shown below are not specified as being horse-drawn, but from the context, and the fact that motorised lorries and railway rolling stock are listed separately, it is probable that these are all horse-drawn:

Guns and carriages	15,889
Trench guns and bomb throwers	27,466
Limbered vehicles	12,103
Four-wheeled vehicles	45,592
Two-wheeled vehicles	74,474
Ambulance wagons	557
Travelling kitchens and field oven wagons	3,594
Water tanks, carts, trailers	1,172
Telegraph cable wagons	129
Pontoons and pontoon wagons	1,152

At the beginning of the war, horse transport in France was based on two main depots. The main depot at Havre was the base where horses and reinforcements of personnel were located and trained. An advanced horse transport depot at Abbeville provided complete 'turnouts' of vehicles, horses and men, and some special teams of animals trained for particular purposes. Other depots were soon set up on the lines of communication.

Pack Transport

The average load for a pack mule is a little over 200lb, with all but 160lb of this being the pack saddle; larger mules can carry up to 320lb in total, smaller ones 120lb. They move at a speed of 2½–3½ miles per hour and can cover around 15–20 miles a day on good surfaces; a day's journey in mountainous country with bad roads was 10–12 miles loaded, 15–16 miles unloaded.

Mules can pick their way easily on bad tracks or steep slopes, and they move faster going uphill than down. However, they do not take kindly to sudden loud noises, such as gunfire or thunder. They will happily follow a leader (usually a mare wearing a bell), and do not need to be tied together head to tail. Some people believe they prefer a grey mare to follow. This loose configuration cannot be used in a baggage train or as part of a mixed convoy, when they had to be tied head to tail and led by a human.

Donkeys are much smaller than mules, can only carry about 100lb, and did not fit standard-sized army pack saddles. Their appetite is commensurate with their size, and they thrive on coarser food than mules. There were three donkey companies with GHQ in Palestine from October 1917, but none on the Western Front.

Pack Saddles
Each type of pack animal needs its own type of saddle, and these also vary according to the load. Most pack animals were mules, which can carry about 200lb and know exactly what that weight feels like, often refusing to budge if the load is heavier. The simplest form of pack saddle for equines consists of a blanket or thick pad, with pairs of sacks over the top, these either containing the load, or stuffed and suspended on either side to form a pad for the load. The first British Universal Pattern pack saddle was called the Otago, after the location in New Zealand where miners invented it, using it for riding as well as carrying their equipment. It consists of a simple saddle shape, held in place with girth, breast plate and crupper, and has additional straps fitted on the side to secure the load.

Another type, known as the Sawbuck, consisted of two crossed pieces of wood, much like a carpenter's sawhorse, with side bars to hold the crossed pieces together. Platforms could be added to the tops of these if required, or panniers on the sides.

A new General Service pack saddle with an adjustable tree was introduced in 1904 and has been in use ever since. The steel arches are quite small and the adjustable part is the way the side boards are attached. They can be turned as far as the horizontal, thus making it possible for the saddle to fit any animal, from a broad-backed horse to a narrow-backed donkey. They could be fitted with a wooden frame to carry machine guns as top loads, with additional lower boards to carry ammunition boxes. When used on a strong horse, they could also carry cacolets (a sort of folding chair attached one each side of the animal for patients who could sit up).

Where possible, personnel who were going to be working with pack animals should practise fitting and loading pack saddles. At home, a gymnasium vaulting horse was useful for this. It was valuable to be able to load and unload the animal quickly, as standing around under a load unnecessarily is tiring; pack animals should always be loaded as close as possible to departure time, and unloaded on long stops.

In the civilian world, columns of mules might be left loose to follow their leader, who wore a bell. This was not considered good practice on active military service, when they might come under fire or have to halt to allow other traffic through, so in most situations mules were led. This was done by holding the reins about 6in below the jaw, but on narrow tracks the handler would walk ahead on a longer rein. Where the condition of the terrain was difficult, the handler should use an even longer rein and go ahead confidently; once the mule had seen a difficult path traversed, he would accept it was possible and follow. A loose head was always preferable, although young mules might need more positive guidance if they became excited. In situations when the mule might want to escape, such as during shelling, one rein should be passed over its nose and back through the other ring of the bit, so that a firm pull would tighten the rein over the nostrils and stop the mule by restricting its breathing. Otherwise it was preferable to attach a lead-rope to the ring on the noseband.

When there was a shortage of handlers, mules might be linked together by attaching a rope from the neck-chain to the lead-ring of the follower, and from there to the saddle of the lead mule. Where the footing was particularly bad, these links should be undone to allow each mule to cross on its own. Steepness or rough footing do not bother mules unduly, but slippery slopes such as loose gravel or dry grass do. In this case the handler should attach a rope to the saddle and an extra man should keep upslope of the mule ready to pull if necessary. Otherwise, it is best to give the mule his head, but allow brief pauses to let him get his breath back. On steep down-slopes, the saddle-rope should be used, with the extra man behind to act as a brake. For narrow tracks on the face of a steep slope, or alongside a steep drop-off, it is essential to keep moving unless there is an obstruction that narrows the track to less than the width of the load. In that case it may be necessary to unload until past the obstruction. This is essential if the obstruction is on the up-side of the path, as if the load strikes the obstruction it may tip the mule over the edge. Steep turns also require care; they should be taken slowly, and the mule should have his head turned so he can see the edge.

With mules, it was recommended that the men should work in pairs with their mules standing by; thus each will have thorough knowledge of the other's mule and saddle. This also means they can perform the loading together, and once on the road the mules, being familiar with each other, will follow without necessarily having to be linked. Columns of more than forty animals should be divided into smaller units.

Harness

There is a simple rule on carrying loads on wheeled vehicles: the heavier the load, the more horsepower is required, whether from an engine or one or more horses. And where horses are concerned, this requires different connections from the vehicle to horse, and different types of vehicle.

Vehicle harness has three functions: to attach the horse and its motive power to the pole or shafts by heavy straps called traces; to provide some stopping power with breeching (in harness use, this is a strong broad strap which fits about 12in below the horse's tail) on which the horse can 'sit' when going downhill; and to connect the horse's best pulling point (the neck and shoulders) to the rest. There are two methods of doing the latter: the horse collar or the breast harness. The horse collar is used where weighty loads are involved. The collar needs to be fitted to the individual horse by adjusting the padding, so they are not used in battlefield situations where the loss of a draught horse cannot be rectified simply by finding a spare horse. The other type is the breast harness, which is easily adaptable to any horse. As its name implies, it is a substantial item which fits round the horse's breast, with straps to hold it in place over the neck just before the wither, and to connect it to the traces. In some cases, where the 'driver' rides, further straps may connect from the traces to a crupper. The harness is kept in place by a girth.

With multiple pairs of horses, some linkages are needed between each pair and the vehicle. The first of these is the swingletree (known as a singletree in America), which is a large triangular metal piece which attaches to the vehicle by a swivel at the apex of the triangle and is wide enough across the base to attach the traces in a straight line. The other is called the whippletree (sometimes called a double tree or, confusingly, a swiveltree). This is a horizontal bar, connected from its centrepoint to the vehicle by a chain running between the two horses, and from its ends to the team in front. They can be hooked up in sequence when using more than four horses. Apart from their use to provide multiple horse power to a wagon, they are essential for moving artillery pieces which often have to change direction at speed. Bridles for draught horses were much the same as those for ridden horses, but with much longer reins.

For some weeks prior to the Armistice, there were few purchases of saddlery, harness and general leather goods and the trade ceased almost entirely from that time. Almost no compensation was necessary as the manufacturers were happy to return to work for civilian customers.

Artillery

As well as wagons to carry goods, horses were used to move artillery pieces until mechanical devices came into use during the course of the war. For the heavy guns, this usually meant vehicles fitted with caterpillar tracks.

Horse artillery consists of two main pieces: the limber (closest to the team) and the gun. Sometimes there is a third part, called the caisson, which is a two-wheeled cart, used either to carry the gun and ammunition or spare wheels and limber poles. The gun, when in action, sits on its two wheels and a rear extension called a trail, which rests on the ground to give the gun stability, while the limber is removed to the rear with the horses. On the move, the trail is attached to the limber, which also has two wheels.

The rough rule for the number of horses required for each gun says that the size of the ball dictates the number of horses: four-pounder guns needed four horses, six-pounders six and nine-pounders twelve. An artillery battery of six heavy guns could involve as many as 200 horses, as well as those for ammunition and supply wagons plus up to ten for the officers and support staff such as surgeons and farriers.

The horses used for guns by the artillery were (and still are) of the light draught type, usually black, dark grey or dark brown. Pale greys and particoloured animals were not used. Most came (and still do) from Ireland.

In the late nineteenth century, some estimates were made for transportation needs for a six-day period. For an 800-strong infantry regiment, thirty-two wagons each carrying 1,200lb would be needed; for a cavalry regiment of 400 men and 400 horses, fourteen wagons; for an artillery regiment of 200 men and 160 horses, twelve wagons; for the RE of about 400 men, sixteen wagons; for the RE's Park, where repairs were carried out, twelve wagons; and for the general's and brigade staff, twelve wagons. So for eight regiments of infantry, three of cavalry, two artillery batteries, the RE's Park, and the general's and brigade staff, a total of 411 wagons were needed, plus twenty-five for the commissariat which included butchers and bakers. Taking three days' provisions with the force, and a further three days to follow, added 360 wagons, and for casualties, breakages, etc., another 193 wagons, giving a total of 964 wagons with four horses each, plus twelve to twenty wagons for shoeing smiths and a forge, plus a carpenter and harness maker, gives ninety-six two-horse wagons, the whole totalling 4,411 draught horses. In addition, there were riding horses for the NCOs (289 horses), command officers (48), the senior officer and his staff (18), and mounted veterinary surgeons (8), giving a total of 363.

In the First World War, Army Service Corps Horse Transport (ASCHT) companies were formed in several categories:

- Depot companies
- Companies in divisional trains
- Companies under command of higher formations
- Reserve park companies
- Small-arms ammunition companies
- Local auxiliary transport companies
- Army auxiliary transport companies

ASCHT companies filled a variety of administrative, recruitment, induction, training and resupply roles. Base companies were in the UK or at the port of entry to a theatre of war. Advanced companies were located further up the lines of communication. There were several of these, based at Aldershot, Catterick, Bradford, Woolwich, Southport, Le Havre and Rouen (Regular Army). Others were formed after February 1915 at Park Royal and Blackheath in London, with base and advance depots in Egypt, Salonika and France; after November 1917, depots in Italy, Ireland and North Russia (a mule transport depot) were added.

In addition, each division of the army had some transport under its own command, known as the divisional train, which carried stores and supplies, providing the main supply line to the brigades of artillery, infantry and other attached units. There were 364 ACS companies of this sort. The train moved with the division.

Convoys and Trains

As far as pack animals were concerned, these were mostly mules, but might include horses and donkeys, as well as other non-equine animals such as oxen or camels, but the latter were not used on the Western Front.

Loading a fresh load from dumps should be done under the supervision of one experienced man, leaving his pair to sort and make up the loads. The animals should be fully loaded, thus reducing the number of animals in use, although some spare animals without saddles should always be taken along. About one spare per thirty animals is the right number. In general, a broken saddle means the load is also damaged so spare saddles are not needed, but when an animal has developed a girth gall, fallen or been wounded or killed its saddle and load can be transferred to the spare. When a column of pack animals is returning unladen, their girths should be loosened by one hole before starting off.

March Discipline

In most military situations, horse-drawn transport was used in large groups (often known as trains) and it was therefore necessary to organise how these moved. There were numerous reports of chaotic marches in the nineteenth century, mainly caused by senior officers bringing vast amounts of baggage with them on campaign. Some thought their seniority and/or social position allowed them to position their wagons at the front of the column of march and there was also much argument about which regiments were most important and therefore should be at the front, so it was necessary to draw up a set of rules on march discipline.

Another booklet on march discipline was issued in the First World War for 'officers who have not as yet had any practical experience, so that when they are called upon to perform any of the duties mentioned, they will have some knowledge of what points require special attention'. This suggests that the topic was not part of the general training for officers. Proper march discipline had two purposes: to ensure the well-being of the animals, and to avoid interference with other traffic.

The first point was the desired location of officers in a column or convoy: the senior officer should be at the front, with warrant officers, company sergeant majors, and company quartermasters (of the Army Service Corps) at the rear. Mounted transport officers should be at the head of their unit, and mounted NCOs should be within the column and not on the flank. These officers and NCOs should drop back at intervals to check the driving and the state of the wagons, doing this by pulling into the side of the road to let their vehicles pass. Crossroads were the best place to do this.

The drivers were to keep their wagons well to the left on roads (except in France where it was the right). This was easy enough on good main roads but less so in France where the camber tended to be steeper, in which case the wagons might have to pull into the ditch. Mechanical transport always took precedence over horse-drawn.

As with columns of motorised vehicles, minimum distances in horse-drawn columns were maintained between units – 500 yards for artillery brigades and other battalions, and 100 yards between all other units, while a gap of of 50 yards should be maintained between each section of twelve vehicles to allow other traffic to pass.

Unless a man was needed on the box to work the brake, it was forbidden for civilians or unmounted men to ride on the wagons; the only exception to this rule was when written (and signed) permission with a time limit had been given by an officer. No weapons or equipment of unmounted men should be carried on or attached to the sides of vehicles, nor should the men themselves hang on to the wagons to aid their progress, especially on hills. No other non-authorised items were to be carried on wagons or motorised vehicles.

One man should walk behind each wagon to operate the brake or a 'drag shoe'; the others should march close up to the rearmost wagon of their unit, leaving no gaps. Dismounted men should not walk idly along where they chose, but should march properly in threes.

The wagon with the slowest horses was to be situated at the front, the others taking their pace from this. However, the pace was never to be more than 3 miles per hour or the marching men would not be able to keep up. If a wagon had to stop for any reason it should pull out of the column, regaining its place at the next halt. If irreparably damaged, its load should be distributed between the other wagons. The proper distance between wagons was 4 yards, and this should be maintained on the march.

On arriving at a steep hill, the column had to halt; the wagons would then be sent on one at a time at intervals which varied with the slope of the hill. Going uphill should not be hurried, or the horses would be out of breath before reaching the top. If they had to stop before the top, a drag shoe or chock should be put under the wheels to prevent the wagon slipping back down. For really steep hills, the teams of the rear half of the column were unhitched and taken to the front where they were hitched in to double up the teams; once at the top, all the horses would be unhitched and taken back to the bottom to bring up the rest of the wagons. Going downhill required a slightly different routine, with a special drag-shoe applied to the leading wagon. Once safely down, it should move along far enough to allow the rest of the column to join it on the flat, and the drag-shoe was taken back up for the next wagon.

Before the column moved off, three spare responsible men were needed, ideally NCOs but experienced privates could also be used. On routes other than main roads, one should go ahead as a scout to find the best way (and remove obstacles if possible), the second should stay at the front of the column to set the pace, taking signals from the scout and passing these back as needed, and the third went to the rear to watch for loose loads and ensure these were put right. Even the smallest columns should not move off until these duties had been allocated. A mounted NCO should be placed at each crossroads, to check that no traffic was coming and to stop any traffic which might try to cut in to the column, with another mounted NCO at the rear of the column to ensure that march discipline was maintained. Another should be available to assist if the road needed to be cleared to allow other vehicles to proceed.

An orderly on a bicycle should attend the column to convey orders and information along the column. If any part of the train should become detached, this orderly should inform the officer commanding the train of its precise location. In the event of 'alarms', any men not in charge of horses should run to the front of the column to receive orders from the officer commanding their company; those of the rearmost company should go to the rear for their orders.

When setting out, there should be a 5–10 minute halt after about 2 miles when the men should check saddlery and harness, tighten girths and check feet and shoes; the horses should be allowed to stale (urinate). After that, halts should be for 10 minutes, and were usually made every hour. For these halts, a spot sheltered from the wind should be chosen and the horses allowed to turn their backs to the wind or driving rain. For especially long marches, a halt of 30–60 minutes should be made at about two-thirds of the way, and the horses given a drink and a small feed of corn, the halting places usually being chosen for their closeness to a water source. On these halts, girths should be loosened and the bit removed from the horse's mouth to facilitate drinking and feeding. At all halts, the drivers should check round their horses, looking for badly fitting harness which might rub and cause galls, and for loose shoes, but otherwise should remain at their horse's head. If it was not possible to move off the road, they should stand on the right side of the road, facing the centre. The section sergeants and NCOs should check that the loads were not working loose, then generally check the horses and wagons and report to their officers. In cold weather, it might be wise to put rugs on the animals. Ridden horses should be unsaddled and their backs hand-rubbed to restore the circulation to the areas where the rider's weight had rested.

The care of horses on the march was of prime importance, in particular the avoidance of unnecessary fatigue (dependant on the military situation at the time) by riders dismounting at short stops and walking with their horses on steep hills, up or down. Every opportunity should be taken for the horses to drink and pick at any suitable vegetation. Wherever possible they should be ridden on the soft roadsides rather than the hard road, unless this would raise a dust which would show the enemy where they were. The pace should be suited to the surface, trotting on soft ground and walking on metalled roads.

During these halts, ridden horses should be allowed to graze. Watering should take place after a couple of hours, ideally three hours after the morning feed and then once or twice more during the day after loosening the girths and taking out the bits. Each wagon should carry a bucket for this purpose, or horses could be unhooked and led to water with an NCO in charge. If watering from streams, the first lot of horses should be taken downstream, and each subsequent group a little further upstream so as not to pollute the water. Public watering troughs were not recommended as they might carry contagion. Where the column was not likely to arrive in camp before 1.00pm, a halt should be made at midday for the animals to be fed. Girths should be loosened, and bits removed before nosebags were put on. However, unnecessary stops, even brief ones to allow those behind to catch up, should be avoided, as it was when starting off from a halt that draught animals had to exert the greatest effort.

It was preferable that the distance should be covered fairly rapidly; too slow meant the weight was on the horse's back for longer. The speed of march by the Royal Horse Artillery, cavalry and mounted infantry was usually about 5 miles per hour, including halts; this required a steady trot at 7–8 miles per hour with occasional walking. Field artillery moved at about 4 miles per hour, including halts, Army Service Corps at about 3 miles per hour. With a long column it was important to avoid checks caused at the front; a distance of 50–100 yards should be maintained between troops and sections. The first and last half hour of a march should always be done at a slow pace. During these slow periods, the men could smoke and talk, but should not be allowed to loll in the saddle as this can lead to sore backs.

A proportion of spare draught horses, harnessed as leaders, at a rate of 10 per cent, should accompany the column.

On long journeys, there had to be overnight stops at designated places. There were two of these between the front and the depot at Abbeville, at Hazebrouck (where there was also a designated stopping place in a field) and at Therouanne. This was a regular journey, arriving at Therouanne on Tuesday, Thursday and Saturday of each week. Advance notice had to be sent to Therouanne of the numbers of wagons, horses and men. At stops in fields, guards were to be posted at night.

Rations and forage were carried with the column for the first night, but at least one spare wagon accompanied the column to carry hay, and there were also travelling kitchens, at a rate of four per battalion. These might have waterproof covers erected if needed, but in that case the cooking pots should be empty.

When a unit or detachment was ordered to change quarters by march, the veterinary officer was to submit a marching-out report listing the sick and lame horses, with a copy of the route. If accompanying the march, he should state with which detachment he would go. At the end of the march he should submit a marching-in report, with details of all the horses listed above, and including any subsequent casualties. This report should show which horses, if any, were left behind and who was caring for them. No horse should be left behind if it could possibly be moved by rail. If the veterinary officer did not accompany the march, he was to send a copy of the marching-out report to the receiving veterinary officer.

Chapter 5

Mechanised Transport

All road transport was under the control of the Army Service Corps (ASC) and was referred to as Horse Transport (HT) or Mechanised Transport (MT).

The army had been taking an interest in mechanical transport since the Boer War, when the Royal Engineers used some steam traction engines. By 1885 driving these was part of the syllabus of instruction for young Royal Engineers officers. In 1903 several engines, with an officer and twelve men known as the 'Dirty Dozen', were transferred from the RE to the ASC after the War Office decided that the responsibility for mechanical transport should lie with the ASC. A couple of years later mechanical transport was included into planning for mobilisation. By 1908 it had been agreed that 900 vehicles would be needed in the event of mobilisation in addition to those already held, but nothing was done to acquire these. By 1913 the War Office had decided against tracked vehicles, although they retained those which they already had. By 1914 several ASC companies were training in mechanics at Aldershot and gradually converting their horsed transport to mechanised transport.

An Inspectorate of Mechanical Transport was set up in 1903 and it was soon recognised that mechanical transport would increase rapidly and by 1907 all young Army Service Corps officers received basic training in its use. The best then spent up to eighteen months as apprentices at some of the great engineering firms. By 1910 most mechanical transport was driven by the internal combustion engine. Later, in February 1918, a Road Transport Board was set up, with one of the members being an officer of the War Office Transport Directorate. Later discussions suggested transferring the Road Transport Board's functions to the Ministry of Ways and Communications. There were three sub-committees, dealing with technical matters, lands and buildings, and the general administration, efficiency and economy of working with mechanical transport.

There were numerous types of vehicle in use by the British Army; these included three armoured cars (made by Rolls-Royce, Austin and Jeffrey Quadrant), ten ambulances (including Argyll, Buick and Crossley), fourteen caterpillar tractors (including Austin, Bulock, Daimler and Foster-Daimler tractors and Holt and Ruston caterpillars), eight cars (including Ford, Rolls-Royce and Sunbeam), twenty-six lorries (including Albion, Daimler and

Wolseley), fifteen steam road locomotives (including Burrell, Foden and McLaren) and three motorcycles (Clyne, Douglas and Triumph). As early as 1914 the BEF used London buses (with internal combustion engines) in transport emergencies to span the gap between the railhead and the battlefield.

There was much discussion on the relative merits of 3- or 5-ton lorries for transporting materiel. Before the war it was thought that the heavier lorry would be difficult to handle on bad roads, but this did not hold good in western Europe where there was a network of well-maintained roads. Attempts were made to add trailers to these lorries, but it was not a success: the motor used more fuel, the tyres wore out more quickly and the trailer slowed down the lorry.

Motor cars were mainly used by senior officers and staff officers, and also by officers in charge of large columns of transport vehicles or marching troops. The preferred cars were the Crossley 20/25 and the D-type Vauxhall, both often in camouflage colours. The Vauxhalls for this task were made at the rate of seven per week.

Motorcycles were gradually coming into use before the war, and in 1911 a motorcycle show was held at Olympia. Several army representatives attended and asked for some samples to be supplied for trial. These machines had a top speed of 40mph. The original idea was that they would be useful for convoy work, when officers had to ride up and down the column ensuring all was well, but it was finally decided that they were not suitable as 'an officer's mount'. Instead, they were mainly used for dispatch work and that was to become their main role during the war.

Omnibuses were used by the British Army to carry personnel, initially from towns and cities in the UK to the Western Front, and then for tactical movements of large numbers of troops within the theatre. They were also used to transport men from the front to their billets, and for this reason (among others) they were kept in a bus park behind the lines. With the seating retained, they were not useful for anything else, however, they could be refitted as ambulances for the slightly wounded. By removing the body, they could be converted into general purpose lorries.

The B-type bus held twenty civilian passengers or, with the windows boarded up, twenty-four soldiers with their packs, rifles and greatcoats. They were also used as wireless and equipment centres, pigeon lofts and covered transport for food, field kitchens, field workshops, armoured cars or anti-aircraft gun-carriages. This last use soon wore out the wooden chassis, often in as little as three months.

There are numerous reports discussing how many motorised vehicles the ASC had, but these vary considerably and do not match up. The only reliable figures are those in the official statistics, which give these figures:

Before August 1914 the War Office had only eighty mechanical vehicles. During the period from 9 August 1914 to 2 March 1919 the following numbers were sent to France:

Motor ambulances	4,921
Motor cars and chassis	13,474
Trailers, vans, tenders	2,363
Motor buses and charabancs	370
Motor store and workshop lorries	38,436
Steam lorries	334
Tractors	1,564
Motorcycles	26,375
Cycle cars (sidecars)	15,920

Several years before the war it was realised that many mechanised vehicles would be needed in the event of war, but the government did not want to spend the money to buy them, so a scheme for registering civilian-owned vehicles was set up, with another scheme for subsidising these vehicles. Owners were paid a small amount for agreeing to surrender their vehicles for a reasonable price if war was declared. A list of approved vehicles was issued and a subsidy scheme was set up to encourage civilian owners to buy these and hand them over to the War Office on mobilisation. When war broke out it was soon found that the approved vehicles would not be enough and others would have to be impressed.

Impressment officers were given, in advance of mobilisation day, various instructions and lists of the vehicles needed. These did not include any in the government's subsidy scheme, which could be identified by the attached tow-hook. The locations for collecting them were mostly in the greater London region, but there were some in Coventry and Guildford. The list given to the impressment officer reporting to the Kensington Gardens depot included twelve powerful motorcars of 45–50hp (Landaulette Daimlers or Napiers preferred), fifty moderately powered motor cars of 12–15hp (Panhard or Napier taxicabs preferred), five vans and one motor charabanc seating twenty-two to twenty-seven persons.

Impressment officers were to encourage the drivers of these vehicles to enlist for one year (at a pay rate of 6 shillings per day). Impressment officers would have a civilian engineer with them to give the vehicles a quick (but not comprehensive) examination. The vehicles should be lubricated and have a full tank of petrol. The Impressment officers were also given a set of printed receipts. The officer commanding the depot had a basic staff of one clerk, two storekeepers and one cook. He had to clothe, arm and equip the drivers who enlisted with their vehicles, and arrange to feed them.

It soon became obvious that the subsidised vehicles would not be enough, so the government took steps to control and increase the output of the vehicle manufacturers in the UK. Manufacturers were restricted to one or two definite types, and the country was divided into areas, each with resident inspectors to liaise between various manufacturers and so hasten production. By the end of 1914 about ninety suitable vehicles were produced each week; by July the following year this number had increased to 250 and by October 1915 production had increased to a point where it was possible to release 1,000 vehicles to government contractors to assist in their work and relieve the railways. However, the following summer 400 of these vehicles had to be recalled for army work.

As well as the vehicles produced by British manufacturers, contracts were placed with American manufacturers. Due to financial considerations some of these contracts were cancelled in 1916, but they soon had to be reinstated, with the Americans supplying some seventy lorries a week. Although Fords were desirable vehicles, owing to the pacifist inclinations of Henry Ford few were supplied, although he had no objection to his vehicles being used as ambulances. Later in the war Ford amended his views and many Ford lorries joined the fleets operated by the ASC.

Soon after the BEF had departed for France, a vehicle reception depot was set up at Aldershot. This soon filled up and the depot was moved to Camberwell. This, too, soon filled and a better location was sought. The main criteria were that it needed to be close to London and near a mainline railway station and main roads for easy access to the mobilisation and embarkation depots. After inspecting many sites, Kempton Park racecourse was taken over and worked successfully throughout the war.

As part of the vehicle subsidy scheme, a reserve of mechanical transport personnel had been formed, and drivers of the subsidised vehicles were encouraged to join this reserve, so that when the vehicle was called up, its driver went with it. As with the vehicles, the supply of skilled men soon fell below demand and training schools were set up for drivers at Hounslow and artificers (mechanics) at Aldershot, Grove Park and Birkenhead. A training school for drivers and mechanics of tractors was established at Avonmouth. Only one of the personnel at this unit (Mr Rose, of Holt's representatives) had any experience with caterpillar work, and he taught there for several months.

To economise on the numbers of men in mechanical work, women were employed and trained to replace men on the lighter vehicles and a special training school was set up for them at Osterley Park. One problem resulting from the general manpower shortage was that over 30,000 mechanical transport men were transferred to fighting arms. This soon led to increased casualties among the vehicles and a strain on repair facilities.

To handle minor problems, each lorry carried its own toolbox, containing:

- 1 adjustable spanner, Seabrook or Billings & Spencer or similar pattern, 10–12in
- 1 adjustable spanner, King Dick or Billings & Spencer or similar pattern, 6–7in
- 1 set of 3 tubular spanners, $^1/_4$–$^5/_8$in
- 1 screwdriver, 9–12in
- 1 pair pliers, side cutting, 6–7in
- 1 fitter's hammer with handle, 24oz
- 1 cold chisel, ½ by 6in
- 1 can lubricating oil, half-pint
- 1 pair 'footprint' wrenches, 8–9in
- 1 half-round file, second cut, 10in
- 1 round file, 8in
- a file handle
- 1 set of three fixed double-ended spanners, from $^3/_{16}$–$^7/_{16}$in
- 1 pin punch
- ½lb soft copper wire, No. 20 SWG
- ½lb tape, rubber primed
- 1 tool bag or roll

A central repair depot for vehicles in the UK was initially set up at Camberwell and others were added as the work increased. By August 1917 it was decided that a much larger workshop was needed and one was set up in Battersea. Even then, it was realised that much larger premises were needed, with a central store. When nothing suitable could be found, a 700-acre site at Slough was taken over and plans to build there were drawn up but for various reasons building was delayed until the scheme was overtaken by the Armistice.

Vehicles in France needing repair were passed to the AOC at Rouen and Amiens, but the numbers of those waiting soon built up to impossible levels. Until October 1914 light running repairs were done by the AOC but after that all repair work went to the ASC, which trained the repair personnel as well as doing the work. Several heavy repair shops were established, the first in Rouen in February 1915. By August 1918 there were five of these heavy repair shops, and a retrieving section; most of this work was done by German prisoners of war under British supervision. By the end of 1918 some 6,700 lorries and tractors, 7,000 cars and ambulances and well over 12,000 motorcycles and sidecars had been repaired.

Obviously all these repairs needed spare parts; at one point the base department held enough spares for nearly 400,000 vehicles of 377 different types. There was a slight difficulty here in that different manufacturers used different names for identical parts, and some even changed the names from time to time. The base mechanical transport department eventually compiled vocabularies for every type of vehicle; this took two years to complete.

Workshop records included a stock register showing receipts and issues with full details of the items (date, voucher number, number received and source) and number issued; a workshop repair book; and a record of unservicable stores. It was not necessary to account for items that were considered 'expendables': bolts, nuts (except special nuts such as gland nuts or union nuts), split pins, washers, rivets and asbestos packing. The records show the workshops were using over 20,000 spare parts per month.

It was decided that demands for spare parts and tyres for motorcycles belonging to signal companies should be dealt with before any others. The equipment for the machines should include a spare set of tyres. Triumph machines were preferred, and each signal company should have as many of these as possible. The alternative was a Douglas.

It was not practicable to take all vehicles needing repair to central workshops, so mobile workshops were fitted out in large lorries, ideally Daimlers or Leylands, using a 40hp engine. The chassis was covered with a platform on which a four-sided closable body was fitted; the two long sides could be opened out and secured horizontally with wooden supports. The top half of each side opened upwards to form a roof extension while the lower half extended the floor space. Mobile workshops carried a crane for removing engines, a lathe and a drilling machine powered by a petrol engine, a tool-grinding machine, fitter's benches and vices and a collection of the necessary hand tools.

One common repair was replacement of rear axle drive shafts. The cause was found to be the vehicle having been towed to start when in first or second gear; only top or third gear should be used for this. Clutch springs, spare leaf springs for lorries and cars, and motorcycle fork springs all had to be changed if any cracks were detected. Maintenance allowed for the replacement of front and rear springs, including front and rear leaf springs.

Tyres of lorries and motorcycles had to be replaced regularly. A variety of tyre presses was kept, including those for American lorries and Foden steam lorries. When wheels were sent loose for re-tyring, they had to be labelled with the make of the lorry, its War Office number, the mileage done and whether it was a front or back wheel. Lorries sent in for re-tyring were to be dealt with in this order: all gun supply lorries first, lorries loaded with ammunition second, and all others third. Although theoretically tough, solid tyres needed to be handled with care and not dropped, as the vulcanite between the steel rim and the rubber could distort and crack.

A fourteen-day supply of expendable items such as oil and grease should be kept by each transport unit. These were presumably used for purposes other than servicing vehicles, as an order was issued that they were not to be used to light houses or billets at night.

Every drum of oils and other lubricants should be inspected by a workshop officer before issue. Units should not be allowed to accumulate stocks and so should draw their requirements daily. Lorries should have a full tank of petrol (about 25 gallons), plus a reserve of 10 gallons in marked tins. Cars had a reserve of 2 gallons and caterpillars 50 gallons, while another 2 gallons per lorry was to be considered an 'iron ration' and stored separately from the issuing stock.

Lubricating oil for American motor lorries was to be used for these vehicles only, as they were designed to use a thin oil. Although it could, technically, be used in other vehicles, the War Office did not approve this use as it was more expensive than the standard British type.

Petrol use records had to be kept; each driver had a sheet for petrol consumption to keep in his logbook, for recording the date, the number of gallons received, and details of each journey when completed, or to make a note if a vehicle was laid up. These were to be handed in weekly to an officer who filled in the mileage column. From this an average mileage per gallon was calculated for each vehicle and checked against a list of consumption for different makes of vehicle; if consumption was excessive, the vehicle went into a workshop for overhaul. The petrol storeman kept a ledger of all amounts drawn by each vehicle (signed for by the driver). The officer commanding was supposed to check this ledger at regular intervals.

Just under 8,000,000 gallons of petrol was supplied through Calais, just under 5,000,000 gallons through Rouen, and just under 1,000,000 gallons through Havre.

There was continued discussion throughout the war on the best type of container for petrol. Initially petrol for lorries was supplied in 50-gallon steel drums, while for other vehicles it came in 2-gallon tins packed in wooden cases. Although many of these tins were lost, they were refillable. The packing cases were also lost, but a move to lighter cases was found to be a false economy as the wastage on cases rose from 10 per cent to 50 per cent. Until the middle of 1916 all petrol used by the BEF was filled in Britain, mainly at Portishead near Bristol. By this time petrol consumption had risen to more than 2,000,000 gallons per month and filling installations were started in France, with tank storage at Rouen and Calais with filling machinery and can and case manufactures. In addition, 4-gallon cans were tried but found unsatisfactory.

By early 1917 the supply of tinplate for cans and timber for cases was becoming difficult and arrangements were made to send petrol in bulk to base supply depots. During that summer 180 railway tank trucks, each of 5,000-gallon capacity, and 200 road tankers, each of 600-gallon capacity, were sent over to France, the petrol being pumped into the tank lorries from the train trucks for onward despatch to unit headquarters. However, it was found necessary to filter the fuel transported in this way and this was done when refuelling vehicles.

Until 1917 all the petrol for home use was bought from the principal distributing firms, and in France from the Asiatic Petroleum Company, both amounting to 2,000,000 gallons of motor transport fuel and 600,000 gallons of aviation fuel per month. After this time most of the fuel came from America.

Drivers were issued with a book of drivers' orders, in which they were exhorted to drive carefully and in a way that would avoid strain on the vehicle, starting and stopping gently and using the brakes as little as possible. The considerate behaviour expected of a driver included not covering pedestrians and marching troops or other vehicles with dust or mud. Troops on the march should be passed slowly, leaving as much room as possible, especially cavalry. There was an absolute speed limit for lorries of 10mph but when in traffic or passing lorry parks this was reduced to 6mph (except for motor cars which could do 10mph). On rough roads, cobble stones or pave, the top speed should be 5mph.

On approaching a steep hill a lower gear should be engaged; likewise, when descending steep or otherwise dangerous hills a lower gear should be engaged to use the engine as a brake. The side-brake (now handbrake) should be used as much as possible and the footbrake only as an emergency brake. On long descents side- and foot-brakes should be used alternately to avoid overheating.

Loaded lorries had precedence over empty ones. Loaded lorries should avoid the edges of roads as these might be too soft for the weight. They should also avoid other soft ground to prevent becoming bogged down. If they did become stuck, chains, ropes, stones or sacking should be put under the rear wheels for traction, or another passing vehicle should be asked to tow them out. Drivers should not allow their vehicle to be overloaded. The load should be equally spread over the floor space. Ammunition should not be carried at the extreme tail end of the body.

As well as always driving on the right (except in the UK), vehicles should pass on the right when overtaking; when meeting oncoming traffic, they should pass it on the left. Vehicles should not halt near road junctions, bridges, abreast of a column of troops or transport, or in any other place that might block a narrow road. When entering a main road, speed should be reduced and the horn sounded.

Drivers should immediately report all defects in their vehicle to their section sergeant, as well as any loss or damage to equipment such as tools or spares. The chief causes of breakdowns and accidents were stated to be:

failure to check that brakes, steering, non-skid chains and lubrication systems were in order and lamps were filled; excessive speed in towns and villages, on cross-roads, around sharp corners, and on level crossings or bumpy roads; driving too close to other vehicles; and failing to sound the horn when overtaking. Accidents were to be reported immediately to the company sergeant major or other senior NCO. Addresses should be obtained for witnesses, owners of damaged property or other vehicles involved, and handed in with the report on the accident and a plan of the scene. When repair work was necessary, work not listed on the driver's transport order must not be undertaken without a written order from an officer, nor should the driver take a vehicle out of the park or garage without orders. Engines should not be kept running when the vehicle is stationary, and no man was to leave his vehicle without permission, leave it unattended or enter any café or estaminet while on duty.

When taking over a vehicle, the driver should check that there was sufficient oil in the engine, that the radiator and petrol tanks were full, that all lubrication reservoirs were filled, that the brakes worked properly and that all the spares and tools listed were present. He should also go over all the nuts with a spanner to ensure they were tight. Vehicles with twin rear tyres should be checked regularly to ensure no stones had lodged between them, as this could damage the tyres. To avoid loss of log books when vehicles were transferred between units, the log book should always be kept in the lorry's cab.

Only the authorised driver of a vehicle should be allowed to drive it, but second drivers should be allowed a turn at driving. There should be a lookout man in the back of the lorry; his job was to warn the driver of traffic approaching from behind, and stand in front of the vehicle when reversing to guide the driver.

Vehicles were to be kept clean. The upholstery of cars was to be looked after and covered if possible when in the garage. Folding hoods should be handled carefully, should not be folded when wet, and should be fastened down securely. Cars that were not garaged with a Motor Transport company were to be brought into the company headquarters for examination at regular intervals of not more than two weeks, this being recorded in the log book. Log books for all vehicles were to be kept up to date.

All motor vehicles had to carry lighted lamps after dusk. One should be placed on the extreme left edge of the vehicle to indicate its position, and rear lights should also be carried on the left side of the vehicle.

Each lorry was to be provided with a fire extinguisher, which was to be kept fully charged, and all the men given instruction on how to use it. Care should be taken when filling petrol tanks; this should always be done with a funnel which was kept with the vehicle. Filling should be done in daylight. If filling at night was unavoidable, it should be done under the supervision of an NCO who was responsible for seeing that there should be no lights within 15 yards (unless electric) and that no one within 20 yards was smoking. Care should be taken that no petrol was spilled onto hot exhaust pipes or on the ground.

In frosty weather, radiators and acetylene generators were to be emptied unless anti-freeze had been added. When radiators were drained, the cylinders, pumps and water piping should also be thoroughly drained. Other methods of protection against frost included putting lighted lamps under the bonnet, or running the engine every two or three hours if there was sufficient petrol and men available to do it. All water should be drained unless anti-freeze had been added. This could be 23 per cent methylated spirits in water (this was prone to evaporating slowly so needed topping up), 26 per cent glycerin, or sodium nitrate at a rate of 4lbs per gallon of water (however, this tended to seep into the joints in the system).

Although railways were the best method of bulk transport, it was not always possible to use them to reach the intended destination. However, large-scale movements by road were subject to complex arrangements, mainly for traffic control purposes. One difficulty that large convoys of vehicles encountered in France was that the French used a circular system of routes for the supply of their troops and frequently changed these routes without informing the British. Sometimes, especially in Belgium where the roads were only paved for the width of one vehicle and had deep mud on either side, convoys of motor vehicles met head on, leaving one group having to fight their way out of the mud.

During the battle of the Somme, when the main road to Verdun was under German fire and the railway line could only carry a small amount of traffic, men and materiel had to be transported over the 45 miles from Bar le Duc to Verdun on the only main road. The volume of traffic moving daily along this road led the French to conclude that the only solution was to take over the road completely and treat it like a railway. The plan was to close a 45-mile stretch of the road to civilian traffic, dividing it into 7- or 8-mile sections, all connected by telephone. Each section would have a traffic controller, and numerous warning signals and signposts, all lit up at night, were provided. Speed limits for each class of vehicle were laid down and a marche table like those used on railways was drawn up. Columns of lorries then entered the section according to a timetable, with their progress signalled ahead. Sidings were provided for relief lorries to pick up the loads of any lorries which broke down, and breakdown gangs were kept available to clear the road. Lorries were never unloaded on the main road but were diverted off it; to save time waiting for horse-drawn wagons to collect it, they discharged their loads into dumps for later collection.

Each unit was divided into three 'fleets' – one of heavy lorries for ammunition and engineer stores, one of lighter lorries and omnibuses for personnel, and one mixed fleet to reinforce the others or carry any loads the others could not take. A similar scheme was planned by the British for a 20-mile stretch of the Arras–Cambrai road, but neither scheme was actually put into practice.

The booklet 'Regulations for the use of the Provost Marshall's Branch' included nine pages of instructions on traffic control and the operation of traffic control posts. Speed limits for open roads and built-up areas were laid down; all lorries were to have a lookout man at the back; a 25-yard gap was to be left between every six vehicles and a 50-yard gap between every twelve vehicles (for any overtaking lorries to go into if meeting oncoming traffic); there should be no double parking when columns were stopped; and if the column had to pause at junctions, cross-roads or other blockages, they should stop at least 50 yards from it, and pull over to their side of the road. A growing number of accidents at unmanned level crossings led to a rule that road traffic should always give way to rail traffic, and no vehicle should start across a level crossing until there was plenty of space for it on the other side. If vehicles were too close together and had to stop, one might be left on the line.

During these operations, as many as ninety men were needed for each division; at other times fewer were needed. There were only twenty-five military policemen for each division, with only ten of these available for traffic control. At first they were supplemented with other men drawn from the division, but since these men had had no training for the role, it was not entirely satisfactory, so a hundred men from each corps were trained and employed permanently.

Control posts were placed at all points where side roads joined main roads, and were issued with cards showing the direction of the traffic circuits at each post. All vehicles were to keep strictly to the laid down traffic circuits, and should not go into other corps' areas without specific orders. All columns or single vehicles had standing orders to comply with instructions given at control posts. There were no restrictions on despatch riders. Large columns should be preceded by an officer to warn all control posts on the route.

A booklet of traffic orders issued by the Second Army in early 1917 included what it called 'Hints for NCOs and men employed on traffic duty'. These included the need for tact, and to stand where approaching traffic could be seen easily. When needing to hold back traffic to allow pedestrians or traffic proceeding in another direction to pass, the left arm should be held out horizontally from the shoulder. When stopping vehicles at cross-roads, the traffic controller should stand in the centre of the road, give the halt signal to the driver he intended to stop, then turn round and signal to the other vehicles to proceed. Main road traffic had precedence over side road traffic, and loaded vehicles had precedence over empty vehicles.

Traffic men were also instructed to look out for staff cars flying flags designating the ranks of the officers within, and to facilitate their progress. The flags were:

Union Jack	Commander-in-Chief
Red and blue	General headquarters
Red flag with black cross	Army commanders
Red flag with white cross	Corps commanders
Red flag	Divisional commanders
Dark blue with a red zig-zag	Artillery commanders
Dark blue with light blue and red	Royal Flying Corps

The main method of moving troops by road (other than marching) was the 3- or 5-ton lorry, the men sitting on benches on each side with their equipment on the floor in the middle. As each group of men sat down, their equipment would be handed in to them (and handed out first when disembarking). They should not lie on the floor, especially at the rear, as this brought a risk of asphyxiation from exhaust gases.

If a lorry held twenty men, a battalion of 1,000 men needed a 'stable' of fifty lorries, plus some extras to replace break-downs. A load master should be in charge to ensure no time was wasted in the process. With practice, and judicious location of the empty lorries, it should be possible to load 1,000 men in twenty minutes. For larger numbers of men, the process would take longer, and the officer in charge needed to contact the commanders of other infantry units to arrange their arrival at the loading points. He must also arrange for his lorries to have petrol and his drivers to have food. He would need extra lorries to carry these, plus a mobile kitchen and lorries for towing when needed. With large columns, each group of thirty or forty vehicles should have an officer in charge, following his group in an open car.

All vehicles should have a description of their unit painted on the dashboard. Apart from this, and the official registration number on bonnets and tailboards, no other markings should be added anywhere on the outside of the vehicle. Details such as 'load not to exceed 8 tons' should be on the inside of the cab. No fancy names or mascots (e.g. horseshoes) were allowed.

It was felt necessary to mark the tail vehicle of each section (defined as twelve vehicles) in a convoy to ensure a proper gap of 50 yards was left between sections. The marker was a red disc. There was some disagreement as to where the disc should be fixed, and what size it should be; this took eight weeks of correspondence to resolve. The conclusion was that the disc should be 12–15in in diameter, mounted on the tail board. Then a front disc of 9in diameter, hung over the radiator cap of the front vehicle of a section, was proposed and approved. The rear disc might cause difficulties as it would not be seen if the tailboard was open, in which case it could be hung from the edge of the tailboard in its horizontal position. It was also suggested that it could be mounted on a stanchion above or to the side of the lorry body. A double disc should be attached to the left hand side of the rearmost vehicle. After a side discussion on whether this scheme should be extended to horse-drawn vehicles, it was decided it should not.

The duties of the officer in charge of ASC transport units included general supervision of mobile workshops; he also had to instigate enquiries into accidents involving ASC MT vehicles. Much of the work of officers commanding mechanical transport units consisted of ensuring that their units were fit for duty, and getting the paperwork done properly. This included an up-to-date register of all mechanical transport in each corps. Any vehicles which were moved to other units were to be transferred in the books; in order to avoid constant changes, this was done on a weekly basis. For this purpose the week ended at 6.00pm on Saturday.

A Senior Supply Officer (SSO) was attached to divisional headquarters and was responsible for everything relating to supplies in the division. He was to live close to the divisional headquarters, and had a car supplied for his own use. Under him were four supply officers (one each for the three brigades and another for divisional troops). They should live with the supply section of the train and were provided with a horse and groom. Beneath each of them was a requisitioning officer and one supply section train officer. They were in charge of the vehicles, horses and personnel of the supply section of the train. There was also an officer commanding supply section trains, usually a major. He was responsible for the efficiency and care of personnel, horses and vehicles of the whole supply section of the train.

A supply officer was responsible for the loading and distribution of supplies on the supply column. He was not responsible for the individual lorries. He was considered a most important officer; he should be a good organiser, cool under pressure and a hard worker, as the efficient and even distribution of supplies to the various units was dependent on his abilities. He had a motor car and a clerk to assist him.

There was a standing order that guns should not be hauled by lorry except in cases of great tactical necessity, and then the lorries must be driven very slowly and only on good roads.

One of the hazards that were faced by men of the supply columns was enemy attacks. By March 1918 the intense enemy bombardment swept practically every road in the Ypres region with 5.9in shell and shrapnel, and gas masks had to be worn while delivering supplies. That July, nineteen ammunition lorries were waiting outside Ypres for heavy shellfire to die down when one of the lorries was hit by an incendiary shell and caught fire. Its ammunition exploded, destroying three more ammunition lorries and twelve siege park lorries. Four others were saved by the swift action of Corporal A.R. Wadsworth, who reversed them out of harm's way. During the rescue of the fourth lorry, he had to wait in a ditch for over two hours to avoid the constant explosions. He was awarded a Distinguished Conduct Medal for his actions.

After the Armistice, vehicles returning from overseas as surplus to requirements or needing major repairs had to be stored at Kempton Park as the new centre at Slough was not ready for them. There was very little cover or hard standing there; the best that could be done was to organise a drainage scheme and remove all stores and parts which would deteriorate from damp.

However, in December 1918 there was much pressure to evacuate Kempton Park to allow the resumption of racing there. The undesirability of moving vehicles on saturated ground was pointed out, but the rapid evacuation was insisted on and the result was as predicted: the ground was badly cut up and the drainage system destroyed. Vehicles became bogged down and much damage was done in extricating them, exacerbated by the reduction in the numbers of skilled drivers and artificers due to demobilisation. The operation took longer than necessary and more damage was done to the vehicles themselves in the process. Eventually enough hard standing was available at Slough for vehicles to be stored there.

Chapter 6

Railways, Inland Water Transport and Docks

At the beginning of the twentieth century the most effective way of moving large quantities of goods (and large individual items such as heavy artillery pieces) over long distances at reasonable speed was by railway.

Railways in Britain were privately owned, but the government took control of them as soon as the war started, doing this through a committee made up of railway companies' general managers. The official chairman was President of the Board of Trade, with the general manager of the London & South Western Railway as acting chairman; the rest of the committee consisted of the general managers of the ten leading railway companies. The purpose was to ensure that the railways' rolling stock, locomotives and staff should be used as one complete unit in the best interests of the state. In all, 130 separate lines were taken over, including those of the twenty-one leading companies. Forty-six very small lines were not taken over.

Before the war, neither the government nor the railways had experience of the amounts of traffic (goods and passengers) that would need to be carried for a modern war. There were many difficulties with shortages of rolling stock, rail repairs and a significant loss of men to the armed forces. This also applied to canals in Britain, about 1,000 miles of these being owned by the railway companies.

Some trucks were privately owned and these might only be engaged for a single, one-way journey. They could only be reloaded with the specific permission of their owners for each train. This situation was not tackled until December 1915, when some railway companies formed groups to pool the use of wagons between them. However, this only applied to open-topped trucks.

Some 185,000 railwaymen enlisted during the course of the war but only about 40,000 of these ended up with the specialised railway troops. Over 21,500 of these railwaymen died during the war. The specialised troops, run by the Royal Engineers, included construction workers. Experienced plate-layers were in great demand for repairing bomb damage and later building marshalling yards and new lines, both standard and narrow gauge. In many places single track lines were widened to create double tracks. One construction company was even sent to Gallipoli, but soon transferred to Mesopotamia to work on the Baghdad–Basra line.

Other branches included the Military Forwarding Department, which handled personal parcels for the troops. These included socks and other small hand-knitted garments from women's voluntary groups and one year there were fifteen trucks full of Christmas puddings. This department was started with two officers and eight clerks. At its high point there were eighteen officers and 500 others. They also dealt with the free daily and weekly newspapers donated by their publishers.

When it first arrived in France in August 1914, the BEF had no control over the French railways or ports, having to use those which had been allocated to them. This became a problem as soon as the numbers of troops increased. There were 81,000 in August 1914, 269,711 by December 1914, and nearly 1,000,000 by the following December. This vast increase in troop numbers led to the splitting of the British Army into five new armies, the first two appearing in March 1915; by 1918 three more had been formed. There was also a sixth army, the Mediterranean Expeditionary Force. Each of these armies was headed by its own general, and had its own base. It took four to six weeks to get a new base into operation.

The French had to be persuaded to allow more railway traffic to be dedicated to BEF use. The attitude of the French authorities to the use of their railway system was firm: in a theatre of war the whole of the railway system was indivisible and had to be under a single authority, not being divided by armies or areas; whilst the military and technical elements should look after their own interests, they should not act independently of one another.

The railways near the front were referred to as being 'in the zone of the armies' and were under the control of the Commander-in-Chief; those at the rear were known as 'the zone of the interior' and came under the Minister of War. In December 1917 this division was abolished and the whole system was then brought under the Minister of Public Works; 'and transport' was added to this title in July 1918.

Shortly after the beginning of the war, the British Inspector General of Communications suggested that the BEF should have its own independent line of communication. This idea was firmly rejected by the *Directeur des Chemins de Fer*:

> As regards the working of the railways, allow me to draw your attention to a principle to which we adhere rigidly. It is that the military railway service must be absolutely independent of all military authorities other than its own, and must be centralised in the hands of the Director of Railways who takes orders from no one but the Commander-in-Chief. It is impossible to hand over to one Army among a group of Armies a line

or system of communication of its own. To do so would render the continual strategical group movements we are effecting impossible. The Commission Regulatrice, the Commissions de Reseau, and ultimately the Directeur des Chemins de Fer must be the sole intermediaries between military authorities and the technical railway service. The same rule applies down to the lowest grade; at stations a military auhority must give no order but must apply to the Commission de Gare ... I shall be very much obliged if you will kindly issue the most explicit instructions on the subject, so that on the French railway system the military railway service may retain the complete independence assigned to it by our regulations.

The basic system for all supplies was that they were delivered to French ports by ship or barge and from there went by railway to base store depots. Some went on immediately to advanced storage depots, also by railway. They were then moved on to a railhead relatively close (i.e. not more than 40 miles) to the front, from where they were taken by road to their destination. Although a high proportion of rail traffic was ammunition, it also included food for troops and fodder for animals, casualty evacuation (often as many as thirty-three ambulance trains per day), engineering stores (between thirty and forty trains per day), road stone, timber and so on. Much of this was bulkier than ammunition (a ton of hay took up much more space than a ton of shells, for example). Specific days of the week were allocated for different kinds of supplies (mainly stores and clothing) and on the days in between items which could not be included in those categories were sent up by lorry.

Railways were the only feasible way to carry the bulk stores required. By 1918 each division of about 12,000 men needed about 1,000 tons of supplies every day. This was the equivalent of two fifty-truck trains, each of which could carry as much as 150 lorries. Problems began about 7 miles from the front, which was within the range of enemy artillery, so main supply dumps had to be established before this point was reached, partly because the gap could not be filled reasonably with horse-drawn transport, as horses could not maintain a daily round trip to and from the railheads. Mechanical vehicles alleviated this difficulty once they were in general use. These convoys were often referred to as 'supply trains' but did not involve railways, being a convoy of horse-drawn wagons or motorised lorries.

Havre and Boulogne provided main bases for supplies and ammunition, with Amiens as the major railway junction on the southern line of communication, through which most *rocade** trains passed. Other depôts soon had to be opened to reduce congestion; several of these held stocks of sandbags,

*A train which connects separate lines to each other.

barbed wire, picks and shovels for the advanced Royal Engineers' parks; another at Paris held blankets and winter clothes.

The French store depots, *stations-magasins* or regulating stations, were operated by a committee known as the *Commission Regulatrice*. All demands were to be addressed to this committee, which arranged for the desired items to be drawn in bulk and sent to the front on the daily supply trains. These trains were to run to their destinations intact; nothing was permitted to be added to or taken from them en route. Troop trains were handled on an equally rigid basis, although they did not all go to the same place. The troop commanders were not allowed any input, merely being told where and when to embark; they were not even told their destination.

Very few, if any, stations in France had platforms level with the floors of goods trucks. Instead, portable ramps were provided and the regulations gave detailed instructions for their use, which included the time to be allowed for loading and unloading. Cavalry and infantry units were allowed one and a half hours, other units two to four hours (with an additional half hour if using ramps). Men and animals were both carried in box trucks, while large items of equipment such as guns travelled on flat-bed trucks, on trains which were made up in set formations and kept available at central locations well away from the front.

Lack of forward planning meant train use tended to be ad hoc. Before the Somme offensive, between five and twelve ammunition trains per day had been sufficient, but after mid-1916 the number grew rapidly to between forty-five and ninety. Many ammunition problems stemmed from the transportation system, which developed from the lower demands of 1914–1915 and the 'daily usage' restrictions. The increase in ammunition production encouraged field commanders to use more and demand more still. But Boulogne could handle only 2,000 tons per day, so sending 5,000 just led to queues of ships awaiting berths to unload.

In November 1916 a shortage of rolling stock began to make itself felt, with as few as sixty-two wagons available each day at Havre. A shortage of maintenance labour led to a reduction in the carrying capacity of lines and a backlog of supplies in the ports slowed the discharge of ships for lack of wharf space. This all continued until it began to look as though the whole system would seize up. As a result Haig, who had previously been amenable to ad hoc changes as his administrators deemed necessary, realised that the difficulties encountered during the battle of the Somme meant that changes were essential. He enlisted a civilian railway expert to sort out the problem.

Eric Geddes (who was knighted in 1916 for his services to the government) was already in government service. Lloyd George had first given him responsibility for small arms production, and then for the filling of shells. Haig was impressed by the man and his achievements, so gave him the rank of major-general and appointed him Director General of Military Railways and Inspector General of Transport. Geddes already had railway experience, gained first in India and later, after his wife's health had dictated a return to the UK, with the North Eastern Railway, where he was made Deputy General Manager in 1911.

Geddes' appointment ruffled a lot of feathers among the military men, partly because he was a civilian (they had already reacted badly to a civilian's report on docks) and partly because they saw him as usurping their positions. Prominent among these were the Quartermaster General, the Assistant Quartermaster General and the Inspector General of Communications. Maxwell, the Quartermaster General, made a great deal of fuss until Haig reassured him personally that Geddes had not been sent to replace him. Haig remarked in his diary that

> there is a great deal of criticism being made at the appointment of a civilian like Geddes to an important post on the Headquarters of an Army in the Field. These critics seem to fail to realise the size of this army and the amount of work which the Army requires of a civilian nature. The working of the railways, the upkeep of the roads, even the baking of bread, and a thousand other industries go on in peace as well as in war! So with the whole nation at war our object should be to employ men on the same work in war as they are accustomed to do in peace. Acting on this principle I have got Geddes at the head of all the railways and transportation with the best practical and military engineers under him. At the head of the road directorate is Dr Maybury, head of the road board in England. The Docks, Canals and Inland Water Transport are being managed the same way, i.e. by men of practical experience in these matters. To put soldiers who have no practical experience of these matters into such positions merely because they are generals and colonels, must result in utter failure!

Two weeks after his appointment Geddes wrote to Lloyd George, laying out what he saw as the two principal problem areas: labour and transportation. Labour was required in road-making and maintenance, quarrying, on the railways and at the base ports, plus forestry and various tactical jobs at the front. The total required for September 1916 was 64,500 men but in August there were only 52,000. The difficulty was in finding enough men to do this work without taking them from fighting units. Amongst the solutions proposed by the new works directorate was the use of women in clerical jobs in France and as cooks, and the use of prisoners of war.

The largest requirements were for road maintenance (17,000 men), at the base ports (24,000 men) and in forestry (11,000 men). Much of the timber needed could be found in France rather than having to ship it in from the UK, but this required both access to the French forests and experienced lumbermen. Wood was needed for the French Army as well as the British, from the humble stakes for wire to fuel, shoring up trenches, railway sleepers, and making huts. Although reluctant at first, the French finally agreed to allocate specific areas of forest to be clear-cut by a special battalion of Canadian lumbermen, with the resultant timber shared between the French and British Armies. This problem alleviated, Geddes was able to turn his full attention to transport.

He regarded transport as encompassing five areas – docks, canals, railways, light railways and roads – and he saw many of the difficulties coming from a lack of policies. Docks as well as railways were being used on an ad hoc basis rather than as part of an overall policy. Geddes found that far from there being a policy on canal use, the BEF only reverted to them when there was a lack of trains. He noted that although the commander-in-chief was keen to use light or narrow-gauge railways, and despite the fact that the French used them extensively, again there was no policy on their use. As far as road repairs were concerned, the Quartermaster General's department had asked for road-stone in quantities based on their guesses of what might be available, rather than asking for what they actually needed. His conclusion was that no central policy on transport existed, and that the whole thing should be under the control of one man.

At the end of 1916, when he found that the detailed work required in the role of Director General of Military Railways and Director General of Transport, not to mention oversight of docks, canals and roads, was consuming too much of his time, Geddes handed over much of the work of controlling the military railways to Sir W. Granet, previously the General Manager of the Midland Railway. Geddes remarked to Granet that his private observations had led him to the opinion that soldiers asked for less than civilians, and actually less than they should have, as a result of the cheeseparing attitude of the Treasury. Geddes began to order vast amounts of railway building and maintenance materials; after the war he was accused of extravagance, and replied: 'All war is extravagant, and provision for the great unseen contingencies of war necessarily involves what must appear surplus provision.'

Originally the BEF had the Railway Transport Establishment, consisting of approximately 100 all ranks, including six deputy assistant directors (mostly captains) and twenty-four railway transport officers (RTOs). After Eric Geddes was appointed Director General of Transport in 1916, the existing directorates of railways and inland water transport were taken over from the Quartermaster General's department, and three new directorates were formed: Light Railways and Roads; Docks; and Transportation. It was intended that Light Railways and Roads would supplement road transport, employ expert personnel to install the most suitable plant and appliances in docks, and generally introduce whatever methods were thought to be advantageous, while Transportation would take over the establishment of the Director of Railways to expand it and make it the medium of communication between the armies and all the various transport services at the front and on the line of communication. The idea was that whatever needed to be moved, the army would apply to the transportation directorate which would select the best medium to use.

Part of this reorganisation was intended to speed up the turnaround of supply vessels at ports. Some 1,000 tons per day were being landed at Havre and Calais, plus food, ammunition and engineers' supplies. One branch of the Transportation Directorate was run by a Director of Docks. This was not entirely successful; rapid emptying of ships was considered more important than careful checking of goods arriving, and much had to be written off as losses in transit.

The organisation of the line of communication between each fighting unit and its railhead was under the orders of the Inspector General of Communications. Once informed by GHQ of where it was to go to refill its supplies, the Inspector General of Communications selected the railhead and informed the unit's mechanical transport columns of that railhead and the rendezvous at which it was to deliver. Having done this, the column returned to the railhead to await orders for the next day. The Quartermaster General at GHQ coordinated these movements between railhead and unit, and, if necessary, establish precedence to avoid clashes. The Inspector General of Communications also selected the type of transport to be used and the coordination of road, rail and water transport. He was responsible for the punctual arrival of stores.

There was also a Director of Railway Transport, who administered the provision of transport and its personnel. The Railway Transport Establishment was under his orders, and he was, in his turn, responsible to the Inspector General of Communications. He was also required to report on any points on the railways which were vulnerable to the enemy. He was also responsible for the inland waterways, with a proviso that if use of them was on a large scale, a separate IWT directorate would be formed. This happened in October 1915.

The routes or conditional timings on which trains might run were known as *marches*. Usually one *marche* per hour in each direction was specified for strategic troop movements, and those time slots could not be used for other purposes. Other *marches* were for mail trains, coal trains, etc., while others were allocated to *trains journaliers* (mixed trains carrying government officials, small parties of troops or small consignments of special goods; if there was room, some passengers might also be given a space). The regular daily supply trains were known as *regulier* or *ferme*; others for irregular traffic such as

Armoured cars and transport camels.

A British motor company at Salonika.

British troops embarking onto French motor transport. Note the equipment on their backs.

A busy field kitchen.

A camel supply train at Kut.

A canteen wagon.

A casualty evacuation barge at Gallipoli.

Clothing being
fumigated at
Gallipoli.

A convoy of
motor transport.

Cooks with Soyer
stoves.

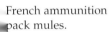

A French provision train.

French ammunition pack mules.

A French wire-cutting automobile.

A Holt tractor pulling heavy ordnance.

Horses at Gallipoli.

Horse barges at Gallipoli.

A horse-drawn ambulance.

A Kegnesse half-track, using a flexible belt instead of metal segments.

'L' beach at Gallipoli.

A Dennis lorry. Note the solid tyres.

A mobile pigeon loft.

A recruitment advertisement for ASC drivers.

An advertisement for Pratt's Motor Spirit.

A repair lorry with lathes, etc.

Troops in Flanders boarding omnibuses.

Unloading supplies at a railhead.

A troop convoy.

Women mechanics at a Women's Volunteer Reserve garage.

Wounded men waiting for transport.

Loading a hospital barge.

Camels carrying wounded men in cacolets.

Dead men's effects.

A refreshment stall near Bazentin on the Somme.

One of the hazards of motor transport. Here sand mats are used to extract a lorry from the mud.

A food convoy in Mesopotamia.

Donkey transport in the Middle East.

A Rolls Royce converted to an armoured gun carrier.

A supply dump.

A train-load of British Army barbed wire.

ambulance trains were referred to as *facultatif*. Any unallocated spaces were reserved for the railway company for civil use, such as empty trucks or long-distance passengers. The make-up of the train was standardised (e.g one passenger coach, thirty covered trucks, seventeen flat trucks and two brake vans; no alteration of this make-up was allowed. These were called 'type' trains; a number of these type trains were always kept empty and ready for use at central locations.

Later, when the movement into Belgium was under way, the 'type' train for personnel was changed to consist of two brake cars (one at each end), forty-two third-class cars (in two blocks of twenty-one, one at each end), two first-class coaches, two covered trucks for goods (or, if necessary, men or horses), and two flat trucks for Lewis guns or other large equipment. These were known as tactical trains.

The voluminous instructions on rail administration given by the French included that petrol should not be pumped directly from railway wagons to mechanical vehicles, and that supply trains at railheads should be fully unloaded within twelve hours.

Metre gauge railways were referred to in an early period as 'light' railways, but this term was properly used only for 40cm and 60cm gauges, the widths used by the French, and for which second-hand rolling stock was rarely available. These light railways were particularly useful when the delivery point was more than 30 miles from the ports, this being the maximum distance conveniently achievable by motorised or horse-drawn supply columns. Indeed, for horse-drawn vehicles, 30 miles was at least two days' distance, more if the loads were particularly heavy.

Light railways, once available, were used extensively. Some of these were known as 'trench' railways, as they could run between the trenches. One line, based in Arras, sent up to 150 trains per night, although some of these had only a few trucks. An initial shortage of small steam locomotives led to ingenious conversions of small cars, such as the Model-T Ford.

Towards the end of 1916 the construction of light railways was under way. By September 1917 the weekly tonnage carried on them had increased to over 200,000 tonnes. Much of this was ammunition carried laterally from other lines close to the front (usually at 6,000 yards behind the front). They also carried a great deal of engineers' stores. These light railways helped bridge the gap but were exposed to heavy artillery fire as they got closer to the front, so smaller dumps were used from which horse-drawn transport took supplies across country, to be collected by soldiers on foot. Much of this had to be done at night to avoid harassing fire. Light railways operated in front of railheads and so were considered to be the army's responsibility. By mid-1917 the BEF was using light railways whenever possible as extensions of standard gauge, and as far forward as possible.

There were a few tramways using hand trolleys or the small trucks used on the light railways, but when loaded these proved too heavy for human or animal traction and so tended, once on the light railways, to stay there. Once the formal directorate of light railways was started, it was decided there should be no connection between the two.

Observing that much congestion on the broad gauge railway system was caused by the difficulties of communication with the body in charge of the French railways, the *Commission Regulatrice*, Geddes negotiated British control of all the railways they used. Although desirable, this raised another problem: the lack of British rolling stock. Geddes thought some 54,000 trucks and over 750 engines were needed and started ordering them through the Railway Operating Division, many of them from Canada; meanwhile he soon rounded up spare capacity in the UK to bridge the gap while new rolling stock was being built.

Geddes ordered 1,200 miles of track and over 200,000 tons of sleepers. He then turned his attention to the light railways, pushing for their extension and improvement. GHQ wrote to the armies, telling them that the Commander-in-Chief wanted the light railways to be used for all supplies along the British front, thereby reducing, if possible, the use of road transport. Roads were vulnerable to shell-fire, and the closer they were to the front, the more likely they were to be damaged. Even so, they were still needed to bridge the gap between the railheads and the front lines.

Besides the road- and rail-building materials, lorries and rail rolling stock Geddes had ordered, the ongoing increases in numbers of troops required additional ammunition and supplies for the troops and other units such as the Royal Engineers. This meant the inadequacies of the ports became obvious. Equipment had been ordered but port efficiency remained static until the new rolling stock came on line, after which the unloading of ships became easier and faster.

Geddes did not remain in post as Director General of Military Railways, but was moved by Lloyd-George to join the Board of Admiralty, but at Haig's insistence he remained as 'a consultant on railway questions'.

The French had begun asking for British locomotives in January 1916, stating that they would need 900. There are some statistics available on the numbers of transport vehicles sent to the Western Front from Britain between August 1914 and the beginning of March 1919. These included 610 locomotives, 547 tenders, 22 passenger carriages, 19,858 railway trucks, 921 brake vans, 394 covered vans, 213 bogie trucks and 333 ambulance carriages. As the need for special ambulance trains grew beyond the point where ordinary passenger carriages could be converted, orders went to the manufacturers to build specially fitted carriages. Some of these remained in Britain, plying between the ports and hospitals, but many were sent to France. This rolling stock was made by the main British railway companies, including the Great Western Railway.

There was one minor problem of incompatibility concerning railway rolling stock; British axles needed grease, which was not freely available in France, where oil was used instead of grease.

Where new lines were built, there was a requirement for a water supply for the locomotives, which needed it to produce steam. Although water was easily available at stops in or near towns, there were some places on new lines where little water was available until pipelines and pumps were installed by the constructing engineers. Until this was done, locomotives either carried their own water in tenders, or were supplied through water trains. The amount needed varied tremendously, depending on the size and type of locomotive, the load it was hauling and the gradient of any hills it had to negotiate. Even the smallest locomotives needed some 500 gallons to fill their tanks.

Northern France and Belgium had an extensive network of canals and rivers, some 50 per cent of Belgian commercial traffic being carried on the canals. Calais and Dunkirk were connected to inland industrial cities such as Lille, while the rivers Somme, Seine and Oise (which was eventually canalised) led as far as Paris and beyond. By September 1914 the possibility of using this canal system to transport the growing volume of war materiel from the railheads to the front lines was being considered by GHQ, and by the following January a Deputy Director of Inland Water Transport was appointed, under the Director of Railway Transport. By that October inland water transport had its own directorate, operating over some 200 miles of inland canals and other waterways.

However, much of this network was behind German lines, including the section between the Somme and the Seine, and so its usefulness was limited. The allies had just three separate canal systems connected only by sea. This connection could only be made in the calmest of weather, as the barges were lightly built and had a very low freeboard. When the Germans did abandon the areas through which the canals ran, it took many months to repair the damage and reopen then.

Although canals had long been seen as a useful way to move non-urgent goods and other slow traffic, in practice they were not. The barges only moved in day-time, but not if there was a severe frost or fog, or if heavy rain had raised the water-level, making it impossible for the barges to get under low bridges. They were, however, useful as floating stores for reserve supplies, and could even be used on occasion as pontoons for bridging.

When air-raids started, canals and especially locks were a prime target. There was little to be done to protect them except for anti-aircraft guns, but there was a stock of lock-gates to enable swift repairs. At Abbeville there was a railway swing bridge over the canal, but rail traffic over it was almost continuous and it could only be opened to canal traffic on rare occasions.

Barge traffic was generally slow, no more than 10mph when horse-drawn or 25mph when pulled by tugs. This meant that canal cargo was restricted to non-urgent items such as building materials (including railway sleepers), hay and corn for horses, and some ammunition, all of which was loaded at the ports by a sort of double quay system, being unloaded from ships on one side and loaded onto barges on the other. These barges were also used to carry drinking water for the troops, and as ambulances and hospitals, giving a much smoother passage to the seriously injured than the jolting of trains.

The Inland Water Transport Directorate had a fleet of over 560 craft, including fifty-eight tugs and seventy-one motorised individual barges, plus 265 'dumb' barges (those with no motive power of their own), saving the need for some 250 trains. In 1916 they carried over 200,000 tons per month. By the end of that year Geddes had introduced numerous men with practical experience in the civilian world to help run the system.

Docks and Ports

As the war progressed, it soon became obvious that more port capacity would be needed. It was suggested that the two northern ports of Calais and Dunkirk would be most suitable. Failing these, Ostend and Zebrugge would be useful, if not already in German hands.

In January 1917 the French Directeur de l'Arriere arranged for an extra British berth at Rouen and two at Dieppe to compensate for the loss of Boulogne after the sinking of the ship *Araby*. She was wrecked near the entrance to the Bassin Loubert at Boulogne. Although she was removed quite quickly, high winds blew her back, this time right into the entrance to the basin, where she sank again, trapping eleven other ships inside the basin. It took the best part of a month to remove her. However, the wreck had forced the diversion of ammunition, coal and coke to Dunkirk, forage, expeditionary force canteen stores and medical stores to Calais, and supplies and case goods to Rouen. In addition, the wreck of the *Araby* blocked the shipment of firewood and forced Calais to deal with leave ships, while sick and wounded had to be diverted to southern ports for evacuation, and extra labour had to be moved to Dunkirk to deal with the additional ammunition being landed there.

One last aspect of port efficiency which needed constant monitoring was that of speedy and accurate telegraphic communications. These often failed to mention when a particular ship was leaving the UK, or complete details of its cargo; worse, many were not sent in enough time for the most appropriate berth for its cargo to be allocated. Sometimes this information did not arrive until after the ship had done so.

Chapter 7

Munitions

In 1913 Lieutenant Colonel Forbes of the Army Ordnance Department, having attended French army manoeuvres, reported to the War Office, comparing the management and supply systems of the French and British Armies. He pointed out that the French system was designed for large-scale campaigns in highly civilised countries, while the British system was based on experiences in what he politely termed 'less civilised countries, where everything had to be got from a remote overseas base', specifically in South Africa. There, with no major battles using large quantities of ammunition and other materiel, troops on long treks replenished their stocks from any Army Ordnance depots they encountered. Since there was no established front, there was felt to be no need for central administration at that point.

Forbes made some specific comparisons in his report; in general these were not favourable to the British system. The French Director of Supplies, with his division ordnance officers, was to be at the front; the British Director of Supplies had an office at the base and a roving commission of inspection. The French supply officers had large staffs and extensive powers of purchase to supply needed items without involving the staff of the lines of communication. The British ordnance officers' duties were mainly advisory except when they had to collect indents and other requests for supplies and send them to the nearest ordnance depot.

The worst deficiency of the British system, as laid down in the manual, was its lack of detail; for instance, whilst units were supposed to make their own arrangements for obtaining stores from a depot, there were no specific instructions on how this was to be done. Since there was a detailed system in place for supplying food and forage, Forbes could see no reason why this could not be used for other items, especially ammunition.

At this time the British ordnance department did not, as did the French, divide its stores of supplies into the relevant classes, merely dividing by provision, receipt and issue work. Whilst this worked well enough in peacetime, in wartime Forbes felt it would be better to make divisions by the different classes of item, one big advantage with such a system being that it would allow the subordinate workers to specialise. While Headquarters staff would have knowledge of planned operations, the whole would be handled by a Director of Ordnance Services at the front. Quite apart from the reorganisation of personnel which this would entail, Forbes was convinced that the manual in current use should be rewritten. Initially the Army Council disagreed with Forbes' recommendations, but it did eventually come round to his way of thinking.

Ministry of Munitions

Before the Ministry of Munitions was created in May 1915, munitions were under the overall control of the Secretary of State for War, then through, amongst others, the Ordnance Department and a Treasury Committee. At the start of the war Kitchener was Secretary of State for War; he remained in that post until his death in June 1916. Lloyd George was Chancellor of the Exchequer until he was appointed to head the newly set up Ministry of Munitions in 1915, then he became Secretary of State for War on Kitchener's death the following June.

The Trench Warfare Supply Department, created in July 1915, began organising deliveries both to the Western Front and to the Dardanelles for the Gallipoli campaign. They also produced and despatched large quantities of mortars.

Guns

In an army context, 'guns' means artillery pieces. During the course of the war their importance increased with the (more or less) fixed front lines. At the beginning of the war the numbers and types of gun were quite small: 30 13-pounders, 324 18-pounders, 24 60-pounders (four per battery) and 108 4.5in howitzers. By 1918 these figures had increased to 5,037 guns in calibres ranging from 6-pounders to 60-pounders, and 3in to 14in howitzers. Most of these guns were fully assembled in factories in the UK, then transported across the channel and transferred to flat-bed trucks; on arrival at the nearest railhead to their destination, they were unloaded and taken the last few miles hitched to horse-teams. This was impractical for heavier guns, and these were sent in sections to be assembled at the railhead before being moved by Holt tracked vehicles to the battery site. The barrel and breach together weighed about 5.2 tons, the carriage, cradle and recoil mechanism about 5.5 tons and the ground platform about 4.25 tons. Ammunition and most of the support items were sent separately. This system did not always work perfectly; one consignment of 6in guns was sent to Russia with the guns' dial sights packed with their spare parts, rendering the guns unusable until the sights arrived.

By the end of 1918 the initial thirty-two heavy batteries and six siege batteries had increased to 117 and 401 respectively. This created some difficulty in moving the heavy guns, as there was a shortage of suitable draught horses, so the War Office ordered more than a thousand Holt caterpillar tractors.

There were also some surplus naval guns which were mounted on train trucks to provide mobile long-range artillery. These included 9.2in, 12in and 14in guns; 12in guns could fire an 850lb shell 12 miles, and 14in guns 18 miles.

These artillery pieces used ammunition on a scale which Forbes described as 'beggaring adjectives'. In the last three months of 1914, 7,131 tons of ammunition were sent to France; during the Passchendale operations in 1917 some 465,000 tons of ammunition were used; by the Armistice the total sent was over 5,000,000 tons. More was used on some days in the First World War than in the whole of the two-and-a-half years of the South African campaign. Over the whole war some 7,500,000 tons of ammunition was used; with the exception of some smaller guns, all this was expended on the Western Front.

Commanders in this war faced a new situation, as everything was expended faster than before. Despite lessons from the Boer War which should have taught commanders that this was going to be a long war, the BEF still based its supply plans on a short war. One example of this, which does not seem to have occurred to them, was that modern rifles and some artillery fired more quickly than before, and thus needed more ammunition at hand. This was exacerbated by the offensive-based doctrine under which the army was operating.

The shortage of ammunition often caused frantic activity. On 14 September 1914, for example, a few wagon loads of howitzer ammunition left Rouen at 8.00pm. By 5.00am the wagons had left Le Mans, arriving at Villeneuve less than six-and-a-half hours later (the usual journey time was twelve hours), this speed being achieved by sending the ammunition on 'light' trains, i.e. ones which carried only the urgent load. However, the vital fuses did not necessarily arrive with the shells, as they tended to be loaded on different ships and had to go to an ammunition depot for assembly.

Ammunition Storage at Home

All the ordnance depots that existed at the beginning of the war were enlarged, and new depots were built near the new hutted encampments. The national filling factories of the Ministry of Munitions at Georgetown, Aintree and Chilwick [sic] were taken over to form the Central Ordnance Depots for the reception of guns, vehicles and general stores from the theatres of war and from commercial premises and docks at home, and these depots were rapidly filled.

Arrangements were made to take over all ammunition from the Ministry of Munitions' factories, thus effectively giving it to the army as soon as it was ready. The original agreement by which the Ministry engaged to hand over all completed rounds of ammunition to the army failed, and it was then changed to sending components, with the army arranging completion on site.

The original storage at the factories was planned to hold a month's output but this never equalled the requirement, so magazine depots at Bramley and Altrincham were completed, capable of holding 240,000 tons, but this too was found to be insufficient and the depot at Bramley was extended to hold a further 125,000 tons. The depot at Didcot was increased by approximately 100,000 tons and smaller depots were set up elsewhere. The site at Bramley, due to the need for adequate spacing between the buildings, covered an area of over 300 acres. The storage shed for filled shells covered an area of more than 9 acres.

Records for each individual gun were kept on index cards; these showed how many rounds were fired. Bores were measured regularly, and the results used to compile statistics of each type and how they reacted to different types of ammunition and propellant. This showed that propellants with high percentages of nitroglycerin caused the most wear. They also showed a tendency for bores to wear into an oval.

After prolonged deliberations, gun parks were approved in March 1917. These were established on the overall basis of one per division, to hold stocks of guns and carriages, with additional space for machine guns and mortars. These gun parks were usually situated next to the 'heavy' repair workshops.

Gun parks were really gun and ammunition depots and workshops, and they tended to expand as time went by. The number of items stocked rose to almost 3,000, not an excessive amount given the number of guns put out of action during heavy engagements. Much time could be wasted in transporting 'wounded' guns to the parks, so advanced parks and light-gun workshops were pushed forward at busy times.

The workshops, as well as effecting necessary repairs to guns, updated all arriving equipment by carrying out any modifications which had been ordered since manufacture, thus reducing the number of failures requiring repair. This included modifications to water carts and mobile kitchens, which were prone to axle failure. They also made from scratch many new inventions or modifications, providing supplies of these before large-scale manufacture could be organised from home. This included such items as mortars and gun components, braziers, tent poles and wheelbarrows.

By the end of the war there were seventy-three of these workshops employing over 10,000 people. On some bases these workers were housed in temporary barracks in warehouses with tiers of bunks; at Havre one hangar for this purpose was rented for £20 per week and provided accommodation for 1,000 men.

The main cause of problems, apart from enemy shell fire, was damage to the recoil buffer, especially in field guns. It needed to be kept full of oil, with any lost by leakage through glands and seals replaced promptly, otherwise excessive recoils could damage associated equipment. In particular, the running-out springs tended to become detempered and misshapen. Fortunately there was a firm in Northern France which specialised in retempering these springs. During periods of heavy fighting as many as 400 springs would have to be replaced each day.

The mobile workshops were so effective in keeping guns working that in May 1915 the allocation was increased to two per corps. These workshops were manned by one ordnance mechanical engineering officer and twenty-one other ranks; each had two (later three) lorries, one to carry materials and the others fitted out as workshops. The heavy-gun workshops had more personnel: one inspector of armourers, two engineering officers and eighty-nine other ranks. Their range of equipment was greater than that of the smaller-type workshops, even including a steam hammer. In 1916, when the allocation of heavy guns was increasing, the personnel for each heavy-gun workshop increased to 180, for medium-gun shops to forty and for light-gun shops to thirty-three.

Some civilian workers were used in all these workshops. There were five heavy workshops employing 900 men, twenty medium workshops employing 800 men, and forty light workshops employing 1,300 men, plus, when tanks were introduced, several special workshops were added for them with a total of 160 men.

Armourers' shops, usually comprised of all but one of the armourers per brigade, were able to accumulate a good supply of tools and usable parts from casualties' rifles. An individual man in his regimental lines could only do light work but in a central shop heavier repairs could be made. All the Lewis and Vickers guns could be overhauled periodically and other equipment such as bicycles could be mended.

The two main types of shell were shrapnel and high explosive (HE). Shrapnel, which was invented in 1784 by Henry Shrapnel, consisted of numerous bullets held within a shell casing and exploded by a fuse. (The term has since come to mean any sort of fragments of metal ejected after firing.) It was a very effective anti-personnel weapon when used against soldiers out in the open, but less so against troops in trenches. It was the main type of shell in use at the beginning of the war but was gradually replaced by HE shells. These could be filled with a variety of explosives, including fulminate of mercury and nitroglycerin (both these were somewhat unstable), cordite or trinitrotoluene (TNT), which were set off by fuses. These could be set for different times, or when the shell struck its target. All these shells were sent on their way by propellants, set off by the firing action of the gun.

By May 1915 the production of cordite was falling behind demand and the factories producing it were ordered to produce more. It was not realised until several months after the start of the war that many of the firms which manufactured HE were run by German directors. Once this became known, these directors were persuaded to resign. Extra supplies were then bought in America.

Various problems occurred with all types of ammunition; the first was that the bullets for British pistols had a flat nose, which caused the same effect as bullets deliberately made to expand. This was contrary to the Geneva Convention and these bullets had to be withdrawn and replaced by a variety with pointed noses. Then there was the small arms ammunition which was difficult to extract from the weapon, and this also had to be withdrawn and replaced. There were some artillery shells which burst prematurely, inside the gun, causing serious damage to both the gun and its crew, and at one time phosphorous bombs were spontaneously combusting. All this required a great deal of skilled work at the bases.

Another problem was that of insufficient care of stocks of ammunition at some of the bases, especially where cases had been opened but not completely used, with the remainder left uncovered. Lastly, there were many soldiers who just did not understand how dangerous their ammunition was. There were several stories of men sitting smoking on ammunition boxes, or lying on straw mattresses on top of ammunition boxes less than 3 ft from a roaring fire, or grenade boxes used as bedside tables holding lighted candles.

Although they lacked experience in the manufacture of shells, many British engineering firms were anxious to assist the war effort by producing them. Early in 1915 a Leicester-based group of manufacturers formed what came to be called the Armaments Output Committee and applied to the War Office for a meeting with the Ordnance Department for advice on how to proceed. The Master General of the Ordnance was dubious about the merits of the committee's plan and five days before the meeting announced that he would not send a representative, and that no further sub-contracts for shell components would be made until the labour needs for the firms already on the War Office list were met. Some hasty lobbying ensued, after which a War Office representative did attend the meeting. This group of potential manufacturers was soon joined by others from such disparate groups as car makers and bridge builders, as well as engineers.

George Macaulay Booth, adviser to Lord Kitchener, was not a believer in the scheme that required labour for the firms to be organised on a local basis. As head of the War Office Output Committee, he would have to oversee the division of industrial organisations into 'A' or 'B' areas. 'A' areas were those where there were major armaments sources; all workers living within a 20-mile radius of these sources were to be reserved to work in them. All other areas were designated 'B' and the workers in these could be moved to 'A' areas or work at other activities. Booth saw this scheme as unwise, since it would denude those areas of all the skilled workers, leaving empty workshops. With the assistance of Sir Percy Girouard, whom Kitchener had persuaded to give up his job as managing director of the Armstrong-Whitworth factory, several possible schemes for increasing the productions of munitions were produced. One of these was to conscript the managers of the great private munitions works for the duration of the war. This scheme was not adopted; instead the government agreed to set up many publicly owned National Factories. A big step forward at this time was that the Committee on Munitions, and later the Ministry of Munitions, was given control of production, without having to refer to the Secretary of State for every decision. This also put an end to the Ordnance Department's insistence that the manufacture of armaments should be restricted to the Royal Arsenal or the firms on the War Office list.

One problem presented itself at this point. Regardless of who was doing the ordering and who the manufacturing, it was essential to know the quantities required sufficiently far ahead to order the necessary raw materials. Some of these came from overseas, and the providers there were not always close to a suitable port. It could take weeks to produce the materials and get them to a port, and then more time for sea and land journeys to the finishing manufacturer. There was a statistics department at the Ministry of Munitions but at the beginning they had no data available. Equally, the Department of Area Organisations had no complete and up-to-date information on the available industrial capacity. The head of that department, James Stevenson, set out to conduct a survey, sending questionnaires to some 65,000 workshops throughout Britain. These surveys asked what machinery each workshop possessed, how many hours per day they worked and what they could do.

Within four weeks the department had received 45,000 replies. On the basis of this information it was then possible to allocate contracts to private firms and give orders to the National Shell Factories. It still took the best part of six months before each area committee had decided what it was going to do; by the end of December 1915 things were well under way, but still under the overall control of the Ministry of Munitions via a branch of the local department of area organisation. These boards ensured that Ministry policies were adhered to, and kept an eye on labour and raw materials supplies. Run by an engineer superintendant, they also included a representative from the inspection department at Woolwich, with authority to reject sub-standard products.

By the end of the war these independent factories were producing about a quarter of all the shells used by the British Army, mostly those for light and medium guns. The shells for the larger guns were more difficult to manufacture, and by the middle of 1915 it had become apparent that the existing manufacturers could not provide sufficient amounts, so a new set of workshops called National Projectile Factories were set up. Armstrong-Whitworth, Cammell Laird and Vickers, among others, provided managers for these factories, who were then seconded to the Ministry of Munitions for the duration.

Most of these factories produced empty shells which went to Woolwich Arsenal for filling. This facility soon found itself unable to keep up, and a series of National Filling Factories were organised: four of these filled quick-firing and breech-loading shells for the light and medium guns, five filled heavy shells, and six others made fuses and other components to set off the shells. Three additional factories were later added for trench warfare weapons such as grenades and mortars.

It was one thing to find out what workshops were available and what they were capable of producing, but another to decide what quantities and types of armaments were needed. For this, it was necessary to know the details of the overall strategic intentions of the war leaders, where they intended to push against the enemy, what sort of troops would be involved and what sort of weaponry they would need. At the beginning the strategy was to aid the Belgians in expelling the German invaders; this involved mostly infantry with a little artillery support in a comparatively small theatre. However, as the war progressed the strategy developed into a series of massive artillery battles intended to soften up the enemy before the infantry moved in to dislodge them from their positions, but it was not until the end of December 1915 that Kitchener reluctantly looked at the artillery requirements to implement these tactics.

For many years the armaments needed during the course of army campaigns had been provided on what came to be called 'pull' systems. The commanding generals in the field asked for what they wanted from the Secretary of State for War, who passed their requests to the Master General of the Ordnance, who in turn arranged for these items either to be sent from stock or to be manufactured by the Royal Arsenal or its listed manufacturers. This system had worked well enough for earlier campaigns such as those in southern Africa, but it would not do for a full-scale general war. By the end of 1914 Kitchener had realised that a much larger army was going to be needed, not only on the Western Front but in other countries as well. As mentioned above, no calculations had been made concerning that army's requirements at that time or in the future, or on the available manufacturers' ability to produce it. Lloyd George went to France to confer with the French Minister of Munitions, representatives from the French War Office and Field Marshal Sir John French. After pointing out that the war was turning into one of heavy artillery use, they estimated that some 750,000 rounds of ammunition would be needed each week. This assumed that the guns and howitzers to fire it would be available. They were not. At that point, the British Army had no more than sixty-one guns of 6in bore or larger, and they were certainly not producing that many heavy shells.

After much prompting from the Ministry of Munitions, at the end of June 1915 Kitchener finally produced, after consultation with Sir John French, a list of what was needed. French had a total of only 1,487 guns of all calibres; he wanted an additional 400 6lb guns, 400 6in howitzers, 250 8in and 9.2in howitzers and 40 12in and 15in howitzers immediately. These would serve an army of fifty divisions.

The Ministry of Munitions produced some different figures, based on seventy divisions. By June 1916 they wanted 5,107 18-pounder guns, 800 60-pounder guns, 1,618 4.5in howitzers, plus 560 6in, 372 8in and 9.2in, and 48 12in howitzers. This was called Programme B. There was also Programme C which required 6,000 18-pounder guns, 920 60-pounder guns, 1,920 4.5in howitzers, plus 980 6in, 462 8in, 378 9.2in and 85 12in howitzers. In September 1915 Lloyd George presented these figures to Kitchener, who made it clear that he was not pleased. The situation developed into a battle at Cabinet level, which ended with Programme C being adopted and successfully maintained.

Ammunition Shortages

By 13 September, partly due to priority issues among the French officials on the railways, who not unnaturally considered their own army more important than the BEF, and partly due to heavy use, ammunition for the 60-pounders and 4.5in howitzers ran out, with no more expected for at least four days. In late October, in the build-up to the first battle of Ypres, the Quartermaster General announced that no more than three lorry loads of ammunition could be delivered to each division each day. Trench warfare created an unexpected demand for HE shells for field guns to replace the shrapnel shells that had proved ineffective for use against enemy trenches. Given that trench warfare on a grand scale was also unexpected at the beginning of the war, it took some time for the manufacture and delivery of HE shells to catch up with demand. Until then, the Quartermaster General would check reports of daily usage and then allocate replacements on a level based on what was in stock. At first there was often as little as six rounds per gun each day. It was not until the summer of 1915 that the situation improved.

Despite the organisation of railway deliveries, this did not provide anywhere like enough shells, and Haig complained in his diary that it was reducing his ability to 'press on' as ordered from above. Meanwhile, more men were on their way: by the end of July as many as a million reinforcements had arrived and by the end of 1916 the number of guns had increased nearly six-fold.

It had been intended that ammunition should be despatched by train in the form of standard packs, containing some of each type of ammunition used, with each train filled with a set number of these packs. This scheme fell down when trains were diverted, as happened with what came to be known as

'Campbell's train', named after the officer whose charge it was. This train, properly destined for Havre, was diverted to St Quentin, then Busigny, then back to St Quentin. Its next adventure was to go to Amiens en route for Creil. While waiting at Amiens for a hot axle to be dealt with, orders arrived to send it to Noyon, where Campbell was ordered by the senior officer to convert his ammunition train into a refugee train. A resourceful man, Campbell sneaked his men off the train one by one and bluffed the station-master into providing him with an engine by threatening to blow up the train, a proceeding which would completely wreck the station. Meanwhile, Campbell managed to annexe some motorcycles and some food.

As with other supplies, at the beginning of the war regulations laid down a scale of ammunition for each gun, working on the assumption that artillery engagements would be of the same type as those in South Africa. Ammunition for each gun was held in stated quantities at the battery, the brigade ammunition column, the divisional ammunition park and in reserve on the line of communication. This was soon found to be inadequate once the action on the Somme started, and inevitably there were shortages; rationing of ammunition meant many guns had to stand silent.

By the beginning of 1916 ammunition production was increasing dramatically but this brought its own problem: that of delivery, when the transport system broke down. It had worked, to a certain extent, by various ad hoc arrangements but these were not enough to deal with the enormous amounts of ammunition needed for the Somme, not to mention evacuation of the wounded on the return trip. Despite this, during the course of the war more than 5,250,000 tons of ammunition was sent to the Western Front.

It was necessary to hold vast stocks of ammunition in France. Depots were needed for receiving the ammunition, but the volumes arriving meant the old depots were inadequate, while the time-scale for creating new ones was stretched by the need for negotiation with the French authorities. At a conference at General Headquarters in July this was slowly thrashed out. The first new depot was at Dieppe and the French also agreed to provide two dedicated berths at the port there. Later more berths, but not a storage depot, were agreed at Dunkirk. More sites, at Rauxmesnils and St Pierre Brouck, were to be constructed immediately and three other existing depôts, at Blargies Nord, Audriucq and Aix-le-Chateau, could also be used, the last of these as an overflow site if needed (which it was, as a result of a catastrophic fire at Audriucq caused by a German air raid). Agreement on these sites took more than two months; it took more time actually to construct or upgrade these depots. There were also stocks delivered to railheads for onward transfer to ammunition parks; there were over a hundred of these, although they were not all in use at the same time. From the ammunition parks, ammunition went by lorry to divisional filling points, where it was transferred to horse-drawn wagons for delivery to units.

At the beginning a base stock was held at Boulogne and sent on by train to bases at Arques and Aire. From there, it was passed on to mechanised ammunition parks and from there to refilling points; from these it was taken on by horse-drawn wagons. The French system of packing each truck with complete rounds (shells, tubes, fuses and cartridges) was adopted; this meant that if a truck had to be taken out of the train, it did not leave the rest short of crucial 'ingredients'. When the BEF was divided into separate armies, the system changed, with the railhead parks moved further forward to St Venant and Strazeele. The other parks remained to hold reserve stocks for reinforcing either army.

In a bid to prevent major accidents, at Boulogne some elements of the stock were isolated and in some cases kept under bomb-proof covers. This was not possible at the depot in Rouen, which was in the middle of the town with no room for expansion, so new depots were built at Quevilly and Audriucq. Quevilly was ready for use in March 1916, but when only the second train was being unloading a box of ammunition exploded and started a fire which spread rapidly, wrecked much of the depot and cost three lives and 600 tons of explosives. This caused much rethinking about stocking situations, with a recommendation that blocks of stock should be situated at least 70yd apart. This reduced the possible levels of stocking, and with the big offensive on the Somme already under way, a greater amount than usual was needed. The depot at Audriucq was full on the night of 20/21 June 1916 when an enemy aeroplane dropped a bomb which wrecked the entire depot and its stock of some 9,000 tons. Over a hundred loaded trucks were also destroyed. One of the resulting craters was more than 60ft deep, and it took several months to clear the debris. The incident did, however, lead to some rethinking about the optimum layout for the depots. The risks associated with such events related to the types of ammunition being held and the way it was packed. Boxed ammunition, consisting of complete rounds in wooden boxes, was extremely vulnerable, as a fire or explosion in one box quickly spread to the other boxes in the stack. The ammunition for field guns came in a single unit, but field howitzer cartridges were sent in separate packages. Trench munitions were perhaps the greatest hazard, as they consisted of boxes full of separate small 'bombs' separated only by their thin metal exteriors. The final type was chemical munitions and incendiary bombs which burned very hot and spread fire very quickly. The resulting design for the depots was for each type of ammunition to be housed separately, with at least a quarter of a mile between each area. There was a master switch for all the lights so they could be turned off if enemy aircraft were detected, and false sites were created several miles away that could be lit up as decoys. Water mains and tanks were buried deeply and a standard size of depot was adopted, with total space for 35,000 tons. Although it had been difficult to find suitable sites, by the spring of 1917 there were three on each of the lines of communication. Constructing new depots was not just a matter of erecting buildings, it also required the laying of new railway lines. One innovation which proved very successful was laying sidings on both sides of each shed, so that receipts and issues could proceed at the same time.

Labour for handling ammunition at these depots initially came from the ASC Labour Companies, but at busy times other nationalities were used, including Kaffirs, Cape Boys, Egyptians, Chinese and others. The Chinese proved to be the best workers, especially when employed on a piecework basis, meaning they could knock off when they had completed their allotted tasks.

Repairs and Salvage

The increase in amounts of gun ammunition delivered to the Western Front, while successful in that it allowed more rounds to be fired, brought with it another difficulty: the guns began to wear out with continual use. Gun barrels were lined with rifled tubes, which wore a little with every round fired. They could be rebored (although this enlarged the calibre), but otherwise the barrel had to be replaced or the whole gun scrapped. In July 1917 Haig reported that a total of 271 guns were unusable. Each major unit had an ordnance corps armourer attached to it, to make minor repairs and adjustments to the guns, but when several units were close together these armourers were able to tackle larger repairs. The ordnance corps also provided mobile workshops and base workshops (four of them on the Western Front) which concentrated on manufacture rather than repairs. They also dealt with defective guns and ammunition, investigating the causes; these were found to be mostly a result of inexperienced manufacturers, but sometimes faulty design.

During one six-week period of fighting in 1917 the sixteen light and five medium workshops overhauled and reissued over 1,600 guns and howitzers of various sizes. In December 1914 it had been decided that a second line of communication was needed on the northern line. This was set up with a base depot at Calais to correspond with the one to the south at Havre. It took some time to divide stocks of heavy artillery and spares. It was then decided in July 1917 to concentrate all the artillery stores at Calais.

Salvaged items, or ammunition returned from the front, were recondi- tioned or repaired if necessary. During the second battle of Ypres a roadside dump was set up, and troops returning from the front line were ordered to search for and bring back any potentially useful items.

Whenever activity paused at the front or moved on, and also at the end of the war, special teams searched for discarded or unused ammunition. They collected what they could and sent it back for the metal and explosives to be recovered. Much of what they found was deemed to be too dangerous to move and had to be destroyed on the spot, but if this was not possible, for instance when shells had buried themselves, a notice was put up next to them saying 'Dud'. The job of recovery was handed over to civilian contractors when demobilisation started; they paid £2,000,000 for the privilege.

Tanks

Although conceived and first used in the First World War, tanks did not achieve their full potential in this war. The precise number of tanks made in Britain during the course of the war is uncertain, as different sources give different numbers, but it seems to have been between 2,200 and 2,600. The French produced some 3,800 but Germany made only twenty, although German soldiers were not averse to using captured tanks. The original suggestion of using armoured vehicles was presented to the government in the autumn of 1914, but it was not until the following January, when Winston Churchill (then First Lord of the Admiralty) took an interest, that the concept of what were at first called landships was developed.

The first working vehicle, by this time called a tank, was built in the autumn of 1915 by William Foster & Co. of Lincoln. It was originally intended to be an all-terrain vehicle, but until they were equipped with caterpillar tracks instead of wheels, and built in a rhomboid shape, this was more of an optimistic hope than an actuality. Their weight made them bog down in soft wet ground, and the early versions were not very reliable mechanically. They were slow, able to move no faster than marching speed (4mph) on a good surface, and usually only 1 mile per hour on broken ground. However, when working properly they could cross trenches or craters up to 9ft wide and flatten barbed wire. They were designated 'male' or 'female', according to their armament: the males carried two 6-pounder cannon and three Hotchkiss machine guns; the females four Vickers and one Hotchkiss machine guns.

Tanks were first used in battle on the Somme in September 1916. They began to arrive in France in August 1916 in small numbers, but these increased steadily to about 700 by 1918. Some early tanks were too wide when fully assembled (13ft 9in) to be carried on trains. Removing their sponsons brought the width down to 8ft 6in, and also had the advantage of spreading the weight of the tanks on the train, as the sponsons weighed 3–4 tons. A lighter (14 tons) and faster (up to 8mph) version called the Whippet came into use by early 1918.

Once tanks came into use, the need for armour-piercing ammunition developed and more of this was supplied by the firms of Hadfields, Thomas Firth, Armstrong-Whitworth, Cammell Laird and the Projectile Engineering Co. as well as the Royal Arsenals. There were some name changes among these firms, for instance BSA became the Birmingham Metal and Munitions Company, and other manufacturers in the Birmingham area joined in, including Ely Brothers, Kynocks, Kings Norton Metal Co., Greenwood and Batley of Leeds and the London Small Arms Co. The three Royal Factories at Woolwich, Enfield (small arms) and Waltham (gunpowder) were all producing large quantities of arms and ammunition before 1914, substantial amounts of which went to the Royal Navy. However, they remained the only Royal Ordnance Factories until 1936, but were greatly extended when the need for vastly increased quantities of armaments was released. The Royal Arsenal at Woolwich employed more than 70,000 workers by 1917, but the greatest proportion of these were for naval armaments.

Trench Warfare Supplies

One other major category of armaments was produced under the aegis of the Ministry of Munitions: trench warfare supplies. This included machine guns, grenades, mortars and other lightweight weapons.

Machine guns

Invaluable though they were in trench warfare, fewer machine guns than needed were produced and only short-term contracts for 3,144, with no continuation clauses, had been issued. There were serious arrears in delivery until Vickers added a special facility at their works at Crayford and another at Erith. A new factory was built at Coventry to make the French-designed Hotchkiss machine gun. These facilities soon caught up with requirements, and by the end of the war more than 250,000 had been produced.

Unlike the machine guns of today, First World War machine guns were heavy and required a team of up to six men to site and operate them. The Maxim gun, which was manufactured by and then modified by the Vickers Company and became known as the Vickers .303, weighed 33lb with another 7lb of water-cooling jacket. It sat on a tripod mount weighing 51lb. Its flexible ammunition belt of 250 rounds weighed 221lb in its box – and as it could fire up to 250 rounds per minute, it needed a steady supply of belts. A two-gun section required a minimum of thirty-two belts at hand, with a reserve in the section's ammunition cart of a further sixty belts. Each of these machine guns was supplied with a set of spare parts including replacement barrels, 2-gallon water cans, oil cans, tools, cleaning equipment, night sights, a slide rule and aiming posts.

Another machine gun was the Lewis 'light' gun, which began to be supplied to the British Army on the Western Front in July 1915. It still weighed 28lb, but was spared the weight of water as it was air-cooled. It used the same bullets as the Vickers .303 (which were also the same as those supplied for rifles). It was produced in Britain by the BSA Co. and in America by the

Savage Arms Co. of Westfield, Connecticut. It had a 'pan' magazine, in 47- or 97-round versions, which could be refilled by hand on the spot.

There was also the Hotchkiss. Mainly used by the French Army, it was also used by the American Expeditionary Force in France in 1917–1918. Its ammunition came in rigid strips of thirty rounds, but unlike the other two guns it used 7mm or 8mm Mauser ammunition. Being the same calibre as the rifles, this simplified making the ammunition. The manufacturers of machine guns and rifles all produced ammunition as well.

At the beginning of the war Britain had just over a hundred machine guns. Orders for more were rapidly placed and deliveries commenced at fifty per week, which soon increased to over 630. By the end of the war machine guns had been manufactured in quantities which steadily increased from 6,064 in 1915 to 129,864 in 1918. Of these, there were more than 71,000 Vickers, more than 133,000 Lewis and more than 35,000 Hotchkiss.

Grenades

Many trench weapons were improvised by the troops themselves, including one called the 'hairbrush' grenade. In the early days of grenade use, one unit asked for elastic to make catapults. A maximum of 150,000 officially sanctioned grenades had been produced, of which only 16,000 were of the latest design. When asked how many grenades were needed, the overall reply was 10,000 rifle grenades, 30,000 Mills grenades and sufficient other types of grenade to bring the total to approximately 500,000 per week. In March 1915 some Mills bombs were sent out for trial; proving successful, they soon became the standard grenade. Other types continued in use and millions were used in the course of the war. The same applied to trench mortars, several types being tested until the Stokes mortar became the standard.

The original British-made grenade, the Mk1, had an attached handle to facilitate throwing, but its design included a contact fuse so that when thrown from a trench, the fused top was likely to strike the trench wall behind the thrower. After several accidents of this type, this grenade was abandoned and replaced by the Mills bomb. The over-arm 'bowling' throw was the preferred style.

Grenades were either designed to explode on impact or had a timed fuse. The type known as fragmentation grenades had a segmented exterior, rather like a pineapple, which everyone thought was meant to break up on detonation, sending lethal fragments flying. In fact this did not happen and some early designers' notes showed that these grooves were actually intended to give a better grip. An experienced thrower could usually manage 49ft accurately, but the fragments on explosion went further than this.

Designed by William Mills of Sunderland, the Mills bomb was made at his Mills Munitions Factory. Several variations were produced, including the

No. 23 which could be fitted with a stick to fire it from a rifle, and the 36M which was coated in Shellac to keep the fuse dry in humid or wet conditions. Just before the end of the war, the No. 23, and the No. 5, both of which could have a rod attached to allow them to be fired from a rifle, were declared obsolete. The original Mills bomb had a fuse delay of seven seconds; this was later shortened to four seconds as it was found that the longer delay allowed the recipients to get away before it exploded.

Mortars

Unlike grenades, which were comparatively small and intended to be thrown by hand, mortars were larger and needed their own launcher. Numerous ideas were submitted for these, and several committees and departments in the War Office were set up to consider and test them. They included the Trench Warfare Department, the Trench Supply Department, the Designs Department and the Munitions Inventions Department.

Mortars, like howitzers, were fired at an angle which allowed the shells to rise high in the air and then drop vertically on their target, making them ideal weapons for attacking the enemy's trenches. Although much smaller than howitzers, they came in several sizes, from 2in to 12in, with the 3in the soldiers' favourite. This version was normally used for high explosive and smoke shells, and the slightly larger 4in version for gas and incendiary shells. Over 12,000 of these were produced. The Livens 'projector', invented by Captain William Livens, was designed to throw poisonous gas canisters. It was not particularly accurate, but was lightweight and cheap enough that hundreds could be set up in a small area and used for concentrated bombardment. The tubes were usually buried in the ground just behind the lines, and could be fired electronically.

The mortar shell was dropped into the tube manually, where it connected with a firing pin at the bottom of the tube which detonated it. It had a range of about 800yd, and a skilled team could fire up to twenty-five bombs per minute. Other methods of firing mortars were available, including a rifle-mounted cup launcher and several variants on the catapult principle.

Mortar launchers needed to be fixed firmly, with base plates and support legs to absorb the recoil, but they could also be elevated to make the bomb drop from a height. Early mortar launchers were very heavy, but in 1915 Sir William Stokes designed a smaller version. This consisted of a metal tube attached to a base plate, with a bipod or tripod mount. Known affectionately as 'Mr Stokes' drainpipe', the whole thing weighed less than 40lb and thus could be carried for short distances by a single man and quickly set up for use in trenches. The first version was mainly used for HE and smoke projectiles, but a later version was also used for gas and incendiaries.

Hand Guns

Rifles

By the start of the war rifles had evolved from large-bore single shot weapons to small-bore bolt action with a spring-loaded clip of bullets. For the British Army the standard rifle supplied was the Short Magazine Lee Enfield (SMLE), so-called because its magazine held only ten rounds of .303 calibre. Designed by the American James Lee, it was manufactured at the Royal Small Arms Factory based at Enfield, just north of London.

When new rifles fell into short supply, the government tried to buy them elsewhere but, with the exception of Japan, could not do so. Some 10,000 abandoned rifles were collected, but when the Canadian troops were re-armed with SMLE rifles in place of their Ross rifles, the latter were brought in but few of the SMLEs as the Canadians had already re-armed themselves with found rifles. Empty shells were returned for refilling, via Calais and Havre, and later Zeneghem.

Supply shortages affected the infantry's rifles, with ammunition supplies rarely exceeding 100 rounds per rifle. With the rapid increase in the demand for rifle ammunition, again the existing facility at the Royal Small Arms factory at Enfield could not cope, so four new National Cartridge Factories were established, three of these being managed by contractors, the other by the Royal Arsenal at Woolwich.

Sniper rifles with telescopic sights were developed, as were high-powered versions to break through loop-holed metal plates. Shotguns to bring down suspected enemy carrier pigeons were also supplied.

In September 1914 Indian troops were brought to the Western Front. They did not use the same rifles as the British troops, and theirs used different ammunition, so all their weaponry had to be supplied, including rifles, bayonets, machine guns and ammunition. The Indian cavalry's swords were specific to the regiment, and would not fit other regiments' scabbards nor those of the British cavalry. At one point a rumour began to circulate that the agent who supplied the swords sourced the blades in Germany.

Pistols

Principally an officer's weapon, pistols were also issued to tank crews, military police and airmen. The standard British pistol was the Webley Mk IV revolver, manufactured by Messrs Webley & Scott in Birmingham. Using 11.6mm bullets, they were very reliable, but needed much practice to achieve accuracy, as they tended to jump when fired.

Bayonets

So-called because they were developed in Bayonne, in France, bayonets were useful in close-combat fighting, when firing a rifle carried the risk of hitting a friend behind the enemy. However, although much used in training, they saw little action in real situations.

Other weapons

Some fashions in weaponry came and went, including daggers and stabbing knives, knobkerries studded with horseshoe nails, and handcarts for Lewis guns, which the General Staff considered were sufficiently important to ship to the front without trial. They proved to be too heavy for the human gun-teams to drag and were promptly abandoned. More useful were stout gloves for handling barbed wire, protective covers for rifles to keep out mud, ear protectors for gunners, and electric torches, not to mention sandbags. As many as a million could be used in a single day, and at one time in 1916 this number increased to 2,500,000.

Chapter 8

Engineering

As with medicine, it can be difficult to see at first glance how engineering comes under the heading of supply, as there were few items which they gave to ordinary army units. But what they did supply was far more important: the infrastructure of roads, railway lines, water supply, buildings, lighting and signalling. For almost all these things, the Royal Engineers maintained and operated them with their own personnel. After the AOC and ASC, the Corps of Royal Engineers was the third most important of all the non-combatant organisations.

Where engineers were attached to headquarters of an army, the personnel consisted of a chief engineer with a staff officer reporting to him, four field engineers, five clerks, a commanding engineer (lieutenant colonel), an adjutant (captain or subaltern), two clerks/draughtsmen, a controller of mines with an assistant and two clerks.

The Royal Engineers were divided roughly into two areas: mechanical and electrical. Within these were branches for signals, inspection, experimental work and a directorate of works in France. At the head office in London, which became so crowded that the mechanical branch moved out to Blackfriars, the head office mechanical division started the war with twenty-five personnel of all ranks and ended it with thirty-nine officers and ninety-seven others. The electrical branch started with three officers and six other ranks and ended with twelve officers and thirty-four other ranks. Overall, in August 1914 there were 1,295 officers and 10,394 other ranks. By August 1918 these figures had increased to 11,830 officers and 225,540 other ranks. A separate Directorate of Engineering Stores was started in the summer of 1918.

Departments within the mechanical branches at home and at the headquarters in France answered technical queries and dealt with technical matters including construction of steel work, special plant and machinery, machinery for pumping and electrical work, machine tools and camouflage, finance, sending engineering stores to France and other theatres, and other miscellaneous areas. Departments within the electrical branches dealt with telegraphs and telephones, pontoons for bridging, water supply and surveying, technical queries and work on committees mainly related to experimentation. The Corps of Royal Engineers also had numerous individual specialised units including electrical and mechanical companies, companies for tunnelling and drainage, companies providing water in Egypt and Palestine, and forestry in France after March 1917; there were eleven of these, with four officers and 110 other ranks, plus four Army Post Office Service base post offices at Boulogne, Calais, Havre and Rouen. In all, there was a total of 1,888 units at the beginning of August 1919, almost half of which (893) were in France.

The Inspectorate of Iron Structures (IIS) was responsible for bridges, plant and machinery for railways, waterways and docks (and the Royal Flying Corps) until late 1916 when the Directorate of Transportation took over. In 1917 the Royal Flying Corps created its own supply organisation.

The work of the Royal Engineers fell into two main categories: mechanical and electrical. Mechanical work ranged from heavy construction tasks to minor repairs of plant and machinery. Electrical work covered everything else, although much of it had no connection with electricity. Much of the mechanical supply system was under the IIS, originally via the Director of Army Contracts or the War Office finance departments, but as the war developed the obvious magnitude of the task led to the IIS being allowed to place contracts directly, merely notifying the Director of Army Contracts of what had been ordered. This allowed the IIS to discuss items with the manufacturers by telephone and order them verbally before following with a written order – a much quicker method than having to go through the Director of Army Contracts. In late 1916 transportation was set up as a separate organisation with responsibility for railways of all gauges, roads, docks and inland waterways, and took the supply side from the IIS. A year later purchases for the American Army in France were handed over to the War Office.

The head office staff sections were reorganised several times, each time ensuring that a specifically experienced officer dealt with every demand. One other major development at the beginning of 1915 moved the loading of engineering stores onto ships from Southampton (which was too far away from London for easy supervision, not to mention often delayed by troop movements) to the South West India Docks in East London. A Royal Engineers shipping officer was based there and was in constant contact with head office, providing him with information on the relevant urgency of items and thus allowing him to prioritise deliveries of cargo to ships. By the end of 1915 it had been concluded that he needed a fleet of ten ships to take engineering stores to France. This soon grew to twenty-two vessels and a number of barges were used exclusively for transportation to France. These ships were not always available and emphasised the need for the docks policy in France that insisted on rapid unloading of ships. In addition to the docks in London, shipments of corrugated iron were sent from Liverpool and cement from Rochester. After submarine activity became a major threat to shipping in

1917, supplies from Liverpool had to be abandoned and Grimsby and Richborough were used instead.

One area where the workload at home increased rapidly was that of inspections and testing. A testing ground in Surrey was acquired in 1916; this specialised in earth-working machines. It was also necessary to send inspectors to check on manufacturers and assist them with tool design and fitting. In peacetime, this work was carried out by three military machinists; this number grew throughout the war to seventy-four by the Armistice.

Engineering stores was a term which covered practically everything the army needed except weaponry, food and equipment for the soldiers. Before the war, everything that might be needed to support an army at home or in the field was exhaustively tested before being approved for use, and added to the official list known as the Vocabulary of Stores. In fact there were numerous vocabularies, each for a specific purpose, such as the mobilisation store table for the expeditionary force for 'Mechanical Transport for a Siege Artillery battery (12 in Mk II Howitzers)'.

It started with the war establishment of the numbers of personnel by type: one captain and three subalterns, a mechanical sergeant-major, a company sergeant-major and a company quartermaster sergeant, twenty-four artificers (foremen, fitters and turners, blacksmiths, wheelers (wheelwrights) and electricians), 146 drivers for tractors, lorries, motor cars and some spares. It then moved on to transport vehicles (caterpillar tractors for howitzers and their equipment, lorries for ammunition, luggage and stores, personnel, workshops and their stores) and cars for personnel.

Other numerous items are listed in sections, covering such kit as hand weapons and their cleaning equipment; water bottles and mess tins, haversacks and bandoliers; axes, kettles and lanterns; all the way down through prefabricated workshops to split pins, nuts and bolts. This store table lists over 600 items in the Vocabulary of Stores, and a further 195 as 'not in vocabulary', which meant they had not gone through the full testing programme but were unofficially approved.

The notes on the front of this booklet include the comments that since the listings are revised periodically, only the current list should be used and the previous listing destroyed. Vocabulary items should be drawn by the unit directly from the Army Ordnance Corps (AOD), and non-vocabulary stores should be drawn from the Mobilisation Depot, Base or Advanced Base, or Mechanical Transport Depot to which the unit is attached. Although not stated, presumably there would have to be a particular reason why the items on the usual list could not be used. However, once the war started and the BEF took to the field, the demand for various articles soon overtook the official lists and could be ordered as 'not in vocabulary'. The AOD was responsible for depots for all these stores.

The types of engineering stores requested was dependent on the usual constraints: the climate and terrain of the theatre, its natural resources and the nature of the operations. In 1914 the emphasis was on siege equipment and full provision of narrow gauge railways, including the lines themselves and the rolling stock, plus repair workshops. Once the armies settled into trenches, by the end of 1915, they needed more than 15,000 hand pumps and 400 miles of hose, plus trench digging machinery (this was found to be too cumbersome and was eventually dropped). One method which did help in digging trenches was originally developed to destroy enemy trenches; this involved forcing 3in and 4in pipes a few feet below the surface anything up to 400ft to the enemy's lines, and filling the pipe with explosives. This was then detonated, creating a rough trench about 6ft deep, and damaging the enemy's lines. This technique was also useful for making communication trenches, but they had to be finished by hand. Another essential piece of equipment for trench warfare was loophole plates. Made of metal and up to .4in thick, with a loophole for observing and firing through, these served to allow outgoing fire while protecting the soldier from incoming fire.

Constant bombardment of the trenches made huts for the troops essential in autumn and winter, and corrugated steel sheets were in demand for this, as well as for revetments, roofing and temporary shelters for troops, animals and stores. In 1916 Lieutenant Colonel Peter Nissen invented his eponymous Nissen hut, consisting of prefabricated sheets of corrugated steel in semi-circles, attached to a light steel frame. The ends were usually made of wood with doors and perhaps a couple of windows. Nearly 50,000 of these huts were ordered in 1917, and a further 50,000 the following year, although delivery was sometimes delayed by steel shortages.

Camouflage netting was in great demand and thousands of yards of fish-nets, canvas, calico and hessian were used. There was some dispute over the specific colouring and patterns demanded by artists but standardisation was finally imposed.

The electrical department provided everything that was not mechanical, including pontoons and mining stores. Before the war the duties of this branch consisted mainly of control of electric lighting for coastal defence (using a type of searchlight) and supplying lighting in barracks. The staff, including those of the inspection division, comprised eight officers and 104 other ranks. By the end of the war these numbers had risen to seventy-three officers and 5,188 other ranks. Very few of these were based at the War Office in central London; there were some at Woolwich but several sub-sections were set up elsewhere.

Before the war the searchlights installed for coastal defence were so well organised and frequently inspected that little attention was paid to development. However, in 1914 the Commander-in-Chief in France asked for small searchlights for field companies. Each company was given an oxyacetylene portable set, with a 60cm projector which took the light about 500yd and could run for five hours on a single charge. It was fitted with signalling shutters, which in good daytime conditions could be seen at a distance of over 20 miles. These lights were not particularly useful in trench warfare and they were eventually withdrawn from the field companies and used for lighting workshops on the lines of communication.

At home, they were used as anti-aircraft lights, mainly in London, once Zeppelin attacks commenced. The first were installed and operated by the Admiralty. In December 1914 it was decided that searchlights should be used in conjunction with anti-aircraft guns. Little was done at this time but the following summer a conference was held with the final conclusion that the number of lights should be increased to a total of 175. Some of these were fitted to 1-ton lorries with generating plants and others to tram cars. Over the course of the next two years the number of searchlights in use increased to nearly 700. Then in the summer of 1917 daytime air raids started and it was realised that night-time raids would inevitably follow. Some experimentation showed that the 60cm lights currently in use were not powerful enough and more powerful 120cm projectors were ordered.

The Commander-in-Chief in France then requested additional anti-aircraft lights and by December 1917 the establishment in France included ninety more projectors of 90cm (some mobile), a hundred more of 120cm with petrol electric lorries and another thirty-six of this type for an independent force in Nantes, making a total of 286. They were formed into ninety-five sections of three lights each. This branch only provided the lights; they did not provide any personnel to operate them.

Large quantities of electric light fittings were provided for home use and in France. It was not until 1916 that the quantities needed increased and in 1916 France required almost 350,000yd of power cable; in the first half of 1917 the amount needed rose to 550,000yd. Overall, some 4,500,000yd of cable was provided.

Larger quantities of surveying stores were also needed; these included some 10,200 levels, 3,300 measuring chains, 3,900 inclinometers, 3,250 sextants and numerous other instruments.

Sandbags were needed on such a large scale for trenches that all the available stocks in Great Britain were bought up, as well as several million bags from America and Canada; arrangements were made for bag manufacture in India, although there was some initial doubt as to whether the jute crop would be sufficient. However, contracts were made for monthly shipments; as the armies in France and their lines grew, the requirement for sandbags also grew, from 10,000,000 per month to 40,000,000 per month. The contracts to supply sandbags were placed with several manufacturers, some of whom used prison inmates to make up the bags. During the course of the war some 1,300,000,000 sandbags were provided. In addition, small bags filled with sand and an explosive charge were used to train troops in the use of grenades. About 1,500,000 of these were provided.

Large amounts of ballast were needed for the maintenance and construction of railways. Mine refuse from Bethune and sand from Calais were transported by rail or road. By August 1917 over 1,000 lorries per day were carrying road metal. (Although referred to as 'road metal', this material was a geological product, including limestone from quarries between Boulogne and Calais, flint gravels from the Pas-de-Calais and 'pierre-de-fosse', a red brick-like shale resulting from the combustion of coal-mine dumps.) There was good gravel near Amiens, and the sarsen stones found on top of chalk deposits in many parts of Northern France. This is the type of stone used by the French and Belgians for pave.

A great deal of timber was used to shore up the walls of trenches and tunnels and to make fascines and gabions as temporary walls. Although both could be made on the spot from material collected from nearby woods, they still had to be carried to the erection site.

Trenches, once dug, needed to be drained, and the Royal Engineers supplied hand-operated pumps for this, as well as heavy duty mechanical pumps for water supply from boreholes, and purification equipment including sand filters. These pumps were mounted on lorries and thus could be easily moved from borehole to borehole as needed.

The Royal Engineers needed numerous vehicles to carry equipment, from tools to building and bridging materials and explosives. Even a wooden building (for a secure store) needed several wagon-loads of timber and other materials, and brick or stone buildings even more. Another large-scale user of wagons (and horses as weight-lifters via pulleys to get materials off wagons and into place) was the pontoon unit. Each pontoon was carried separately on a four-wheeled cradle pulled by four horses; they also needed stout timber for the platforms over the pontoons, and rope and other materials to hold it all in place. The Royal Engineers also needed to carry materials for trench digging and tunnel building and mining under walls, plus explosives to bring down walls and bridges.

Signals

Before the war what was thought to be an adequate reserve of electrical signal stores was maintained but, as with almost everything else, the actuality proved this to be incorrect. As an example, it was thought that 8,800 telegraph poles, 2,300 miles of field cable and 900 portable telephones would be enough; in the first two years of war the actual use of these was 334,000, 165,000 and 51,000 respectively. There was particular difficulty with obtaining portable telephones as the type used before the war was deemed unsuitable for field work. A new type was undergoing trials when war broke out. It took time to organise manufacturers to produce this new type, and it was fortunate that the Post Office, which had taken over the National Telephone Company some years before, had large stocks of various apparatus which could be utilised until adequate numbers of the new type were available.

In October 1914 the Commander-in-Chief in France proposed some improvements in telephone communications between artillery units and the divisional artillery commander. One of their problems involved the light-weight cable used to connect artillery brigades, which wore out very quickly. There were several types of field cable available but few of these were found to be completely satisfactory; the difficulties involved in manufacturing a better pattern ranged from shortages of factory space and machines to shortages of labour and material. Despite this, production eventually rose to more than 47,000 miles of cable a week.

Other items which were difficult to obtain included signalling lamps and electrical cells (batteries) and telephone switchboards. Eventually the task of providing these items was given to the Post Office, which also stored and issued them. A liaison officer was appointed from the Controller of Post Office Stores to attend regularly at the War Office, and another officer from the Post Office engineering branch was given a temporary commission and made regular visits to the signal service in France. The War Office was able to hand over the design and provision of these stores to the Post Office for the dura-tion of the war. Items provided this way were valued in excess of £6,000,000, and included switchboards for trenches, base offices and lines of communi-cation, mobile line-testing equipment, trench telephones and numerous other items.

Other signalling activities included the use of despatch riders, who rode motorcycles (Triumphs for preference) and carried, as well as a small tool kit, a pistol for defence. There were also large numbers of carrier pigeons, carry-ing messages in small tubes attached to their legs, or rolled maps strapped to their backs. Pigeons have a natural urge to return home (espcially males with a mate and eggs in the nest) but they seem to forget where home is after seven days, so have to be released and replaced with a new batch. They could be carried in baskets on the back of a motorcycle, but most were in mobile lofts, either horse-drawn or built into a lorry (or omnibus) chassis. Sixty horse-drawn lofts, each holding seventy-five birds, were used at first, this number increasing to 120 lofts in 1917 and again to 150 by the end of the war. The message tubes were small and lightweight, and the paper used for messages was flimsy. Message pads were issued to the operators, each sheet designed to be folded into eight and rolled to fit in the tube. The tubes had one part which was fastened to the bird's leg; the other part, which held the message, then screwed into place. Messages were always sent in duplicate, using two different birds with a time delay between the releases, in case one bird met with an accident or was shot down.

Stores

The Royal Engineers' personnel included an inspection division for the stores branch. As well as the obvious tasks of checking and passing (or rejecting) batches of stores, they also prepared drawings and specifications of stores for Royal Engineers units, light fittings and lamps. Amongst the items designed by the division were double-skinned pontoons, cable drums, field cables and telephone cords. They maintained a watch on timber prices and were able to circumvent a shortage of Oregon pine (the most suitable for bridging super-structure and telegraph poles) by purchasing a large quantity when staff saw that prices were starting to rise. It bought at 3*s* 10*d* per cubic foot and the price subsequently rose to 10*s* per cubic foot. This was a new concept for the War Department, who had previously left the supply of raw materials for various work to the contractors who did the work.

The inspection division took on experimental work on wireless equipment and eventually a separate sub-division was formed to deal with this work and some civilian experts were recruited. Much of this work, especially communications for Royal Flying Corps aerial observations for artillery guidance, grew rapidly and the division was moved from the RFC establishment at Brooklands to Woolwich, where a portion of Woolwich Common was taken over, with a permanent mast and numerous huts. The division was also responsible for providing propaganda balloons. Made of paper, these were packed with leaflets and a length of tinder which burnt down and released the leaflets. Each balloon carried 4lb of leaflets; they were packed at Charing Cross.

As the work of the division increased, the space at Woolwich became over-whelmed and sub-sections were started in Manchester, Birmingham and Bradford. The inspection division found that several of the factories used to make items which had been designed by the division and needed to be made in conditions of secrecy were failing to meet their targets and it was decided that they should be taken over. These included firms at Soho, Teddington, Kilburn, Cricklewood and Southall. After a while their work was reorganised and some premises at Raynes Park were acquired for a machine shop to make essential parts.

A couple of months after the war began a purchase office was opened in Paris, then store and equipment parks at Strazeele and Berguette. These were run by the Director of Works, France, who indented for stores from the War Office to be delivered to Boulogne, and sent on from there. A base workshop for bridging items was set up at Havre.

Store base depots were set up early in 1916 at Les Attaques and Abancourt. Havre and Rouen became subsidiary store depots. The depot at Les Attaques received its stores from Calais, Dunkirk and Boulogne. It supplied the three northern armies and lines of communication. It was situated between the Calais–St Omer canal and the railway. Branches of the railway were brought into the depot and wharves were constructed along the canal for items brought in by barge. The depot originally covered some 50 acres, but was soon enlarged to 65 acres as the quantity of stores built up. A large timber depot of some 150 acres was created on the other side of the railway.

At Abancourt there was no canal, but the depot was located at a junction of railways from Havre, Rouen and Dieppe. It received its stores from Havre, Rouen, Dieppe and Fecamp, and supplied the two southern armies and lines of communication. It soon grew from the original 32½ acres to 163 acres. A further wharf was acquired at Rouen where most of the timber from overseas arrived.

The base workshop at Havre was enlarged and manufactured bridging supplies as well as repairing machinery. Further workshops were opened at Rouen and Abancourt for converting timber into stores for trenching and hut construction, and other wooden items requested by the armies, including floors for tented hospitals.

Bridging

At the beginning of the war there were few bridges in Flanders capable of carrying the amount of traffic needed for a serious advance. Steel spans were needed as wood was not strong enough to carry heavy guns or tanks. The 8in howitzer had 13 tons weight on a single axle and the 6in Mk VII gun was even heavier, at 17 tons per axle. The introduction of tanks in 1917 required modifications to many of the existing bridges to enable them to support a 30-ton load.

The first order, placed in October 1914, was for enough material for sixteen steel girder bridges; the maximum length per girder was not to exceed 25ft, the maximum width was not to exceed 7ft 6in, and the maximum weight was not to exceed 3½ tons. Further amounts were ordered in March and October 1915, April 1917 and May 1918.

Each of the new armies included one horsed bridging train, and one mechanical transport bridging train. By the end of February 1917 the Engineer-in-Chief in France had ordered 188 bridges of spans from 16ft to 85ft. Despite this requirement being considered excessive at the time, during the advance later that year supply had not caught up with the demand and special efforts were called for to hasten supplies from England.

When the expeditionary force was mobilised, it was provided with equipment including airbags and superstructure to construct rafts. Then the

Commander-in-Chief in France requested a collapsible boatful of equipment to create a light bridge capable of taking any horsed vehicles with the cavalry.

There was some discussion on the necessity of providing bridging pontoons to carry heavy loads across wide rivers, such as the Rhine. Heavy pontoons for this task were designed, some 45ft long, 4ft deep and weighing approximately 5 tons, but they were not made as it was decided that there was little likelihood of having to cross the Rhine to carry operations into Germany. Some 2,700 ordinary pontoons were provided during the war.

Bridging was mostly done with pontoons, either using custom-built pontoon boats, or whatever local boats were available. These were moored facing the current, at equal distances, all made fast to one or more cables stretching from bank to bank. They also had to be lashed together and individually anchored. Then baulks of timber were laid across them and planks nailed across those to make a roadway. When on the move, each pontoon's stores were carried inside it, to a usual weight of 1,200lb; this required a team of at least four horses, more likely six. This was only effective if trained men were sent with the pontoon train. It was suggested in the First World War that the General Service wagon would make a good pontoon, but one officer who tried it remarked that the experience had made him decide he would rather swim.

Barges were also used to fill gaps in bridges. Fitted with turntables, they carried a double roadway for floating bridges, one 60ft through span erected on the turntable, and a set of shore trestles. The barge was put in place, the turntable swivelled round, and then water was pumped into the barge until it had lowered enough for the span to rest on the existing abutments. Barges were also used as pontoons.

The types of bridges needed were designated Class B (to carry a 13-ton axle load), Class A (to carry a 17-ton axle load) and Class AA to carry tanks.

Charles Inglis, a Royal Engineers officer, invented what came to be called the Inglis Bridge. It was constructed with steel tubes (rather like modern scaffold tubes), bolted together in triangular shapes, either with the sides leaning in to touch each other at the top, like a pyramid or at a less acute angle and connected at the top by horizontal tubing. They could be erected quickly and dismantled equally quickly to be reused elsewhere. The pyramid shape was principally intended for marching infantry, but it was not suitable for mechanical transport as it narrowed too much near the top. The rectangular pattern could carry anything, but was not substantial enough for heavy guns or tanks. However, these bridges were in much demand.

Heavy bridging depots were located at Havre and Les Attaques; each had a fleet of 280-ton barges, comprising one fully equipped workshop barge, two store depot barges each carrying two 60ft spans, two 30ft spans and two 13ft spans with launching gear, roadway and erection stores, two timber depot barges with pile drivers and 30ft lattice steel derricks, as well as timber and two turntable barges. By the end of 1915 three of these fleets were completed and a fourth was nearly ready.

Early in 1917, when it was realised that canal transport was not useful for carrying bridging material during an advance, the barge depots were discontinued and the barges given to the Inland Water Transport department, which had a desperate need for transport barges.

However, the fact that many areas of the front lacked canals meant that smaller bridging store depots were needed in those areas and these were duly set up. In addition to the stocks of spans, the store depots held piles and trestles, steel cube piers, hand, petrol and steam pile drivers and an air compressor plant for repairing salvaged girders for reuse. The stock spans were transported by special lorries with trailers and a 5-ton steam Foden tractor to carry loads up to 24ft long, a 5-ton Clayton steam lorry, shorter than the Foden, to take loads up to 18ft, and 3-ton petrol lorries for everything else.

The numerous canals in northern France made it necessary to install lifting bridges. These were made with a standard span of 21ft 6in. There were several types, none of them particularly effective for various reasons, including tendencies to twist and stick in operation.

The total value of all engineering stores supplied throughout the war was approximately £32,250,000.

Army Postal Services

In 1907 the Territorial and Reserve Forces Act required the General Post Office to provide additional detachments from amongst its numerous employees for the four newly created territorial divisions; it already had four such units. Worried that this might impact on the civilian postal service, the Post Office asked the War Office to 'consider and report' on the current and future situations between the existing civilian postal and telegraph services and the army. A committee consisting of members of the Post Office, the War Office, the Royal Engineers Telegraph Reserve and Lieutenant Colonel William Price (who had experience with the Army Post Office Corps in the Boer War) was duly set up.

The committee's final report was not delivered until June 1911. It said the committee thought cooperation between the Postal Corps and the Army Signal Service was important, and they should be put on a common basis. It continued by saying that because the Army Signal Service was a branch of the Corps of Royal Engineers, the Postal Service should have the same status. They put forward three main reasons for this: mutual assistance and cooperation would increase economy and efficiency; administration would be simplified, as would transfers of personnel between branches; and personnel of both services would have the same conditions of enlistment, service and rates of pay. This would help with recruitment and prevent jealousy between the services.

The result was that in February 1913 the existing Army Post Office Corps and the proposed Territorial Army Postal Service joined the Royal Engineers' telegraphists and were renamed the Royal Engineers Special Reserve (Postal Section) and the Royal Engineers Territorial Force (Army Postal Service). Price was appointed as director and remained in that post throughout the war.

Almost all the personnel of the Royal Engineers (Postal Section) were recruited from the General Post Office; at the start of the war there were 300 of all ranks. By the end of the war this figure had grown to over 7,000. In May 1917 the first women from the Women's Army Auxiliary Corps joined and worked at the base army post office, some of these also serving on the Western Front. These women were also recruited from the General Post Office.

When war was declared in August 1914, all but two NCOs and twenty-eight other ranks went to France with the BEF. It was thought the workers left in London would recruit and train additional personnel as needed, while the actual mail handling would be done by the civilian post office, but as the army grew so the amounts of mail grew to such an extent that the Home Depot had to take over mail handling as well. The growth continued: in the first week of October 1914 they handled 1,616 bags of letters, 8,249 registered letters and 8,249 parcels; four years later, in the first week of October 1918, those numbers were 44,648 bags of letters, 118,121 registered letters and 479,667 parcels. By the first week of April 1919 there were still 30,816 bags of letters, 36,268 registered letters and 202,951 parcels. There had been a reduction in the number of parcels in 1917 when the weekly number dropped from 1,026,684 to 645,084 as food rationing took its toll on presents of cake.

The growth in amounts of mail for the forces required more space to handle and the Home Depot moved out of the single room it had occupied at Mount Pleasant. Its activities were separated into a letter office and a parcels office, each in different buildings; these continued to expand onto additional floors. A further move then took them into hastily built wooden premises in Regents Park. Even so, yet more space was was needed and by the end of 1917 there were additional offices in use in Bristol, Glasgow, Leeds, Manchester and Sheffield.

This all needed more personnel. By November 1914 the original two NCOs and twenty-eight other ranks had been joined by two officers and 145 other ranks; by May 1915 the establishment was increased again to five officers and 563 other ranks. More people came, including some civilian women and some disabled soldiers; at the height of the war the Home Depot had over 2,800 employees. There was some internal reorganisation, creating a General

Correspondence section, a Recorded Letters section, a Locations section (which kept records of the locations of all army units, and a Returned Letters section. This latter section dealt with letters returned by the units of deceased men (parcels sent to them were retained and the contents spread among their chums); the numbers of letters they handled increased dramatically for each major offensive, sometimes to as many as 3,000 a day.

During the first year of the war mail was moved around London and from the Home Depot to railway stations for the ports by using the same contractor who provided the transport for the London Postal Service. In the autumn of 1915 this contractor had to pull out due to labour shortages and after an appeal to the War Office the 620th Company ASC (MT) was attached to the depot. This company grew to over 500 men equipped with 220 3-ton lorries.

The team which went to France with the BEF established the first British Post Office at Havre, with an Advanced Base Post Office at Amiens; two more, at Rouen and Boulogne, quickly followed. At Havre the mail was sorted into unit bags which were sent on to their final destination via Amiens and the railways. A railway guard accompanied the trucks, and handed the mail over to the Field Post Office at the refilling points where regimental transport gathered. From there it went to the regimental postal orderlies who distributed it. A further Base Post Office was opened at Calais in June 1915, and this, together with the offices at Havre and Boulogne, continued to provide an exemplary service to the BEF right through to the end of the war. There was one minor hiccup in September 1914, when the retreat from Mons disrupted service for three weeks, so a temporary depot was opened at Nantes.

Army post offices also dealt with internal mail, and registered letters and parcels. They also sold war bonds.

Chapter 9

Food and Drink

An army needs to be fed if it is to remain fit to do its work, whether that work is marching, serving a gun or manning a trench. For the British Army it was the AOC which had the responsibility of doing the feeding. It purchased stocks of food stuffs, stored them in its depots and passed them to the ASC for delivery. The nutritional thinking of the day was that calories were critical and the items that mattered were protein (including fats) and carbohydrates. They did not know about vitamins, which were not discovered until 1924.

At the beginning of the war the daily ration per man was:

- 20oz bread
- 17oz meat
- 4oz bacon
- 9^6/$_7$oz vegetables
- 3oz sugar
- ^{6}/$_7$oz butter or margarine
- 3oz jam
- ^{1}/$_2$oz tea
- 2oz cheese
- 1oz condensed milk
- ^{1}/$_{36}$oz pepper
- ^{1}/$_{20}$oz mustard

This ration was changed after a few weeks, and again early in 1917, the second time reducing the amount of bread to 16oz.

As an example of the vast amounts of food delivered to the army, during 1918 these totalled:

- 129,204,000lb of biscuits, costing £3,394,000
- 52,203,000lb of margarine, costing £3,163,000
- 167,234,000lb of sugar, costing £ 2,281,000
- 38,262,000 tins of meat and vegetable ration, costing £2,190,000
- 168,745,000 rations of preserved meat, costing £8,916,000
- 14,409,000 lb of tobacco
- cigarettes costing £2,765,000 (of which one-third was tobacco and the rest cigarettes)

The numbers fed during the war rose from 324,000 in 1914 to 2,973,690 in 1918, and the amount of bread issued in an average month rose from 5,974,382 in 1914 to 58,717,114 in 1918.

During stressful periods, such as the retreat from Mons, supplies did not always find the men, and there were a couple of occasions when the ASC could do no better than hand out food at random, or even dump piles of it on the roadside. Although an unpleasant experience at the time, this did stimulate the army to reorganise its supply chain with more care and planning than it had done before.

Some food items, such as potatoes and onions, which were liable to rot if stored in bags, were spread out on a warehouse floor until needed and then bagged.

The rum ration was delivered in stoneware jars marked SRD for Supply Reserve Depot, but the letters were variously interpreted by the troops as Service Rum Diluted or Seldom Reaches Destination. These jars, when empty, made desirable drinking water containers.

At the time of the Armistice more than 7,000,000 tins of pork and beans were purchased each month from the USA. As an alternative, rations were obtained from British packers; of these 261,000 rations of beef or pork and beans, valued at £8,500, were cancelled. The average value of meat and vegetable rations purchased during the three months ending 30 November 1918 was £140,000 weekly; approximately 2,250,000 rations were cancelled, equal to a week's supply. All supplies from biscuit manufacturers, valued at £54,000 per week, were stopped on 30 November 1919. On 11 November 1919 the total quantities of flour shipped to France, Italy, Salonika and Egypt was 35,790 tons per month. After a reduction in quantities, 20,400 tons was sent to France, 350 tons to Italy, 7,500 to Egypt, 2,500 to Rotterdam and 2,100 to the Black Sea.

The large stocks of rum at the cessation of hostilities allowed the Supply Department to sell 893,195 proof gallons to the trade at an approximate profit of £190,000. Tea had been purchased for the Department by the Ministry of Food, and it was found possible to transfer to that Ministry over 12,000,000lb to the value of £353,202.

Supplies of condensed milk sent from America directly to the theatres of war were terminated by nine months' notice from 30 June 1918. Deliveries of jam were slowed down, as surplus amounts were available in eastern zones, and current contracts for 7,000,000 of marmalade would cover requirements until the next fruit crop was gathered.

Few local contracts had been made after the Armistice. Many of the products, especially Egyptian meat, bread, forage and hospital food supplies, had been purchased by a central authority during the war and it anticipated that a return to the peacetime situation could only be gradual. None of the contracts for food and forage supplies contained break clauses, but in view of the universal utility of these items and the world shortage of food, reversion to peacetime production would not be a problem.

To make it easier to store, handle and collect, it was decided that the meat supply should be frozen; however, to provide against emergencies, some pre-served supplies should be maintained. During the first few months of the war the meat was shipped to England, inspected and sent on to France, but as the size of the BEF increased, it was sent from the River Plate to base depots in France. Due to the loss of ships and increased freight needs, the practice of using meat ships for storage at the ports was stopped as soon as adequate storage was constructed.

All the frozen meat from Australia and New Zealand in the reserve stores was allocated to the army, along with some of the frozen meat from the USA, Canada, South America and South Africa. Only chilled meat and some items of offal were kept for civilian consumption. Civilians were encouraged to substitute sausages, fish, rabbits and brawn for other meat. Bacon was always popular with the troops, and a supply of excellent quality was obtained through a firm of brokers.

Cheese was purchased through the Board of Trade. It became difficult to obtain sufficient when Holland was cut off, and the ration for troops in the trenches was reduced from 3oz per day to 2oz, with other items substituted.

Despite the shortage of supply, it was thought unwise to reduce the sugar ration for trench troops, but the sugar shortage, combined with a failure of the fruit crop, allowed a reduction in the jam ration.

As well as hay, potatoes were managed by the Forage Committee. When the full quantities became difficult to obtain, arrangements were made in Ireland and Jersey to ensure a regular supply, and seed potatoes were sent out to Egypt and Salonika.

Enemy prisoners received slightly less bread and meat, and salt herrings or sprats, potatoes, rice and oatmeal. The bread, originally white, was changed to the black bread the German prisoners were used to.

One small problem lay in providing food to Orthodox Jews. There were three Jewish battalions recruited in Palestine who were granted the right to kosher food but those in the general army population had to abandon their Orthodoxy for the duration or forgo much of the ration (or exchange items with their friends). The same applied to vegetarians, although there were few of them at this time. There were also some complications over food for the troops from India. Hindus would not eat beef, Muslims would not eat pork, while Sikhs and some other Indians wanted what was euphemistically called 'Indian treacle' (opium).

British soldiers carried an 'emergency' ration. Originally this was just choc-olate, but after it was realised that it was insufficient, this was changed to a small tin of preserved meat, 16oz small biscuits, 3oz cheese and 4oz bacon, with tea, sugar and salt. Known as the 'iron' ration, it was only meant to be eaten when an officer ordered it but, despite frequent inspections, hungry men inevitably ignored this rule.

Once the War Office had decided to take a serious interest in feeding the army properly, it began to specify the quality, sizes and packaging of the food and other commissariat supplies. The first edition of the *Handbook of Specifications for Supplies* was issued in 1908 and, as with the *Manual of Military Cooking*, it was reissued at regular intervals, updated as necessary.

The packaging required was either tins (and for a couple of items, glass or stoneware pots) packed in wooden cases made to War Office specifications or was to be obtained from the Reserve Supply Department at the Royal Dockyard, Woolwich. All products were subject to inspection before, during and after manufacture and packing, and had to comply with the approved sample which was submitted to the assistant director of supplies. This meant that the contractors needed either to be based in London or to have an agent there.

Bags also had to be obtained from the Reserve Supply Department for granulated sugar and salt, both to be in double bags with the inner bag of calico and the outer of jute. All items packed in bags had to be sewn up, not tied. Oats and bran could be in single bags, as could rice, flour and imported cane sugar. There was an attempt to pack biscuits in papier mache, partly because there was a shortage of packing material, but also from a desire to reduce the weight of the packages in the field. This was not a success as the biscuits soon deteriorated. The biscuits themselves were made by Messrs Huntley & Palmer, with their name stamped on one side.

Bacon came as sides, middles or bellies, each piece to be wrapped and sewn into stout canvas, then packed into iron-bound wooden cases, each containing a maximum of 60lb. Compressed bran and forage for horses were to be supplied in 80lb bales and covered with canvas and iron hoops for export. The forage was to be made of the best English meadow hay and crushed oats, in the proportion of 13lb hay to 12lb oats.

Meat essence and meat extracts were to be in sealed glazed earthenware or glass pots, containing 1 or 2oz, packed in wooden cases of 160 or 320 pots. Candles were to be wrapped in stout paper, white or brown, packed in wooden cases containing 60lb, and oil for lamps was to be supplied in 5-gallon tinned iron drums. Lime juice, brandy and whisky were to be in casks; jars for the lime juice and bottles for the whisky, with bungs or corks, were to be supplied separately. Wine for hospital use was to be in black glass bottles, all packed with straw in wooden cases.

Everything else was to be in tins, made of best quality steel coated with pure tin; 112 of the steel sheets, 14in by 20in, should weigh 122lb. The tins for preserved meat should be tapered with a key opening (just like corned beef tins today) and the tins for biscuit, although not specified, must have been square or rectangular, as were the actual biscuits (4½in by 3in, weighing 2oz). All other tins were to be hermetically sealed, soldered throughout with resin and tin solder, stamped from the inside with the date of manufacture, and to be thoroughly cleaned before filling.

Preserved meat could be beef or mutton, the beef from animals between two and four years old, and the meat to be from the fore- or hindquarters. No neck, shin, flank, head meat or scrap meat was to be used. Much the same applied to mutton: the beasts to be no more than four years old, and the meat should not include head, neck, breast or skirt. There should be no less than 10 per cent of good hard natural fat distributed among the lean meat. The tins were to contain 12 or 24oz of meat, with not less than ½ or 1oz of clear jelly made from soup stock and soup bones; gelatine was not permitted.

Corned beef or mutton should contain no preservatives except salt, saltpetre and sugar. Roast or boiled beef or mutton should be in tins containing 12 or 24oz, with no more than ¼ or ½oz of salt. The meat was to be fresh, not frozen. 'Meat and vegetable' ration was to consist of 12oz beef without bones, 5oz potato, 1oz haricot beans, 1oz onions and 2oz stock gravy. The tins should ideally be tapered (but Maconochies came in round tins) and packed in wooden cases of thirty tins.

Roast chicken (or as the tins stated 'roast fowl') was in 12oz tins, so must have been either a very small bird or one with the bones removed, but no neck, liver, gizzard or offal. Even if packed in the UK, foreign birds were not allowed. They were packed in wooden cases of ten tins and must have been for hospital use only.

Tea was to be a blend of two or more types of pure China, Indian or Ceylon tea, the blending to be done in a public bonded warehouse. Coffee was also to be a blend, either of two-thirds Santos and one-third either of Costa Rican or Columbian, or two-thirds Santos and one-sixth each of the other two types. It was to be roasted and ground before being packed into tins holding 25lb, packed two to a wooden case. Cocoa powder was to be made of pure cocoa, equal in flavour and quality to such soluble cocoa as Cadbury's Cocoa Essence or Rowntree's Cocoa Extract, and packed in 1lb tins, forty to a wooden case. Condensed milk sweetened with cane sugar was to be in 15oz tins, with an unsweetened version of 12oz, both packed in wooden cases of forty or sixty tins.

Jams of soft fruit (gooseberries, strawberries or blackcurrants) or stone fruit (plums or apricots) were to be made of fruit and sugar only without juice, glucose or colouring; the fruit was not to be pulped until after the first inspection. Marmalade was to be made from the present season's best bitter oranges. Jam and marmalade were to be in 1lb tins, packed in wooden cases of fifty tins.

Dried fruit could be raisins and sultanas, apricots, pears or plums, packed 50lb to a tin. There was no mention of apples, either dried or as jam, although the most common jam (indeed, at some times, the only jam) was plum and apple, much to the troops' disgust. Made by the Grimsby firm of Ticklers, this jam was the subject of several ironic marching songs.

Although always dried, vegetables might be labelled 'dried' or 'preserved'. They could be onions, potatoes or a mixture with other vegetables, but in that case they should not contain potatoes or parsnips. They were to be packed in 5lb tins in wooden cases of ten tins. Butter was in 1lb tins, thirty or forty tins to the case, as were arrowroot, pearl barley, oatmeal, Patna rice, sago, tapioca and pepper. Mustard was to be in ¼oz tins, also forty to the case.

Despite the efforts of the historian R.H. Beadon, who worked for the ASC, to claim that army food was good and plentiful, diaries from the front told a different story. (It was forbidden to mention poor food in letters home as this was thought to have an effect on morale.) Adverse comment was prevalent in recuitment camps, where the shock of army life first struck the new soldiers. They, and those in the field, were particularly unhappy about the use of biscuit instead of the white bread they were used to. There were some short-ages there, too, as the government had not expected the enormous response to recruitment campaigns.

There was rather a fuss concerning the Vesteys, a family of ship-owners and meat suppliers. The government had introduced a tax on 'excess profits' aimed at companies whose businesses enabled them to profit from the war. On being refused an exemption from this tax, the brothers William and Edmund Vestey moved to Buenos Aires and ran the business from there. As if this was not bad enough, in 1922 William was made a peer, ostensibly for his services during the war, but less visibly, according to gossip, because he had paid Lloyd George £29,000 for the peerage.

Back in Britain, there was a problem with opportunistic pricing. Attempts to introduce requisitioning in the annual Army Acts had always been refused, and prices soared during 1914. One example of this was with sugar. Priced at 12*s* 3*d* per cwt two days before war was declared, the price quickly rose to anything between 56*s* and 75*s*. General Long, the director of supplies at the War Office, called in the principal sugar merchants and told them that he knew from customs' officials exactly how much sugar was in store or in bonded warehouses. He had already posted guards at those places to prevent anything leaving, and had customs' agreement that they would release nothing from bond until the army's requirements were met. He said he was prepared to pay 12*s* 3*d*, or he would seize the sugar and pay for it at the end of the war, assuming that the British won. He applied the same method to the meat cold-stores in Liverpool and Bristol, going to the finance secretary at the War Office to tell him that an Act empowering seizure of essential supplies must be passed immediately. Despite some initial protests, it was done by 10.00pm that night.

Meanwhile, all the members of the public who could afford to were buying up stocks of food such as hams, jam and sugar, or, as Long deemed it, were hoarding. Some of these people had their hoards requisitioned by the Board of Trade. The government requisitioned all ships with insulated holds and required all military meat to pass through central control. The meat packers tried importing inferior meat which they knew would be rejected by the army, allowing them to put it on the open market at inflated prices. Long's response to this was to have the meat rejected as unfit for human consumption and he arranged with local authorities to condemn it. The meat packers tried to evade this by sending the meat to London, but Long had already arranged for the London health authorities to seize it and condemn it. Condemnation meant a total loss to the meat packers, who had to abandon this ploy.

Realising that the amounts of food coming through the manufacturing factories would be more than the existing inspectors could cope with, the head of the medical department of the local government boards was asked if the medical officers of health would take on the inspections. They were given copies of the book of specifications and within forty-eight hours every food factory in the UK was being inspected.

It took a while to get enough trained cooks for the army, and some female civilian cooks were used at first. New cooks spent six weeks at the Army School of Cookery at Aldershot, learning not only how to cook for large numbers, but also how to maintain the desired cleanliness and how to complete the numerous forms. One of these was the 'dripping and by-products diary'. These were considered very important and the money received from their sale went a long way towards paying the cook's wages. Dripping derived from roasting meat and from bacon was kept and might be issued in lieu of margarine if there was a shortage, or used to make pastry, puddings, or for frying. All the rest, and other waste fat, was sold to be processed to extract glycerine, which was then processed into nitroglycerine for high explosives. Packed into tea or biscuit tins, and marked with the unit's number, they were handed in and in due course the payment received for it went to the unit where it was used to purchase extra vegetables, spices and herbs, etc., or for new cooks' clothing, mincing machines and so on. Even the fat in waste water was saved; it was not to be thrown down the drain as the fat could build up and block pipes. The best method was to set up large galvanised tanks with taps at the bottom. All waste water was dumped in this and allowed to cool. After the fat had risen to the top and set, it was skimmed off and the water drained. Swill tubs for table refuse and peelings were also kept, at some distance from the cookhouse to prevent smells and flies gathering. The swill would be sold to a local pig farmer with the proceeds going into the mess accounts.

A report on the commissariat in the Boer War included information on the best way to stack supplies, which was still valid in the First World War: grain, flour and other supplies in 4-bushel sacks should be formed into a rectangular stack, the sides being three sacks lengthwise or five endways. The layers should alternate direction, and stand on a base of stones or tins of meat, with gaps to allow for circulation of air. They should be stacked ten high at the front, less towards the back to create a slope for rain to run off, then a tarpaulin should be put over the whole thing.

Theoretically, the cooks should not have shown any favour among the men, but inevitably some did; others took the chance to 'get their own back' against men they disliked, hence the saying 'never argue with a cook'. One of the favourite jokes of the time was the one about the man who was getting a medal for saving his battalion by shooting its cooks.

There were numerous versions of recipe books issued to army cooks, but most of these recipes were just variations on the theme of 'meat with something'. 'Sea pie' was a meat pie in pastry and contained no fish; tomato stew was actually a meat stew with tomatoes; fish paste was tinned sardines mixed with bully beef. There was Irish stew, brown stew, plain stew, curried stew, rabbit stew, meat pie, rabbit pie, meat with haricot beans or peas, meat puddings, meat minced, meat boiled or meat fried as fritters or rissoles. Bully beef would appear as 'spring soup' with vegetables and stock, 'bread soup' with stock and bread, or 'fish cake' of bully beef minced with tinned herrings, mashed potatoes, breadcrumbs and pepper, rolled into rissoles or flattened into cakes, rolled in breadcrumbs and then fried.

As well as the booklet issued to cooks at home, another was issued for the cooks in France. These both started with the importance of hygiene and the cleanliness of the cookhouse, utensils and the cooks themselves. They were given a free issue of two suits of cook's clothing, which were replaced twice a year; if they needed more spares could be purchased from the proceeds of selling the cookhouse by-products.

The booklets also emphasised the importance of variety in the diet. Failing to provide this brought a great deal of grumbling from the troops, who perhaps did not realise the difficulty of obtaining anything else. It was usually possible to provide a pudding every day for the men out of the trenches, and sometimes for those in the trenches as well. This was often done by using spare bread, biscuits, flour, dried fruit, rice, suet and oatmeal, so all bits of those items which were not consumed were meant to be returned to the cookhouse. There should not have been an excess of bread, but when it was issued direct to the men instead of the messes it tended to be left lying around in the billets and became dirty and inedible. The men also used it to wipe their cutlery and then threw it away.

There were other faults listed in the handbook: issuing cheese raw, for example, instead of using it in cooking when it would go further. Bacon rind was often thrown away instead of being rendered down for dripping; jam tins were not always scraped clean, thus wasting the small amounts that could be used for puddings; potatoes were peeled before cooking instead of being cooked in their jackets; and a build-up of surplus food was not allowed as if there was a need to move hurriedly, the spare food could not be carried and would have to be thrown away.

The idea of proper cooking for the troops had been growing slowly, and in 1895 the first edition of the *Manual of Military Cooking* was issued. It was updated and reissued at regular intervals, covering everything from hygiene and kitchen equipment to recipes. These included various ways of cooking meat (mutton or beef) as roasts, steaks, rissoles, stuffed or potted. There were curries, pies, stews and soups, and for puddings, suet pudding with currants, dates or jam, bread pudding, bread-and-butter pudding, rice, tapioca, treacle tart and baked custard. Dried fruit made its appearance in 1910 (apple rings, figs and prunes), and there was a range of sauces.

This was more or less what the average housewife cooked for her family, but there is a big difference between cooking for a few and cooking for a regiment. There were no precedents, not even the big restaurants in London, and it was not until factory canteens were started by industrialists that the machinery that was needed for large-scale catering made its appearance. J. Fry & Co. fed 2,000 people each work day in their canteen, the engineering company Tangyes employed contractors to feed 3,000, and Cadbury's factory at Bourneville fed almost as many.

The *Manual* was comprehensive, including a section on butchering cows and sheep. It did not mention horses, although many horses died in the field and these were often added to the meat ration, although some men refused to eat horsemeat when they found out what it was.

Cooks were recommended to keep a brine tub for preserving meat. The brine was just salt and water, strong enough to float the meat (which then had to be weighed down to keep it under water). Brisket and flank were best for brining, taking from five to ten days to preserve. The need to keep a stockpot was also emphasised, not only in a camp or barrack cookhouse, but also in one of the boilers in a travelling kitchen when on the move. A haybox could also be used for stock, as well as for other cooking, as long as everything went in boiling, but they did not work for those things which needed a fast boil or were usually cooked in an oven. The handbook included a table of times for haybox cooking. A smaller version of the haybox was the back-pack container, made by pressing hay round a 2-gallon petrol or lubricating oil tin. Despite being well scalded out, the taint of petrol was difficult to eradicate and the tea tended to carry the taste. The back-pack container could be carried to the trenches by one man, and might contain soup or tea, which would be kept hot for up to twenty-four hours.

The *Manual* included instructions on how to start and maintain a stockpot. This consisted of filling a large saucepan or boiler two-thirds full of cold water, adding salt and meat scraps and/or bones, and keeping it simmering for seven or eight hours a day. Clean peelings of carrot or onion could be added, but not cabbage or potato. Every night the pot should be emptied, the contents strained and put back in a clean pot, then a little more water and more scraps could be added. Once a week, a fresh pot should be started and the older pot contents strained and reduced to one-third by boiling, skimming if necessary. The end product should be dark brown and of a glue-like consistency; this could be poured into small pots and left to set. If it was to be kept any length of time, the pots should be sealed with a layer of lard or dripping. It could then be turned into soup or meat 'tea' by the addition of boiling water.

The bakery at Calais was near the docks. There were four officers and 1,020 other ranks, plus 100 workers from the docks who could be attached when needed. It consisted of four field corps bakeries and could produce a total of 450,000 2lb loaves per day, of which 60,000–80,000lb were for the French. It had sufficient racks for two days' production.

Although it was not really suitable, the only building available for the bakery was an old paper mill. The ovens were on the ground floor, but the dough was made on the upper floors, from where it had to be carried down all the way across the floors to the chutes to send it down. The work was done in three shifts, day and night, and each shift made dough and baked it. There was a conveyor to raise the flour and water to the upper floors, but no machinery for making and working the dough, so all the bread was handmade. The ovens were made by the firm of Hunts, and stood in blocks of four, each taking 150 loaves per shelf; there were also twenty-four blocks of smaller ovens, each taking 98 loaves per shelf. The actual baking took an hour and each oven baked seven lots per shift. There was no mechanical temperature regulation, there being some variation both in the temperatures on different parts of the floor, and also in the flour, so they were dependent on the skill of the bakers.

The bakeries at Havre loaded for fifteen sections daily, with a daily turnover of 1,000 sacks. In addition, there were issues to six out-stations. The maximum possible daily output was 364,000lb and the actual was 337,000lb in one shift. Dough making was done at night and baking during the day. To prevent warm loaves being piled up and crushed, special duck-board racks 2ft 9in square were made which restricted loaves to two in a stack.

The bakery at Boulogne was larger than that at Havre, turning out 530,000lb of bread per day. There were actually two separate bakeries, each with two bake-houses, and a total of 132 ovens. Work consisted of two shifts of nine hours, starting at 4.00am. They used 108 tons of flour per day, which was delivered from the bulk stores and stacked near the dough mixers. Four Foden lorries carried the flour from the bulk stores. Bread was not baked at night as a precaution against air raids.

There were fourteen bread stores at Boulogne, each with a capacity of 900,000 2lb loaves; these were then packed for issue in bags containing twenty-five loaves. Bread issues to trains started at 4.00am and took until 1.30pm. There were no sidings in the bakeries, and the bread was taken to the trains in lorries; issues to local hospitals were made direct from the bakery.

The bakery personnel consisted of five officers and 971 other ranks; of these, two officers and 265 other ranks were Canadian. The labour required was supplied by about eighty Chinese coolies.

One sack of flour needed 15 gallons of water. Fresh yeast was used, and in case of emergencies there was a small brewhouse which could produce more. The flour came by rail from the docks to the flour hangar, which could hold up to 4,576 tons. From there it was issued daily, being carried by coolie labour.

Traditional loaves had a cross cut in the top, but it was found that this left them susceptible to damage on handling, so they were made with smooth tops. Each loaf weighed 2½lb and was intended for two men. The bread, once cooled, was packed in what were known as 'offal sacks'; these were cheap, loosely woven jute sacks, used in the butchery trade for packing offal when it was sent off to specialist factories. Used only once for offal and then washed, these sacks cost 4s per dozen. Each held fifty loaves, and ten sacks were sufficient for a battalion.

Aldershot ovens were used in bakeries in France until early 1915, when steam ovens were introduced. Then, to save manpower (and money), automatic machinery of the type supplied by Messrs Baker & Sons of Willesden was introduced into the largest bakeries in England and France. By the end of the war this had saved some £381,000. A substantial sum was also obtained when this machinery was sold after the war.

The Aldershot oven was introduced in the 1860s; each could produce up to fifty-four 2½lb loaves (the ration for 108 men) or cook dinners for 220 men. It consisted of several cast-iron sections which could be transported by wagon and erected quickly on the chosen site. The ideal site was clay soil on a gentle slope, never sandy or marshy ground. The sections were two arches 3ft 1in high and 3ft 6in wide, two ends, four bars to connect the ends, a bottom piece and a door. All this weighed 374lb (or 208lb without the bottom piece). They came with nine bread tins and a peel. Usually erected in a row, the ovens should be positioned so that the mouths faced the prevailing wind, but ideally with a slight slope towards the back to carry off rain. They should be located in a shallow trench 18in deep, 2ft wide and 6ft long for each oven. After erecting the metal pieces, the top should be covered with the clay from the trenches and rushes or leafy twigs and any available sods, beaten down well to at least 6in thick. After that the door could be fitted and a preliminary firing done to bake the clay. This took about four hours and used 300lb of wood; when the oven was in regular use, the first heating of the day took two hours and 150lb of wood.

The principle of using such ovens is that a fire should be lit inside, kept burning until the oven is hot enough, then drawn out leaving just a few embers. Meat could be put in straight away, bread after waiting about thirty minutes for the top heat to cool down. The door was wedged shut with a piece of wood against the door and the front trench and sealed with clay. When the day's cooking was finished, the wood for the next day was stacked inside to dry out. Brushwood was the preferred fuel, made up in bundles called bavins. These were made up in 4ft lengths, with the twigs at one end and the thick ends at the other, so they could be stacked alternately.

An alternative was to use a beer barrel. This only worked in clay soil, as the method was to dig a curved trench for the barrel to sit in, then cover it with clay, well packed down, and light a fire in it until the wood had been burnt away and the clay had baked, supported by the barrel's iron hoops. Other possibilities were biscuit tins, opened out and fixed together, a hollowed-out ant hill or just a large camp kettle.

Another variation was to cut a fireplace into the side of a solid bank. This would be a little wider than the cook-pot, with a narrower deeper section below in which the fire would be lit, so the pot stood on the wider section above the fire. In the trenches these fireplaces could be cut out of the trench wall. Other methods of cooking in the trenches included little braziers, which were issued with charcoal, but these had to be properly ventilated to avoid carbon monoxide poisoning. Otherwise, the men improvised cookers out of whatever was available. Biscuit tins or buckets with holes punched in them to let air get to the fire could be used, with something laid across the top so smaller tins of food or a frying pan could be balanced over the fire. Toast or kebabs could be made with the aid of a bayonet.

Lucky soldiers had a Primus stove or a 'Tommy cooker'; the latter consisted of a tin with a solid gel fuel cake. The gel was lit and, after cooking was complete, the fire was extinguished by putting the lid on. When the gel was used up, strips of cloth or wood chips soaked in candle wax could be used. These cookers were so useful they were adopted as an issue item, but they were always in short supply.

Another cooking method, although not suitable for baking bread, was the Soyer stove. Designed for use in the Crimea, its design was brilliantly simple, consisting of a large drum with a fire at the bottom and a removable cooking pot fitted into the top. It had a flat lid and an external flue which prevented light escaping and alerting the enemy to its presence. Part of its popularity was that it used no more than a tenth of the fuel needed for other cooking methods. Both the Soyer stove and the Aldershot oven were still in use throughout the First World War. Later in the war some other ovens were introduced, including Perkins' and Hunt's steam ovens, each capable of baking 150 loaves at a time; both these types were used at the base bakeries, usually in sets of four.

There is a considerable difference between what can be produced by trained cooks in permanent kitchens and eaten at a table and what can be done with a field kitchen and eaten from a mess tin on the knees, not to mention the ad hoc meals the troops cooked for themselves. The main difference was in the availability of cooking stoves. In the unit cookhouses at home, cast-iron cookers with ovens, boilers and hotplates for saucepans or frying pans were used. These were fired with coal and were manufactured in sizes to feed 50, 100 or 150 men. In the field such cookers were impracticable and cooking methods were restricted to what could be boiled, stewed or cooked in the Aldershot ovens.

There were also field or 'travelling' kitchens. The purpose of these was to provide a hot meal when required. Infantry battalions each had four travelling kitchens which marched with the troops. Each consisted of a cook-cart drawn by two horses, made up of two separate parts: the body and the limber. The body had a fire box at the back with a fuel box on either side. There were four boiler holes with 5-gallon tanks for cooking, each with a lifting rod on either side, and struts which could be dropped to hold the body rigid when stopped. The limber was fitted with four asbestos-lined chambers to hold the tanks full of hot food and keep it hot for up to twenty-four hours. There was also a cupboard with the door hinged at the bottom so it could be laid flat for preparation work; it had four pull-out bowls, two for sugar, one for tea and one for salt. Two small lockers for storing small utensils and stores were fitted under the axle of the limber.

The food was cooked while on the march and the cook-carts were not allowed to stop while the troops were on the move, so they had to organise their cooking to fit in with the march. There was usually a 3-mile march taking fifty minutes, followed by a ten-minute halt, during which the cooks could attend to the food, usually moving the cooking containers so the food did not overcook during the next fifty minutes, and stoking the fires as needed. The food could only be of the stew or thick soup type, which could be ladled straight from the cooking pot into the men's mess tins or a dixie pot for a small group of men.

When the troops were in trenches, the cook-carts were stationed in the reserve and transport lines behind the trenches, preparing hot food and tea which were carried forward over the narrow duckboards through the narrow communication trenches. If these carts were not available, a trench would be dug, a narrow fire built along the middle and the cooking pots placed either side of it with another row on top. Other containers for hot food might be the bigger 'dixies' but these were difficult to carry through the narrow communication trenches, especially if the carrier had one in each hand.

At the docks two officers and their staff of talliers and weighers worked on the discharge of frozen meat, often working out of all six holds of a ship simultaneously. Special nets were used for mutton, each taking twenty cut carcases. The maximum permitted load per net was 14 tons. The meat was transferred from dock to train by lorry. The term 'cut mutton' meant that the carcass was halved and the hindquarters were put inside the forequarters to save space.

On the Western Front groceries were sent up on a daily train to the nearest railhead, where they were unloaded and sent on by 'train' – either a convoy of horse-drawn wagons (usually 200, using 400 horses with 400 accompanying men) or lorries accompanied by warrant officer 'conductors'. The groceries changed hands several times on the way to the final destination, from the railhead to the supply train to the divisional supply column and finally to refilling points where they were often dumped on the side of the road to be collected by each regiment and taken to the quartermaster sergeants who divided it into bags for each unit. If the ground was dry enough, hand trolleys could be used from there, but otherwise it had to be carried on a man's shoulders through the mud. There was often some difficulty in finding secure routes for the train, especially if the enemy were close. The Germans would have loved to get their hands on British supplies, so the standing order if they got too close was to shoot the horses and burn the supplies (assuming that there was time).

Animals for the Indian Army troops were processed at Marseilles, where they butchered sheep and goats, the greatest number of these being 26,096 in 1915. These animals were raised on farms close to Marseilles and Rouen. Although kept in sheds, they also had outside runs. These farms were run by civilians who lived on the sites. A pig farm was started near the base at Etaples, the animals fed on the food waste from the base. Several other bases did the same, and several also kept chickens at the bases, for the eggs. Sometimes the men kept their own animals in dug-outs in the trenches, including chickens, rabbits and even, in one case, a milk cow.

Vegetables and potatoes were often in short supply, and in some fixed locations attempts were made to grow them. The problem with this was that if the front was moving, there was no guarantee that the people who had planted and tended the crops would be there to harvest them. However, this worked both ways and there were some instances of British troops harvesting crops sown by the enemy. One medical officer, concerned by the lack of vegetables, sent out parties to pick the nettles and other wild plants which grew near the camp, which worked well enough if the party doing the harvesting were diligent in their selection. If not, they might pick poisonous plants and the result would be stomach problems all round.

Many Frenchwomen did their bit in feeding the troops by opening estaminets in their houses. The favourite dish was egg and chips, which would have provided a welcome change of texture from the inevitable stews turned out by the army cooks, but part of the charm must have been that someone was taking care to cook for the men.

Soon after the beginning of the war it was realised that canteens were needed in France and a new organisation, the Expeditionary Force Canteens, was set up with the managing director of the main supplier, Sir Anthony Price of Richard Dickson & Co., appointed honorary director. More contractors were needed and a Board of Control of Regimental Institutes was set up. This quickly made some rules: only approved contractors could supply the troops and retail price controls were fixed. A branch of the Quartermaster General's department was set up to make inspections and enforce quality standards. By April 1917 there were over 2,000 canteens at home and in June of that year the Navy joined in, and in April 1918 the Air Force joined too. In 1921 this organisation was transformed into the NAAFI.

In France the EFC began its work at Le Havre in 1915, operating out of a single second-hand car. At its peak, there were 577 branches, operating out of a fleet of 249 lorries and vans, 151 cars, 42 motorcycles and 14 trailers. They took over the mineral water factory at Etaples for general army supply, making lime-juice cordial as well. They also brewed beer and bought wine from suppliers in France, Spain, Portugal and Italy.

Other organisations, including the Salvation Army and the YMCA, also provided canteens and what were called 'rest huts', providing tea and buns and a comfortable place to relax.

Scrounging or 'winning' (i.e. thieving) was a useful skill adopted by some men, who were adept at picking up fruit or vegetables, eggs, or even an unwary chicken or duck; some even managed to grab a pig or sheep, although these were obviously difficult to conceal. There were a couple of recorded incidents of troops of soldiers coming across herds of pigs in oak woods. Turned out by their owners to forage for acorns, they soon found themselves turned into roast pork.

Items had a habit of disappearing from the supply trains en route to the front line, pocketable small tins being the commonest, and of those, the most 'popular' was tinned fruit. The people in the best position to help themselves to extra rations or portable items in tins were the cooks and those working on the supply trains, and there are numerous reports of their doing just that. The statistics of courts martial during the war shows 9,322 relating to theft. Among the men, there seems to have been an unofficial set of 'rules': it was one thing to steal from the army itself, or from local civilians, but not from other soldiers and never from a comrade. Scrounged food should be shared with mates. Some men drew the line at food taken from corpses, although when a dead man's belongings were returned to his family, any food or other immediately useful things were retained and shared out.

Biscuits and home-made cakes (especially rich fruit cakes) were a popular gift from home, although some donors had to be told that sending soap in the same package was not a good idea. Chocolate and peppermints were always welcome, as were small tins of fish or meat relishes, even curry powder which added a different taste to the ubiquitous bully beef. Letters home frequently requested such things as OXO, Bovril, sardines or other tinned fish. Perhaps best of all were Christmas puddings which, as with all other edibles, were carefully shared out among the recipients' mates.

Officers usually ate better than the men, mainly because they could afford to pay for additional items. They, like the men, received food from home, although this was more likely to be in the form of hampers from one of the big London stores such as Fortnum & Mason. These would include tins of fruit such as apricots, pears or pineapple, pâté de foie gras, Gentleman's Relish (a dense paste of anchovies) and bottles of brandy, port, wine and champagne, not to mention cigars. Those with friends or family in the countryside might receive game birds such as pheasant, partridge or grouse, and in some rural parts of France they even managed to shoot their own game, including deer and wild boar. In fixed locations they had officers' messes, where they ate with all the regimental ceremony of home; elsewhere they had dugouts where the batmen could prepare and serve meals.

Fortnum & Mason stocked a number of 'hampers' (which they called boxes) listed in their 'war catalogue'. They also offered 'monthly' boxes. These contained fairly ordinary items such as tins of peaches, but also some exotic foods, such as tinned grouse, devilled ham, turtle soup or lobster. These boxes were priced at 15*s*, and there was also what was called the 'Guinea Box', which could be sent direct to France for £1 2*s* 4*d*, or the 'Mediterranean' for £1 4*s*. Fortnum's also advertised 'Specialties', which included galatine of chicken, Guard's Mixture tea and crystallised fruits. Fortnum's also offered boxes which they thought were suitable for officer prisoners of war. Priced at between 4*s* 6*d* and 15*s*, these boxes were less exotic, and one, the 'T' box, contained fewer eatables but included a khaki handkerchief, shaving soap, bootlaces, coal tar soap, tooth powder and a toothbrush.

In the appropriate seasons, such things as cauliflowers, asparagus and tomatoes were also sent. There was also a 'Camp Pie', which was less popular. One officer wrote home that 'there was rather too much of the dog about them. Peter Crawford's dog seemed to recognise an old pal in the one we had last night.'

Christmas was always treated as an occasion, with a special meal, and officers from regiments with a national identity (Welsh, Scottish, Irish) would celebrate their saints' days. The traditional format was followed: soup, a roast, Christmas pudding and mince pies, and perhaps oranges and nuts, with beer for the men. In the other ranks' messes, it was traditional for the officers to wait on the men.

Serving Food to the Sick/Wounded

When serving food to hospital patients the first rule was scrupulous cleanliness. The cloth on the table or tray should be spotless, the place and glass polished until bright. Plate covers should always be used to keep hot food hot, and portions should be small, as a large plateful can be off-putting. It was felt that the content of meals should come as a pleasant surprise to the patient, but if they had expressed a strong dislike for any food item, this should not be ignored.

Chapter 10

Uniforms and Other Supplies

For many decades before the First World War British soldiers in the field wore the famous red coats. It was not until the campaigns on the north-west frontier of India that the wisdom of wearing less conspicuous uniforms was realised and khaki was adopted instead. Khaki is the Urdu word for 'dust', and describes the colour. The khaki serge uniform, known as the 1902 Pattern Service Dress, was introduced in 1902 and remained the standard throughout the First World War.

Service dress (i.e. that which was worn in the field, as opposed to cere-monial dress worn for major parades) consisted of thick wool, dyed khaki, most visibly in the jacket (also known as the tunic) and trousers. For cavalry regiments the 'trousers' were referred to then as pantaloons, but are now known as breeches. The tunic had two breast pockets for the man's pay book and other personal items, two other pockets at hip level and another sewn inside the right flap for the First Field Dressing. There were rifle patches above the breast pockets to prevent wear from the webbing equipment and rifle. Shoulder straps were sewn at one end and fastened with brass buttons. Rank insignia for other ranks was sewn onto the upper sleeve and Long Service and Good Conduct stripes were on the lower sleeves. The trousers had vertical pockets in the side seams and 'provision' (i.e. buttons) for braces.

Puttees were in use from 1902. Made of wool and fastened with tapes, they were worn over breeches or trousers and short boots, wound spirally and tightly, up from ankle to knee in infantry regiments and down in cavalry regi-ments. However, if wound too tightly, they could restrict the blood flow to the feet so that trench foot and even gangrene could ensue.

The tunic worn by other ranks buttoned right up to the neck and had a 'stand-and-fall' or 'Prussian' collar. The outside pockets were closed with a buttoned horizontal flap, and the tunic had five vertical buttons, sometimes of regimental pattern.

Amongst other minor variations, tunnelling companies wore the heavy working jackets with leather reinforcement across the shoulders that are still in use today and are known now, as they were then, as donkey jackets.

Scottish regiments wore a tartan kilt or trews instead of the khaki trousers, and the front of the tunic was cut away to allow space for a sporran. However, the sporran was for ceremonial occasions only, and in the field it was replaced by a thick cloth apron with deep pockets. With a kilt, no underpants were issued, and although short puttees were worn above the boots, long socks were added. The Highland regiments wore a Glengarry or Tam O'Shanter cap instead of the peaked cap.

Six sets of bagpipes per battalion were also issued as regimental equipment to Scots Guards and other Scottish battalions, including, rather incongruously, the Scottish cyclist battalions. These were not just used in ceremonial situations, but to cheer on the men as they advanced; their wailing sound frightened many of the enemy.

Unauthorised alterations of dress were forbidden. For example, men would cut off the skirts of greatcoats to avoid mud but officers were instructed to stop this, and to remind the men that the skirts of the coats could be buttoned up to keep them clear of the mud. It was also reported that in some Highland battalions the front corners of jackets were being cut off and rounded, another practice which was to cease forthwith.

The total quantities of clothing ordered on War Office contracts from 4 August 1914 to 31 March 1919 were as follows:

Ankle boots	46,973,000 pairs
Jackets	31,764,000
Trousers	28,297,000 pairs
Pantaloons (breeches)	9,874,000 pairs
Frocks, khaki drill	3,624,872
Trousers, khaki drill	3,695,254 pairs
Cardigans	20,059,000
Great-coats, dismounted	8,733,000
Frocks, khaki drill	3,624,872
Trousers, khaki drill	3,695,254 pairs
Cardigans	20,059,000
Great-coats, dismounted	8,733,000
Great-coats, mounted	91,849
Coats, warm, mounted and British warm	2,714,834
Leather jerkins and fur undercoats	4,362,500
Caps, service dress	23,549,000
Puttees	34,535,762 pairs
Flannel shirts	57,121,000
Cap comforters	13,030,877
Drawers, cotton	11,090,558 pairs
Drawers, woollen	41,818,577 pairs
Drawers, flannel	960,628 pairs
Drawers, cotton, short	14,044,936 pairs
Drawers, woollen, short	1,228,621 pairs

Gloves, woollen	19,501,986 pairs
Socks, worsted	136,764,000 pairs
Vests, woollen 20,331,597	
Vests, flannel	1,298,650
Blankets	41,143,938
Ground sheets	16,255,715
Fabrics (by the yard)	
Serge	66,463,501
Tartan	43,204,112
Cloth, great-coat	32,584,107
Bedford cord	4,523,508
Barathea	2,361,006
Whipcord	17,322,307
Flannel for shirts	231,075,317
Flannel, other	11,198,268

Some of these quantities may seem excessive, even for such a long period, but the War Office was also supplying uniforms to the allied armies. The total spent on clothing as listed above was £295,000,000, vastly more than the normal £850,000 per year in peacetime.

Provision, storage and issue were dealt with by the Chief Ordnance Officer's Royal Army Clothing Department. It started the war with a central depot at Grosvenor Road in Pimlico but this soon proved inadequate. As well as all the usual clothing for the rapidly expanding army, there were additional items ranging from cold weather to very hot weather uniforms, rubber boots and gas masks. At least they did not have to provide and stock dress uniforms, just standard service dress or khaki drill.

Additional premises were opened in London in Battersea Park, Olympia and White City, and further afield in Leeds, Manchester, Edinburgh, Glasgow, Dublin and other places where textile industries were located. Further depots were created for the sole purpose of clothing the Home Commands; the final number was eighty-five depots. By the end of the war there was total floor space in these clothing depots of over 2,000,000 square feet.

Badges of the regiments to which the troops were assigned were worn on the hat. There was a special badge for soldiers who voluntarily came from their homes in South America, Central America and Mexico to enlist in the army. The badge consisted of the letters BVLA (British Volunteers Latin America) in a diamond shape in yellow on a blue ground. A free issue of two badges was given to officers and other ranks. A version of this badge was given to members of the Nursing Services, QMAAC and other recognised women's army organisations. Wound stripes and overseas chevrons were issued free, but replacements had to be paid for.

Officers' dress was different from that of other ranks, except in colour. The cloth was of better quality (and thus more expensive) wool, and the whole thing was tailored to fit. After 1908 the tunic had longer skirts, and the Prussian collar was replaced by open lapels, more like a jacket than a tunic. A shirt and tie were worn under the jacket, both khaki from 1913. The breast pockets were pleated with scalloped flaps; those on the hips had straight edges. Rank insignia, which had formerly been on the cuffs, were moved to the shoulder straps, as they were thought to be less easy for snipers to see in that position. Like those for other ranks, where the higher ranks had more stripes, those for officers also had a varying number of stripes and stars and/or crowns.

The trousers or riding breeches were worn with brown leather riding boots, even in infantry regiments as many officers were still mounted. Officers of mounted regiments wore Bedford cord breeches and spurs on their boots. They wore a Sam Browne belt, black for rifle regiments, brown for others. Their peaked caps were like those of other ranks but better quality. Officers had to pay for their own uniforms, pistols and swords, but grants were available for the less well-off officers. Officers who had the money obtained their uniform from tailors in the London area of Saville Row, or the large London stores such as Gamages.

There was an authorised list of tailors, manufacturers and wool merchants who were approved to make officers' uniforms. There were some 4,000 of these on the authorised list. As well as reasonable prices and good quality work, they had to agree to observe certain working conditions, including fair wages. Yarn was issued to these manufacturers at fixed government prices, and it was to be used only for the fulfilment of the orders specified in the merchant's application. Prices of all sales from mill to wearer were on a fixed basis, and manufacturers and merchants had to supply monthly lists of all sales.

Officers could choose between sixteen cloths. The selling price of these was fixed at a rate that still allowed the best London tailors to do their bit. In fact, it turned out that 85 per cent of tailors were selling below the authorised price. In 1918 this scheme was extended to include officers' caps. It was discovered that these, which had been fetching from 18*s* 6*d* to 30*s*, could be produced at a standard price of 15*s*. Control of officers' badges and buttons followed.

At the end of 1918 cap and collar badges for officers of the Machine Gun Corps were changed from bronze to white metal. Bronze badges did not have to be changed and bronze badges in stock were to be used up. At the end of 1918 the wearing of officers' gloves became optional, except on ceremonial occasions. If worn, they should be of the brown regulation pattern.

In November 1914, when the winter set in early, there were queries about why winter clothing was taking up to three weeks to reach the troops when ammunition took forty-eight hours. The need for warm winter clothing was often not anticipated until the time for issue had almost arrived. Amongst the other items required for this were 3,000,000 goat and other skins, and many million square feet of sheep-skin; fur clothing had to be purchased in the USA and Canada. Inevitably, there was something of a shortage of winter clothing at the beginning of the war. One novel but successful solution to this was to pay a 'bounty' to recruits who brought their own greatcoats, boots and a good suit of clothes to wear during training and until a proper uniform became available.

Some special winter clothing was issued to certain units. Guards and brakes-men on broad gauge railways had leather jerkins, sweaters and leather gloves, and drivers of long-rein horse transport units working in forests had leather jerkins and greatcoats instead of a sheepskin-lined coat. Other units had oilskin suits, but these were to be regarded as unit property and should not be taken away by departing personnel. There were two types of oilskin: either a long coat or trousers and frock, in each case with a hood or sou'wester.

Extra blankets were issued to men of the British West Indies regiments and to 'Cape boys' with army auxiliary horse companies. These were marked in the men's paybooks.

None of the uniforms was waterproof and they became very heavy when wet, nor were they warm enough to withstand a really cold winter such as that of 1916/17. A rubberised waterproof cape was issued in 1917; this had a collar and button-up front. It could be used as a ground-sheet, or attached to another to form a shelter.

The standard great-coats were not waterproof either and became very heavy when wet. Goatskin jerkins were issued in 1915, but these were very smelly when wet. A later version of the jerkin made of plain leather with a blanket lining was issued in 1916; these were comfortable and durable.

As well as the issues of warm clothing for winter, many items of woollen clothing were sent from home by soldiers' families, volunteer women's organisations and the Red Cross. Collections of knitting patterns were available in book form, such as *Good Housekeeping* magazine's *Forces Knitting Book*, in other magazines and from wool shops. Patterns included balaclava helmets, scarves, caps, mittens and pullovers.

There were also 'trench comforts'. These comforts included thigh-length gumboots, fur undercoats, woollen underclothes and sheepskin waterproofs for the drivers. The cold winter of 1915 resulted in some cases of frost-bitten feet, so the men were issued with thick socks to wear in boots that were a size too large, plus an extra pair of socks to carry in their greatcoat pockets. There were braziers in the trenches near which wet socks could be dried, but there was no way of effectively drying soaked boots. Extra boots were not issued, so when the boots got wet in the constant slush and mud they stayed wet. In very wet conditions extra socks were issued in waterproof bags. Other trench stores included stretchers, periscopes and gumboots.

By the summer of 1918 a weekly ration of additional clothing and other articles was issued, on the basis of twelve jackets and fifteen pairs of trousers, twelve pairs of puttees, five caps, five mess-tins and four ground sheets per 100 unmounted men; or twelve jackets and twenty pairs of pantaloons, twelve pairs of puttees, five caps, five mess-tins and four ground sheets per 100 mounted men. Every autumn winter clothing and blankets had to be issued, and then collected up for repair and cleaning six months later when summer versions were issued. This involved so much bulk that special trains had to be arranged to carry it all.

During a twelve-month period in 1916–17, the following items were issued and returned:

	Issued	*Returned*
Jackets	2,912,530	1,523,435
Trousers	2,844,150	1,306,671
Greatcoats	284,317	221,483
Pantaloons	1,556,685	375,539
Shirts	5,934,158	1,445,356
Cardigans	1,478,128	524,644
Drawers	4,907,245	1,062,854
Socks (pairs)	12,724,340	3,883,110
Puttees (pairs)	3,631,899	714,166

No reason for the discrepancy between the two columns is stated in the official statistics, but those items not returned may have been worn out, damaged or perhaps lost when their wearer was killed.

Lightweight summer uniforms were known as khaki drill. They were a lighter shade of khaki and had only the breast pockets for other ranks. Trousers might be replaced by Bermuda shorts. A helmet known as the Pith helmet was worn; this was made of pith or cork with a cloth cover which included a wide pocket. Intended to shade the wearer's face and neck from the sun, they were worn in the Middle East and Africa.

At the beginning of the war there was a shortage of khaki material for uniforms, mainly because the khaki dye had been produced in Germany and it took some time to find other sources; however, there was plenty of dark blue serge available and this was used to provide 500,000 sets of clothing. Known as Kitchener's Blues, these uniforms were issued to recruits during initial training. They had no breast pockets or shoulder straps. There was also a shortage of buttons at this time. Greatcoats in blue and grey and some 500,000 civilian pattern greatcoats were bought, and 1,300,000 jackets and trousers, with 900,000 obtained from the US and Canada.

During the war period over 250,000,000 yards of woollen material, equivalent to 75 per cent of the country's production, was purchased by the government. The production of blankets in 1918 was two and a half times the pre-war output. The British wool clip was obtained direct from farmers, and arrangements were made with the Australian and New Zealand governments to buy whatever was not required for their home mills. The East Indian government made an arrangement whereby their wool could only be exported to Britain. Despite these measures, a shortage of shipping caused a shortage of wool and restricted amounts were made available to the civilian trade. This shortage became so extreme that unemployment benefit had to be given to workers in the combing trade. The British government spent £92,000,000 on wool in the year 1918.

The Board of Trade had set up a Cotton Control Board, but this proved inadequate to the task, so a Cotton Textiles Office was set up in Manchester and took over the whole of the government's purchasing.

Flax, from which linen is made, had traditionally been purchased from North Russia, but became difficult to obtain through Archangel during 1918; less than a third of the previous year's production was available. The Flax Control Board applied itself to finding adequate substitutes before the supply was cut off completely.

Because of the difficulties in leather supply caused by shipping problems and adverse exchange rates, it became necessary to control the use of leather. One of the measures used to conserve stocks was a prohibition on manufacturing ladies' boots with uppers over 7in long. Another was that from 1 April 1918 leather supplies to manufacturers using leather for civilian purposes was rationed and supplied only on production of a certificate of intended use. Goatskins for high-quality glace kid was obtained from America, this being sufficient for over 14,000,000 pairs of gloves in 1918. Hides from South America were used for army boot soles. The shortage of leather for boot uppers meant the government had to sanction orders worth £4,000,000 for this leather from America. Almost 2 tons of hides and tanning materials are needed to produce 1 ton of leather; about 360,000 tons of these were used during 1918. All but a quarter of this was produced outside the UK, and restrictions on its use were imposed.

Due to shortages, the government had to continue the control of imports of hides and tanning materials in 1918. Much of these came from India, but some also came from South Africa at fixed prices. All these contracts were cancelled without the need for the British government to utilise the break clauses; this was done by the Indian government. Surplus stocks were disposed of through pre-war channels.

The normal peacetime use of boots for the army was about 245,000 pairs, produced by some twenty-five firms in Northamptonshire. Once the war had started, the firms producing boots included some from Leicester, Bristol, Leeds, Scotland and Ireland. All work connected with boots, including repairs, was handed over to Edward Penton (later Sir Edward), the head of one of the leading firms of leather manufacturers. He coordinated all the work of the UK's bootmaking industry in making army boots. While most of these were for the British Army, Penton also supplied our allies.

Ankle boots for other ranks were known as ammunition boots because the contracts for them were sent out by the Munitions Board at Woolwich rather than from Horse Guards. They were unlined ankle boots, usually brown for field service and black for parades, and all were finished with hobnails except for those worn by storekeepers in ammunition stores for fear of sparks, or by lorry drivers as the nails might damage the pedals. Early versions had leather laces but in 1915 this was changed to woven cotton.

Just before war broke out, a new type of boot made with chrome tanned leather and machine-riveted seams was tested and approved, but there was a delay in production until the necessary machinery was made in sufficient numbers. These boots could also be re-soled and re-heeled by machine.

Gumboots were issued to certain companies, short ones for water tank companies and long ones (thigh-length) for mobile repair units and other motor transport units. The long ones were intended for use only when working in deep mud or water to recover ditched vehicles. They were to be regarded as part of the unit's equipment and not the individual's.

Ankle boots which could not be repaired at the front were to be returned, tied together in matched pairs. Failure to do this wasted a great deal of time at the receiving depots, and eventually a large collection of some 200,000 individual boots built up. At divisional boot repair shops, each man's boots could be repaired and returned to him, but there was an understandable reluctance to wear 'dead men's boots'. If the boots were too badly worn to be re-soled or re-heeled, a wooden sole would be fitted and the resulting 'clogs' were used in muddy lines.

A soft peaked cap, with a wire support to keep it in shape, and covered in the same khaki serge, was worn. The wire was often removed by the men to make their hat look battered. Later, a soft cap with ear-flaps, known as the 'Gor Blimey' was issued, then a soft cap without ear-flaps, known as the trench cap. This was easier to fold or roll and put away when the steel (officially known as the shrapnel) helmet was worn. It had a leather chin strap held at each side by small brass buttons. A regimental badge was attached at centre front above the peak. Some men liked what was called a cap-comforter, which was basically a woollen tube that could be worn as a cap or pulled down to form a scarf.

'Brodie helmets', protective soup plate-shaped helmets with a rounded top, were first issued in 1915, but it was not until the summer of 1916 that enough were available for a general issue. They reduced casualties with head injuries by as much as 80 per cent but were criticised as being too shallow, too reflective and too sharp at the rim, while the lining was too slippery. The second version addressed these complaints and had a separate folded rim and a two-part liner, and was finished with matt khaki paint and sand, sawdust or crushed cork to give a non-reflective finish.

In February 1918 contracts for just under 670,000 cork helmets were placed to meet urgent demands.

Salvage

An order issued in August 1918 showed the financial benefits of salvaging unserviceable clothing. For six months' worth, this totalled over £1,000,000. Most of this related to items sold to the rag trade, but it also covered some articles which were cleaned and re-issued, including buttons, and rags for cleaning purposes. However, a further order commented that many items of clothing were being exchanged for replacements before they were completely worn out; items for replacement were in future to be inspected by an officer who should ensure that they really were worn out beyond possible repair. Such items that were really unserviceable were to be returned in sacks or bundles, marked with details of the unit returning them; they, and the packing cases for re-use, were to be returned to the base ordnance units.

The salvage units operated a 'don't leave the front empty-handed' rule, which meant picking up any potentially useful items which had been abandoned by any of the combatant armies. Salvaged boots were repaired if possible and re-issued; damaged puttees were cut up and the good bits sewn together.

On the Western Front great warehouses, full of salvaged clothing and boots, acted as clearing houses. After cleaning and mending, these depots gave immediately usable items to the nearest units, or passed others to a repair workshop if a little more skill was needed. Only items or parts which were completely useless went in the scrap piles. At home a warehouse was set up at Dewsbury to receive rags shipped home from overseas, and condemned or repairable clothing from home commands.

Bath Houses

Bath houses were set up wherever possible, using beer barrels cut in half as baths. Periodically topped up with hot water from coppers, they were emptied when they became really foul and refilled with fresh water. While the men were bathing, their underwear was dumped into a big vat of creosol and their uniforms were ironed along the seams to kill lice. The men, once out of the bath, dashed upstairs where they were issued fresh underwear and given their uniforms back. The dirty underwear was boiled for four hours, then repaired if necessary.

Equipment Sets

Usually referred to as 'Equipment', these were basically a set of belts with shoulder straps and the items that were hung on them. The simplest was the Bandolier Equipment. This consisted of a set of five ammunition pouches worn diagonally over one shoulder and across the chest, with a belt round the waist with other pouches, a water bottle and a haversack. It proved inadequate for infantry but was retained by cavalry; this version had four more ammunition pouches on the back. Each pouch held ten rounds.

As well as their uniforms, men were issued with what were known as 'accoutrements', or equipment sets. This meant everything carried outside the clothing which was not a weapon (although it did include a pack of 150 rounds of .303 ammunition): belts, pouches, bandoliers, slings, mess tins, water bottles, entrenching tool and a haversack. The latter was to carry the greatcoat and a blanket.

The alternative was known as the 1908 Webbing Equipment, the webbing made of strong woven cotton. Like all other army supplies, the requirement for equipment sets was much greater than the existing supply. Only two firms possessed the machinery needed for making the webbing. When these companies had difficulty in keeping up with demand, a leather version was produced. This was initially intended for training only, to be replaced by webbing on leaving for active service, but in practice many reinforcements arrived at the front line still wearing the leather version.

The webbing itself was made by the Mills Equipment Company, which also made Blanco. This came either in a cake or as loose powder in a tin, and was used with a brush and water to clean the webbing and maintain its colour. With the exception of the version for ceremonial duties of military police or men on traffic control, it was not always white, as the name implies, but could be khaki or tan.

This equipment consisted of a wide belt with ammunition pouches holding seventy-five rounds on each side, and braces which went over the shoulders and crossed over the back. On top of these crossed straps was attached a large pack, meant to carry a greatcoat and blanket. Other items were attached to or hung from the belt: there were loops for a bayonet and entrenching tool handle, with the entrenching tool head in a canvas or web cover, a water bottle, a gas mask, a small haversack and a mess tin in a cloth cover. The haversack carried a rifle cleaning kit and personal items such as a knife and a rolled cotton pack of cutlery, shaving kit and comb. The demand for the items comprising this equipment soon outstripped supply and agents were employed to buy supplies from America and Canada.

All this weighed over 70lb, or more when the steel helmet was added. It might include a holster for men carrying a pistol. The whole thing could be assembled so that the wearer could put it on in one piece before fastening the belt. A joke of the time was that a young boy asked his father what soldiers were for, and the answer was 'To hang things on'.

Anti-gas clothing (combination suits or long coat and trousers) was issued in large quantities. Once contaminated, it was not to be returned to base until it had been hung up for exposure to the air or washed with soap and water. There were also anti-gas gloves, either leather or cotton.

After the Germans started using gas, it became a matter of urgency to produce respirators. The first version was a simple wire frame which covered the mouth and nose and contained a chemically treated fabric. This proved ineffective and was replaced by a copy of a German mask filled with cotton waste, and finally by what was known as a 'smoke helmet', which was long enough to tuck under the jacket and had celluloid eyepieces. The celluloid was produced from the cinema industry, but the gas-repelling chemical tended to evaporate and had to be renewed after a few months. Well over 7,000,000 masks were re-impregnated at special workshops before the smoke helmet was replaced by the PH helmet, so-called because the fabric was impregnated with a solution of phenate hexamine, which operated through a non-evaporating filter in a tin canister.

At the End of the War

Each man on his release, having handed in his arms, was provided with a full set of uniform and boots, a complete set of underwear and other necessaries. They were only meant to wear uniform for twenty-eight days after their discharge. This scheme involved the Ordnance Corps, which had to handle issues and returns, not only the returns from individuals but also those returned by units and those left in stores. Between the Armistice in November 1918 and October 1919 some 650,000 suits and 250,000 overcoats were issued to discharged soldiers.

On the cessation of hostilities, steps were taken wherever possible to reduce or terminate contracts for clothing and other items of equipment. Those reduced were generally on four-week termination clauses, but an additional proviso banned the cutting of materials supplied by the government. Other contracts were reduced progressively over an eight-week period. The reduction of khaki clothing contracts was offset by the demand for demob suits.

As soon as the Armistice was signed, the Royal Army Clothing Department (RACD) cancelled various orders for cloths and flannel; this was done with care to avoid unemployment. Many manufacturers were concerned that this process would lead to surplus stocks which they wanted the government to accept; this required careful negotiations as the RACD already had surplus stocks.

The contracts for cotton textiles included a break clause, but after some negotiation it was mutually agreed that it would be better to fix a period to the contracts, and not deliver any items which were in arrears. This meant that orders for 5,000,000lb of cotton yarn were cancelled without the government having to pay compensation.

No contracts for tanning materials were placed after the Armistice, and contracts for 500 tons of chestnut extract and 50 tons of hemlock were cancelled.

The only contracts which were difficult to cancel without compensation were those for boot half-soles, as these were not known in the civilian trade and there was some unemployment as a result.

The makers of hobnails and boot studs had been given permission to reduce their rates of delivery before the Armistice, but most were able to revert to civilian trade. Only a few makers were dependent on government orders and they were given orders for tips and tip nails for repairs.

One week after the Armistice, a month's notice was given to terminate contracts for the three principal types of glove. Contracts for motorcyclists' gloves had already been terminated as sufficient reserves had accumulated. Orders for aviators' gauntlets were cancelled with two months' notice. A notice was issued to the trade that no more skins should be cut up for fingerless sheepskin gloves, and another to the makers of anti-gas gloves. These manufacturers were anxious to return to their peacetime markets and so no compensation had to be paid, except for small amounts to the makers of tapes used in those types of glove.

In August 1918 orders for 250,000 pairs of rubber boots had been placed with two firms. It was agreed with both firms of bootmakers that supplies should cease as soon as possible, and only about one week's supply from each was delivered after the Armistice. Both firms had civilian contracts outstanding, so no compensation was required. However, a large claim was lodged by the makers of the waterproof cloth used for the top parts of the American trench boots (also known as Pershing boots, as General Pershing had approved their design), as there was no market for these boots in the UK. For high quality officers' boots, the firms making them were only too happy to revert to civilian trade where they could obtain higher prices.

Chapter 11

Medicine

At first glance it might not appear that medical services count as 'supply' for an army, but the supply of medical equipment and personnel trained to use it to keep the fighting and administrative men of that army fit is every bit as important as the other two of the oft-listed trio of 'beans, bullets and bandages'. During the course of the war medical teams in France handled 1,183,290 wounded men.

Four weeks before the Armistice, all new demands for medical and surgical dressings were carefully scrutinised. On 9 November manufacturers of dressings who had already been warned that outstanding quantities might not be required were notified that they should immediately cease production, and were requested to provide full details of stock in hand and the amount of undelivered quantities under contract which they were awaiting and which could be cancelled. A few of these contracts were subject to break clauses, but these involved minimal amounts of compensation.

On 8 August 1914 medical and surgical equipment and stores were ready for issue for the BEF and there were reserves in the main stores at Woolwich and two subsidiary stores at Southampton and Dublin. Contractors were warned to make arrangements to meet very large demand for medical and surgical stores, and stores were warned to maintain stocks of 100,000 wound dressings, vaccines and sera including anti-typhoid, anti-tetanus, anti-sepsis and cholera. A million doses of anti-tetanus sera (used as a prophylactic, as tetanus was one of the common problems associated with gangrene) were held in the medical stores at Woolwich. This store covered 21,495 square feet at the beginning of the war; this was soon trebled during the first year by erecting another sixteen sheds and hiring the Plumstead skating rink. In the second year more space was acquired at an unused tram depot and in the first half of 1916 nine large sheds were erected on Woolwich Common. More depots followed at Bristol, Liverpool, Reading, Northampton, Edinburgh, York, Aldershot and Dover. There were sixteen medical base supply depots in the field: five in France, three in Salonika, three in Egypt, two in North Russia and one each in Mesopotamia, Bombay and Italy.

More than 800 firms were given special contracts for 109,000,000 bandages, 87,721 miles of gauze and more than 7,251 tons of cotton wool. About this time it had been discovered that sphagnum moss (*Sphagnum cymbilio-folium*) has antiseptic properties, and when dried was an excellent absorbant for wounds, allowing cotton to be diverted to explosive manufacture.

Many standard drugs had been manufactured in Germany before the war, including aspirin, and British manufacturers were encouraged to produce more. Quinine, mostly in tablet form, was in much demand in theatres where malaria was prevalent. Some 5½ tons were needed each month.

The medical services also used a great deal of chloroform, ether and nitrous oxide for anaesthetic. Over the five years of the war 413,198lb of ether and 249,041lb of chloroform were used. Much oxygen was needed after the Germans starting using gas; the metal cylinders which held it in gas form were very heavy and so it began to be supplied in liquid form.

The average annual spending on medical supplies, which before the war had been £28,500, rose steadily through the war years: £475,962 (1915), £2,656,335 (1916), £3,961,932 (1917) and £3,009,028 (1918).

The overall control of the medical services in the war was through the Army Medical Service, which was part of the Adjutant General's Department. It was headed at the War Office by the Director General Army Medical Services, who had the rank of surgeon general. This rank was retitled Lieutenant General in 1917. Below him, in the field, were the Director General Medical Services (also a surgeon general); on the lines of communication the Director Medical Services, a surgeon/major general; with each corps there was a Deputy Director, usually a full colonel; and at division level there was an Assistant Director Medical Services, a colonel or lieutenant colonel. These officers were all qualified doctors but controlled the medical services' administration rather than performing medical duties.

The actual 'hands-on' medical work in the field was provided by the Army Medical Service Corps, subsequently the Royal Army Medical Corps (RAMC). With the exception of quartermasters, all officers of the RAMC's field units were doctors. This organisation was 'manned' by officers and men of the RAMC, female nurses of the Queen Alexandra's Imperial Nursing Services, some mobilised reservists (qualified nurses) and the Territorial Force Nursing Services, usually referred to as sisters. There were also male and female members of the Voluntary Aid Detachments, and the staffs of voluntary hospitals, both provided by the British Red Cross and the St John Ambulance Association. Ambulances were driven by men of the Army Service Corps and in some base and line of communication areas by women of the First Aid Nursing Yeomanry (FANY).

The Queen Alexandra's Imperial Nursing Service, most commonly called the Red Cross, consisted of ladies who had been trained as nurses, and who, when approved by the Nursing Board of the Medical Service, were admitted into the army as nursing sisters or as staff nurses, the former being the higher of the two ranks. Non-commissioned officers and first-class orderlies of the RAMC also underwent special training in connection with the Imperial Military Nursing Service, and these, when qualified and passed as such, were known as Queen Alexandra's Staff men. The total number of matrons, nursing sisters and staff nurses of the Imperial Military Nursing Service at the outbreak of war was about 300, distributed among the large military hospitals at home, in Mediterranean stations, South Africa and Egypt. The nursing sister went no nearer to the firing line than the base hospital. The services of fully trained lady nurses were invaluable in cases requiring prolonged treatment, and especially in cases arising from disease, as distinct from the surgical cases.

The headquarters of the RAMC was at Aldershot, where three depot companies were devoted to the training of recruits, and there was also a training school for medical officers and a school of army sanitation. Aldershot was also the location of the record office of the corps, which dealt with all statistical matters concerned with enlistment of recruits, communications with reservists and all that might be classed under the head of the corps' business organisation.

The *raison d'être* of the medical services was the maintenance of the army, both at home and in the field, firstly by the prevention of disease and secondly by the treatment of the sick and wounded. To this end, the work of the officers of the RAMC included the supervision of sanitary precautions, the collection of the sick and wounded and their delivery to dressing stations and hospitals and their care whilst there, the compilation of records, and the maintenance of surgical and medical supplies.

What they could not deal with was dentistry, which was much needed. When the BEF went to France in 1914 it took no dentists. Then General Haig had a terrible toothache at the height of the Battle of the Aisne in October of that year; no one was able to help him and he had to wait until a French dental surgeon arrived from Paris. Haig contacted the War Office to ask for dentists to be recruited for the BEF. Twelve arrived in November and eight more in December.

Teeth were checked at recruitment centres, but some men with poor teeth were passed. This left them unable to eat the hard biscuit, and they were also vulnerable to the early stages of scurvy which affects the teeth, loosening them and causing the gums to swell. This was due to the lack of food containing sufficient ascorbic acid in the rations.

The officers of the RAMC also had the same duties of care and discipline for their men as did any other type of officer. These included providing food, clothing and housing, transport and fitting them into their allotted place in the line of march. And of course they had to have the requisite qualifications to perform their actual duties as doctors and surgeons. They were required, in peacetime, to attend lectures on the principles of staff duties in the field. These included how an army was organised in the field and how its various departments worked; a general outline of strategic and tactical operations to allow medical officers to work out the best arrangements for those operations; how the lines of communication worked, with a view to evacuating the wounded; the systems of communication and the desired format of messages; plus map reading and field sketching, using scales, the conventional signs and use of the compass. This was intended not only to teach the officers how to reach a specified point on a map, but also how to submit locations and plans of proposed hospitals and dressing stations.

There were separate training syllabuses for NCOs and men, which included the use of semaphore signalling. They would have already gone through basic training, which included the use of firearms, but as medical personnel they did not have any involvement in actual fighting, except when necessary to defend themselves or their patients. These syllabuses included improvised carriage of patients, such as making hand-seats between two carriers, plus stretcher exercises, the preparation of general service wagons and other vehicles to carry wounded, and the preparation of operating and ward tents. All these exercises took place in the morning. In the afternoon instruction was split between that for officers and that for NCOs and men. For the latter, this involved learning about sanitation in the field, preparing field ambulances and dealing with necessary paperwork, plus mounting and dismounting injured men from horses and basic horsemastership (necessary for the care of the horses who pulled the wagons). It included pitching and striking tents: a standard small circular bell tent took two men. They had a single pole and twenty-two or twenty-four bracing lines, depending on the model. Each tent came in a large canvas valise, with forty-seven pins in a smaller bag and two mallets (with separate handles). The whole thing weighed 83lb.

The hospital marquee had internal dimensions of 29ft long by 14ft wide and required an eleven-man team to erect it. Marquees came in several pieces, including a four-piece waterproof base. There were four poles, plus 184 tent pegs, eighty-two bracing lines and two mallets as above. The whole thing weighed 512lb. A larger version of the hospital marquee, with internal dimensions of 35ft long and 17ft wide, weighed 1149lb. Operating tents were smaller than the marquees, but rectangular with a doorway at each end. They had two upright poles and one ridge pole. They were fitted with six small ventilators and one large ventilator on each side. They weighed 181lb.

Training courses also taught methods of water purification. It was well known that bad drinking water is a fruitful source of disease in military forces. Each field artillery brigade had three men of the RAMC and each infantry unit had five to ensure the purity of the water supply by sterilisation and the thorough preparation of all drinking water. These men were under the orders of the medical officer attached to the unit concerned, and were intended to assist in the care of the sick and wounded when necessary.

For the officers, there were lectures on field medical organisation, duties in camp and on the line of march, how to select suitable sites for camps, billets, hospitals and dressing stations and ensure they were away from hazards such as rifle and shell fire. If time permitted, advanced training included working as a unit in the field, collecting wounded and treating them; whenever possible this training would be combined with field exercises of other troops.

The first discussion in the training manual was on the incidence of sickness in the army and how attention to good sanitation practices made a difference. The first thing which affected the health of troops was the individual's age; one might suppose that older men were more prone to sickness, but the opposite was in fact true, especially relating to enteric fever (typhoid). We would now explain this by saying that the older men had built up some immunity through prolonged exposure. Over the five years of the war 49,890 officers and 952,921 other ranks with illnesses (rather than wounds) were evacuated from France and Flanders.

The next discussion was on locality, especially where this coincided with a hot climate. As well as enteric fever and other digestive problems, malaria and pneumonia were prevalent in hot countries, especially in the wet seasons. Interestingly, the hospital admissions records of troops showed that battle wounds were the cause of only one in twenty-five cases, the others being due to disease. The only situation in army life where life in the field was healthier than life in a garrison was that of venereal disease, on a ratio of one case in the field to four in garrisons. Even so, over 18 per cent of the common diseases in sick patients were due to venereal disease. The other major problem was that of trench foot; this is caused by prolonged immersion in dirty water which causes deterioration and destruction of the capillaries and morbidity of the surrounding flesh. Left untreated, it usually results in gangrene (and amputation). The best prevention is keeping the feet dry, warm and clean. The incidence of trench foot was reduced by the introduction of duckboards in trenches, and by pairing each man with another: they then mutually inspected each other's feet every day.

The longer a campaign lasted, the more admissions there were to hospital for disease. The holding of a position for any lengthy period, siege works and actions which demanded the retention of a considerable body of men in one place for a length of time invariably increased the proportion of disease among the total of the force employed, so there was much emphasis on disease prevention. Vaccination was used, mainly against smallpox and typhoid, although the latter was only effective for a couple of years. More important was personal cleanliness; baths at least once a week were advocated, and daily washing of crotch, armpits and feet. Fingernails should also be attended to when washing the hands. The hair should be kept short and brushed at least once a day, as should the teeth, although some recruits had to be taught the use of a toothbrush. The hairbrush should be washed or rinsed in cold water with washing soda. Underclothes should be changed weekly, and a separate set used for sleeping. Each man should have at least four pairs of socks, two in the wash and one each for morning and evening wear. When it was not possible to wash clothing, it should at least be brushed or shaken and left in the open air for a while.

The necessity of fresh air and good ventilation was emphasised. One point of great interest in this and other contemporary manuals is that they show what was the norm in various equipment and building methods of the time. This manual, when discussing good ventilation, suggests that the top window sash should be lowered a few inches to allow air flow, which suggests that hinged windows were less common.

The need for cleanliness in barracks and hospitals was well established, as it was in kitchens and canteens. There were a few basic rules as far as food was concerned: no food should be kept in barrack rooms, tents or hospital wards. If it was absolutely essential that it should be there, it should be kept in a covered utensil. All meat or bread stores should be kept free from, and inaccessible to, flies. All areas used for preparation of food should be kept scrupulously clean, as should the hands and clothing of mess orderlies and cooks.

Associated with this cleanliness was the disposal of refuse and the use and care of toilet facilities. There were special receptacles for kitchen refuse; wet and dry materials should be kept separate, but both should be covered to keep out flies and should be emptied and cleaned daily. Paper should be kept separate. Latrine accommodation as discussed in the training manual is another area which throws light on what was considered the norm at the time. In most barracks at home water closets were provided, these being flushed automatically or by hand (with a bucket of water, one supposes). In the newer barracks there were water closets with individual flush tanks; the users of these were advised to seat themselves carefully to avoid fouling the seat and to see that the contents of the pan were properly flushed away by pulling the chain of the flush tank.

Toilet paper should be torn or cut to the size of a hand; despite this being provided, it was apparently not unusual to find that whole sheets of newspaper had been used. In a few places at home and most commonly abroad, dry-earth closets were used; a box of dry earth or sand was kept in the closets with a scoop to facilitate its use. The buckets were to be emptied regularly and scoured out. Much the same applied to urinal buckets.

In the interests of cleanliness of clothing and bedding for the sick, field equipment included portable steam dispensers. For items which were too large to be put in the body of the steamer, such as soiled mattresses, a solution of formaldehyde was sprayed on. As with everything else the British Army did, the procedures for medical services were laid down in the Field Service Regulations, and RAMC officers were expected to be familiar with them. They included a requirement to deal with the pay and discipline of the men under their care until they were discharged back to duty.

The general structure of each army consisted of divisions, each of three brigades, each of which comprised four infantry battalions. Each battalion had its own medical officer. Each brigade had a field ambulance, each of two sub-sections, one tent sub-section and a bearer sub-section. The tent sub-section manned the advanced dressing station, close to the firing line, and also staffed main dressing stations further in the rear. Bearer sub sections, divided between the four battalion aid posts, received the wounded from the regimental MO and took them to the advanced dressing station; from here, after receiving further treatment, they were sent by ambulance to the main dressing station, which then sent them on to the casualty dressing stations and then on to hospitals.

Whenever the fighting arm was planning an attack, the Chief Administrative Medical Officer was to be included in the plans so he could organise the medical arrangements, such as the number of field ambulance units, the areas allotted to them and thus specific locations at various times, and, if possible, the numbers and sites of dressing stations. He then drafted paragraphs to be included in the divisional operation orders for the information of troops, and arranged routes for the medical units and the time and order of march. Those of the wounded who could not be returned to their units would be evacuated on the returning supply wagons. Arrangements would also have to be made to feed troops under the care of the medical corps.

The organisation of the medical services in the field was divided into three zones: the collecting zone, the evacuating zone and the distributing zone. The first of these contained the field units, field ambulances and regimental aid posts and dressing stations. The second, situated on the line of communication, contained clearing hospitals, ambulance trains, advanced depots of medical stores and sometimes hospitals. The third consisted of hospitals, convalescent depots and the means of moving patients to a more permanent and suitable facility. This was known as the chain of evacuation; it operated on the general principle that the sooner a man's wounds were treated, the better his chances of survival.

The first thing to be done when a man received a wound was to put a dressing on it and get him to the regimental aid post. Each man carried a 'first field dressing' in an inside tunic pocket and this would be applied by himself, his comrades or a stretcher-bearer. The 'first field dressing' consisted of a cloth packet containing two dressings (one each for entry and exit wounds) made of 2½yd of bandage, some gauze and a safety pin. At the start of the war an ampoule of iodine had been included with the first field dressing carried by every soldier, but it was later discovered that it had no useful purpose and tended to cause blistering. The white bandages of the first field dressings were soon replaced by khaki versions once it was realised that white was too conspicuous. At the aid posts, casualties received basic treatment such as ensuring they could breathe properly, immobilising injured limbs and stopping bleeding. These aid posts were also known as dressing stations.

Sometimes the casualty would be able to get himself to the regimental aid post, but if not the unit's stretcher-bearers would carry him there. Every major fighting unit organised a regimental aid post close to the front line, ideally in a sheltered spot such as a barn or abandoned house. These posts were run by the unit's regimental medical officer, with two orderlies as well as the attached stretcher-bearers. These regimental aid posts usually had fifty stretchers and a hundred blankets, plus splints, shell dressings, and means of heating food and water, with sixteen stretcher-bearers allocated from the regiment, with a reserve of another sixteen at the start of an offensive.

The term 'field ambulance' did not just mean a vehicle for carrying the wounded, but was a self-contained mobile medical unit, three of which were allocated to each division. It was commanded by a lieutenant colonel. Its 234 personnel included ASC ambulance drivers as well as RAMC personnel. It had ten horse-drawn ambulances, seven of which were soon replaced by motor vehicles, with the other three retained for use on ground too rough for motor vehicles. It included a bearer division for the collection of wounded, and a tent division for their reception, temporary treatment and care. As well as the ambulance wagons to carry the wounded, transport wagons were included to carry medical and surgical stores, equipment and a supply of water. Each unit was meant to be able to deal with 150 casualties before they were moved on.

Although they do not seem to have used the term 'triage' at the time, this clearly took place, with serious cases being dealt with first. Priorities were to stop bleeding, apply field dressings and support broken limbs. Pain relief could be achieved by applying morphine under the tongue, from where it is quickly absorbed, but this could only be done under the orders of a medical officer. Each wounded man had a tally attached to him, listing his name, regiment, rank and number, and specifying the cause of the wound and its location. There were twelve classifications of gunshot wounds, starting with those to the head and face and going on to those of the limbs, plus three other types of wound (by sword, lance or bayonet, and 'miscellaneous'). The tally also included whether an opiate had been given and the amount. The tallies used were coloured red for the seriously wounded or white for slightly wounded. Cases where a tourniquet had been used were automatically classified as seriously wounded.

Once placed on a stretcher, the wounded man was not to be moved from it on reaching an ambulance vehicle; the stretcher-bearers were provided with another stretcher for the next patient. When motorised ambulances had to go into a workshop for repairs, their stretchers should first be removed.

When collecting patients, their weapons should also be collected. Ideally their ammunition would have been taken from them before they were sent to the rear, but when this had not been done, it would be collected and handed over to ordnance depots. Later in the war, when America had joined, American troops who were sent to casualty clearing stations had their clothing, arms and accoutrements taken with them. When they transferred to ambulance trains, these items were to be passed to the base ordnance depot at Havre or Calais, the package clearly marked as containing American equipment or clothing. On arrival, the contents of the packages were sorted into quartermaster's property such as clothing and shelter tent halves, poles and pins, or ordnance property such as accoutrements and pistols, mess tins, water bottles, entrenching tools and bayonet scabbards, and were then passed to the American quartermaster or American ordnance depot. When an American patient needed to be reclothed on discharge from the hospital, he was given British underclothing, puttees and boots, and American uniforms, blankets and accoutrements such as haversack, canteen and cover, mess tin, and cutlery. As stocks of American clothing were short, the hospitals should not demand more items than would be needed in the next four or five days.

The training manuals for RAMC personnel suggested that dressing stations should ideally be located in a building, but otherwise in a tent. They should be positioned as far forward as was safe from rifle and shell fire. Low ground was better than high as it generally gave some protection, water was more easily obtainable, and the wounded did not have to be carried uphill. Casualty clearing stations should also ideally be in a building, situated well behind the front line or artillery positions, near water if possible and easily accessible to wheeled vehicles. However, care should be taken not to block roads needed by fighting troops and supply wagons. Plenty of space was desirable as it might be necessary to encamp the entire ambulance unit. Suitable buildings, if available, should have easy access, be clean and readily cleanable, have good ventilation, and ideally offer facilities for lighting, heating and cooking. Schools were generally considered the best.

On arrival at the designated site, the medical store cart should be unpacked, groundsheets, blankets and the necessary medical and surgical equipment prepared for use, and distinguishing flags erected. If there were no permanent kitchens available, temporary fire trenches should be dug and simple shelters erected for the feeding and treatment of the wounded. Everything should be made ready for receiving and dealing with the wounded as they arrived. Although operations were only to be carried out in cases of dire necessity, an operating room or tent would be prepared with sterilised instruments.

As well as basic wound dressing supplies, the regimental medical officers carried a box with items for the relief of simple ailments such as headaches, coughs and colds, and stomach upsets.

Since system organisation was considered to be of the greatest help in dealing with large numbers of wounded, the dressing station should be arranged in separate departments: one for receiving, recording and classifying the wounded on arrival and also for recording their transfer or discharge; another for severe cases; another for slight cases; and one for the dying. There should also be marked places for cooking and boiling water, receiving arms and accoutrements, latrines, urinals and refuse disposal, a mortuary and a park for transport.

The evacuation zone consisted of hospitals, ambulance trains, advanced depots of medical stores, and sometimes stationary general hospitals. The space required for tented hospitals for up to 200 patients was 204yd by 190yd, but there should be extra space available in case of larger numbers. These tented hospitals were more or less stationary, but might have to relocate depending on the ebb and flow of battle. There was some degree of specialisation involved, and one location might have several casualty clearing stations, each dealing with, for instance, certain types of wound or infectious diseases. While every effort was made to aid the recovery of casualties, many wounds were beyond the skill of the medical officers, and these cases moved from the clearing stations only as far as a military cemetery.

There were sometimes difficulties over moving sick patients with infectious diseases during an epidemic. It was essential to separate these patients quickly from the healthy troops, but the usual method of sending them back on returning supply transport was not advisable as there was unlikely to be sufficient time for this to be properly disinfected before reloading with supplies.

From the dressing stations, casualties were moved to a casualty hospital; these were renamed casualty clearing stations in 1915. They were originally meant to be a link between dressing stations and base hospitals but when trench warfare became established many gradually developed into field hospitals. On the basis that the sooner operations were done the better, from 1915 many operations were performed at these casualty clearing stations. These stations were located close enough to the fighting zone to allow early treatment but ideally were beyond the range of enemy artillery fire. They were also preferably close to a railway so that casualties could be evacuated by rail to base hospitals and on to a port for transport to a hospital at home. In northern France ambulance barges were used on the canal system. These barges had a kitchen, a dispensary and a toilet, with one medical officer, two nursing sisters, nine RAMC orderlies and three Royal Engineers of the Inland Water Transport department for navigating duties. Each was wide enough to provide two rows of beds. They were mainly used for men with head and chest wounds and gunshot fractures of the thigh, for whom the jolting of road transport was contra-indicated. These barges mostly moored up for the night.

When it came to transferring patients, they were divided into those who could walk, those who could travel sitting up in a wagon, severe cases who had to lie down in a wagon, severe cases needing hand carriage on stretchers, and very severe cases who should not be moved until stabilised. These latter tended to be those with penetrating abdominal wounds. These were exacerbated if there was food in the stomach, as partially digested food escaping into the abdominal cavity tended to cause a high mortality rate from infection. This problem largely derived from the practice of giving the men a good breakfast before they went into action.

As well as the light ambulance wagons, there were also some heavy ambulances, drawn by six horses. These were specially constructed to serve as temporary shelters for up to four patients, as well as transport. They were like small hospitals for serious cases and if necessary could be parked in a safe place with an orderly to care for the patients. Each of the five armies had a mobile x-ray unit and at least one mobile laboratory.

Services in the distributing zone consisted of stationary hospitals, general hospitals, some convalescent depots on the line of communication, ambulance trains, hospital ships and finally the military hospitals and convalescent depots in the UK. These were for patients who were expected to be fit for duty in six weeks and could then be returned to their units. There were six main convalescent hospitals in the UK, each dealing with patients from hospitals in a specific command: Eastern and Aldershot; London; Southern Command; Western Command and men from Lancashire regiments; Irish Command and men from Irish regiments; and Northern and Scottish Command and men from Scottish regiments, in each case assuming there was space. If not, they would go to the nearest convalescent hospital with space.

Stationary hospitals were located at certain points on the line of communication, often including railway posts. They were mobilised on a ratio of two per division in the field and were organised for 200 beds, but had to be prepared to expand in emergencies. Buildings were preferable, but tents were acceptable if no buildings were available.

General hospitals were much like the larger military hospitals in peacetime; some had convalescent facilities attached or close by. Most were at port locations, with a capacity of 520 patients, and were staffed by about 170 personnel. By 1918 some had grown to a capacity of 2,500 patients, with over 450 personnel, of whom forty were medical officers and 125 were female nurses. In

1917 the American forces took over the running of six of these hospitals, which were then known as American General Hospitals. When the war started, only 900 beds (for British patients only) were provided in hospitals in France, but by the end of the war, after it had been decided to treat more minor cases in France, this number had grown to almost 90,000.

Medical statistics for this war are sparse, and those that are available do not include the men who died before they received medical care, or those who were killed outright. Some 2,273,000 men were wounded in action, of whom over 1,454,000 (64 per cent) were able to return to full duties, with nearly 410,000 (18 per cent) returned to light duties or sedentary work. Just over 1,000,000 were evacuated to the UK from the Western Front, but this figure includes the sick as well as the wounded. A total of 118,541 officers and 2,245,050 other ranks were brought home to hospitals in the UK. Not surprisingly, the numbers of men suffering from illnesses were greater amongst those serving in hot climates: East and West Africa, Gallipoli, Mesopotamia and Palestine.

A sample of those admitted to casualty clearing stations showed that just under 40 per cent were wounded by rifle or machine-gun bullets, and most of the rest by grenades, shells or trench mortars. The most frequent wounds were to the head, face or neck at nearly 16 per cent, the legs at over 15 per cent, and the arms at 11 per cent.

Meanwhile, more military hospitals were set up in the UK. Some Territorial Force hospitals were taken over, and several mental asylums were converted to military hospitals after the residents had been moved elsewhere. Some private auxiliary hospitals, including one at Highclere Castle, were started by rich individuals and staffed by volunteers; others were run by the Red Cross.

The British wanted all sick and wounded who were to go to England to go through Calais, but the French were using this port for goods and were reluctant to allow this, so most hospital ships from the Western Front crossed the Channel from Boulogne to Dover or Southampton, from where the men were transferred first to trains and then to road vehicles to reach their designated hospital. Much of this transfer work was done by volunteer first-aiders.

Base depots of medical stores were provided on the Western Front in a ratio of one for every two divisions, mostly near the ports and on the lines of communication. They supplied and replenished the medical and surgical supplies of all the medical units in their designated area.

Much attention was paid in the training manual to removing the wounded from the field both with and without the use of stretchers. Where a single man was to carry the patient, he could do this pick-a-back (piggyback) if the patient was conscious and able to hold on. This method was eased for both parties by improvising a seat. The best of these consisted of twisted straw wound round a stick, with loops added for the carrier's arms; these connected with a horizontal piece at the front which sat across the carrier's chest so he could hold it in place. The patient faced forward with his head alongside that of the carrier and his arms over the carrier's shoulders. Obviously this method was not suitable for patients with wounds on the front of their body. These would be better carried by the back-lift, where they were positioned with their back to the carrier's back, and held by the armpits. The fireman's lift involved the patient lying face-down across the carrier's shoulders, with one of his arms extended backwards across the carrier's chest and his own thigh, and the carrier gripping his wrist to keep him in place.

Puttees could be used to assist the carrying of a patient on the carrier's back. The puttee was taken off the patient's leg and placed at the top of his thighs in front of the buttocks, then tied in a reef knot to form a long loop. That loop was then placed across the carrier's forehead. If needed, a second puttee could be placed outside the first, across the patient's back, under the carrier's armpits and tied across his chest. This was a particularly useful way of carrying in broken country as it left the carrier's hands free.

When there were two carriers available and the patient was unconscious, one carrier put his arms under the patient's armpits from behind and clasped his hands across the chest. The other carrier took the patient's legs, standing between them, and they proceeded with the patient moving feet first. However, this method might need some modification if a leg was injured, in which case the legs should be tied together. When the patient was conscious and could be moved sitting up, he could be carried using what was known as the 'hand-seat'. Here the two carriers faced each other, each put one hand on the other's hip and they grasped their other hands together. The patient was seated on the gripped hands and supported behind by the crossed arms. This method could only be used for short distances.

There were various types of stretcher available. As with most other bits of equipment, the design changed over time and with experience. All could be rested on the ground or on a wagon on four small feet and all consisted basically of two long poles with carrying handles at each end; these were connected by a short pole known as a traverse, and they had a canvas 'bed' and a wedge-shaped pillow with leather thongs to hold it in place. The side poles were 7ft 9in long, and the canvas bed 6ft long and 1ft 11in wide. The whole thing weighed about 30lb and was usually carried by four men. Some versions had a hood for use as a sun or rain screen. The patient's position depended on the nature of his injury but in general the head should be kept low and not pressing on the chest. With head injuries padding was organised so the injured part was not pressing on the canvas.

Stretcher-bearer teams practised together to keep the stretcher level; this was best done up and down steps. The poles should never be carried on the bearers' shoulders, as it was essential that the patient could be seen, and if one bearer tripped or was wounded, the distance from the stretcher to the ground was likely to cause further injury. The patients were usually strapped in so they could not fall out. The stretcher should never be lifted over walls or fences; instead, these should be broken down if there was no opening available.

Where there were no normal stretchers available, they could be improvised with poles (or even rifles) and blankets, great-coats or stout sacks, attached by twine passed through holes and round the poles. If nothing else was available, puttees could be tied diagonally between the two poles. Doors, gates or hurdles could also be used.

Animals could be used to carry stretchers, with the stretcher attached to the tail end of one beast and the head of another. When camels were to be used for this, they had to be trained to rise from their sitting position together and walk smoothly. Each was led by an attendant. Mules or camels could be used to carry cacolets but this was very tiring for mules due to the weight involved.

Wagons used as patient-carrying vehicles could be either purpose-built or adapted. In either case, the standard size was for four patients lying on stretchers (two on the floor and two on rails set higher up). They should be wide enough to permit an attendant to move down the middle aisle. The wagons were four-wheeled with a frame for a canvas cover. Some wagons had seats fastened to the sides for patients who could sit up, with two seats at the front for the attendant and the driver.

A resourceful team using General Service or other similar wagons could either devise a method of holding stretchers in place, or provide a soft springy 'bed' of hay or bracken covered with blankets. If mattresses were available, they could be added. The French provided a 'Brechot' fitting (a three-tiered frame to support three stretchers). Each wagon, with one of these in each corner, could carry twelve stretcher cases. At least one wagon fitted with these frames was added to every supply train from Amiens. These wagons were painted with a red cross (known at the time as the Geneva Cross).

As the war progressed, mechanical ambulance vehicles came into use; as with the horse-drawn wagons, these might be purpose-built or adapted from other uses. Motor lorries used to deliver supplies, for example, were frequently adapted to carry wounded men rather than returning empty. A 3-ton lorry could carry fourteen men sitting up with their backs to the sides, or eight lying down. Motor omnibuses were also used.

In cold weather ambulances had to be heated and most were fitted with a system of heating based on pipes leading from the exhaust. The pipe led vertically upright from the silencer or exhaust pipe and was carried round the inside of the ambulance in a 1½in pipe and then out of the back of the vehicle.

When these were fitted, great care had to be taken that there would be no escape of exhaust gases inside the ambulance, and commanding officers were to make periodic inspections to check this.

Ambulance trains were used whenever possible to carry patients long distances; up to 230 stretcher cases and 60 'walking wounded' cases with about 40 medical staff could be accommodated on each train. Those with purpose-built carriages were used for serious cases; the trains were also equipped with coaches for medical personnel, a dispensary, supplies and kitchens as well as storage for food. They had corridors end to end and were basically well-equipped rolling hospitals. The carriages for patients were designed to allow easy access and egress for stretcher cases. These trains had sixteen cars, and those for patients had three tiers of beds on each side, the middle one of which could be folded back to allow sitting patients to use the bottom tier. The trains were heated by steam, but also generated their own electricity to drive ceiling fans. British passenger sleeping carriages usually had six compartments, each of which could hold six minor cases. The larger British railway companies already had sleeping cars, and a plentiful supply of bedding material.

At the beginning of the war, one ambulance train was to be allocated to each division. Congestion on the railways led to ambulance trains often having to take a very roundabout route, and including the necessary stops for meals and dressing the patients, it could take up to seventy-two hours from front to hospital. Despite calls for more trains to be provided, the General Staff ruled that there should not be more than thirty ambulance trains per day, with any additional patients being moved by road or held near the battle area until trains were available.

Field ambulance vehicles, like static medical establishments, were marked during the day by a flag bearing the Geneva Cross on a white ground and a Union Jack alongside, and at night by two white lamps, placed horizontally.

The training manual seems to define civilised countries as those which had signed the Geneva Convention, while those which were not signatories were considered uncivilised. As far as the medical service was concerned, the main difference was that wounded British personnel in 'uncivilised countries' could not be left on the field in the expectation that the enemy would care for them. The medical units might need an armed escort and their personnel might have to go armed to defend themselves and their patients.

RAMC troops were not really soldiers, but had to go through basic training on enlistment as soldiers, so they learned the habit of quick, intelligent and obedient response to orders, were taught to march and execute military formations, and learned other matters which might have seemed to the men to bear no relation to their real work; then, under a drill sergeant, they were instructed in stretcher drill, and the routine of hospital work. The actual care of patients was taught last, although this went on throughout their service. Making beds for patients was done in such a way that changing sheets and all else that might be required was carried out with the least possible discomfort to the patient. Later in training, the RAMC men were promoted to second class and then to first class orderly, when they learned the various ways of bandaging, how to take temperatures and pulses, and everything required for the nursing of serious cases. If satisfactory, they might be recommended for a course of training in Queen Alexandra's Imperial Nursing Service, from which they emerged with an extra sixpence a day on their pay, which they retained in all ranks.

The working day of a first class hospital orderly (known to the rest of the army as 'poultice-wallahs') started early, at 5.00am. On arrival at the ward, he turned out the convalescent patients and gave them various tasks in connection with the routine of the ward, drawing rations for patients on ordinary diet, sweeping and other cleaning tasks. The orderly took particulars from the night man, then washed the patients that needed careful attention and prepared them for the day. He would have the help of another man for making the beds of those patients too ill to be moved, then saw about getting breakfast for the patients. They needed to be carefully watched at mealtimes; some were often half-starved in their own interest and would attempt to get a little more if possible, perhaps by trading a cigarette for some bread with another patient.

After all this, the orderly had half an hour for his own breakfast, then had to prepare the ward for the visit of the medical officer. He had to be on hand for this, ready with diet sheets and temperature charts; after the medical officer had gone, he would sit down and make out the indent forms for the various diets and extra food and drinks ordered for the patients. By the time he had done this, it was time to fetch the patients' dinners from the cookhouse. Generally there would be convalescent patients to help fetch the trays; if not, the two ward orderlies would have to do it all. Some of the seriously ill patients needed help eating. Finally the orderly could go and get his own dinner.

The afternoons were usually quiet, so one orderly stayed on the ward while the other attended lectures, or went out on stretcher drill. If none of this was organised, he could usually have a snooze until 4.00pm, when the patients had their tea. Then there was getting his own tea, washing patients for the night, perhaps cooling patients with a high temperature and generally getting ready for the evening visit of the medical officer. Then he had to set about squaring up for the night orderly, then, at last, he could go off duty. Night duty was easier, except in summer when the night man would get the patients washed before going off duty to make things easier for the day orderlies.

Chapter 12

Other Supply Activities

This chapter covers numerous other supply activities which don't fit into any of the other major categories.

Army Printing and Stationery Services (AP&SS)

At the beginning of the war this was originally a small base stationery store, which went to France with the BEF. Its equipment, supplied by the Royal Engineers, included a small hand-printing press manned by three officers and seven other ranks. Although its personnel establishment was never large, the AP&SS fulfilled its function with branches operating in theatres overseas as well as on the Western Front. It was controlled by a director stationed at GHQ and reporting to the Adjutant General; he was also responsible to the Air Ministry, as the department offered facilities to the Royal Air Force, these being handled at the respective headquarters by a deputy assistant director.

The director administered all branches in advance of General Head-quarters, with the assistance of a deputy director and a deputy assistant director. Each branch at the army headquarters was headed by a deputy assistant director. The detailed administration of all branches on the line of communication was handled by a second deputy director who was assisted by two assistant directors, one each for the northern and southern lines of communication. To cope with the increase in the forces on the Western Front, the personnel grew from ten men in a single stationery depot in August 1914 to sixty-two officers and 860 other ranks in thirty centres by November 1918. There were additional branches in other overseas theatres.

Although there had been a directive to contract for printing services locally, this proved impractical due to the confidential and secret nature of many of the publications, while printing in England inevitably meant some delay, so a printing press was established at Havre in July 1915 and another at Boulogne in January 1916. The printing and photographic work soon expanded and was divided into a headquarters and general headquarters section at General Headquarters, another section with each army headquarters, a process section for illustrations needed for training pamphlets and technical instructions, a machinery gang for the erection and repairs of all printing machinery and two large presses on the lines of communication. The General Headquarters plant included eight linotype machines. As an indication of the type of work done there, the 'Order of Battle' – which consisted of 120 foolscap pages closely filled with tables – was printed and issued in thirty-six hours. At the other end of the scale numerous forms were produced, including several hundred forms designated 'non-army', as well as over 1,100 army forms.

A photographic section, equipped to produce 5,000 whole-plate prints per day, was established for the Fourth Army in October 1916. This proved so successful that a similar section was established for the other armies. Their work, much of it from aerial photos, included maps and stereoscopic photographs for operations, graves registration, photos of deserters and escaped prisoners of war, as well as general outdoor photography for training and record purposes. The number of photographs taken and reproduced grew rapidly, from 25,000 in 1916 to 2,244,750 in October 1918.

The publications department started in May 1915. It was important that training pamphlets and other pamphlets were issued automatically without delay to all concerned. This soon extended to producing other booklets, informative circulars and printed orders.

The Typewriter Inspection and Repair Service maintained a workshop at each depot and a system of travelling mechanics, many of whom used motorcycles to transport themselves and their light repair workshops. This kept 7,500 typewriters in good repair; as a result the total scrapped as being of no further use (which included those lost as a result of enemy action) was only 2½ per cent of the total number of machines in use.

The service ran a rubber stamp factory, which produced numerous stamps, including those required for censorship of letters. In the year to October 1918, over 57,000 stamps were made by this factory. It also maintained stocks of technical supplies such as parts for printing machinery and the plates and chemicals used in photography.

There were branches of the AP&SS in Italy, Salonika, Egypt, Palestine and Mesopotamia, all performing the same functions as above.

From March 1916 the AP&SS also started handling the salvage and collection of waste paper, and this expanded into a separate all-purpose salvage organisation, using the AP&SS's paper baling presses.

The Army Spectacle Department

This department was originally intended only for fulfilling spectacle prescriptions but eventually produced artificial eyes, optical tools and ophthalmological equipment, including cases of trial lenses, fitting sets, trial frames, maps and test types. They also designed and bought a special type of sun-goggle, sending 300,000 of these to Egypt and Mesopotamia in 1916. There was some difficulty in getting an adequate supply of glass eyes, as most of these had come from enemy countries. There were only six makers in the UK, and they were averse to teaching others their trade.

Forestry

A great deal of timber was needed for various purposes on the Western Front, including railway sleepers, huts for the troops, trench shoring, duckboards and firewood, not to mention the large quantities needed at home for packing-crates. The principal source of wood for Britain was (and had been since the early eighteenth century) the countries of Scandinavia, but once shipping was targeted by enemy submarines this became impractical. There was some standing timber in Britain, but little skilled labour to harvest it, and as soon as it was sent to France the submarine problem arose again.

There were vast forests in Northern France and the British Army began to use them, in some cases without first obtaining licences or permission, or recompensing the owners properly. In 1915 the French Military Command responded to complaints by setting up a forestry department in its military liaison commission, and through this put pressure on the British Army which then set up a forestry directorate reporting to GHQ. French foresters were given power to authorise or prohibit felling in both state and privately owned forests. The amount of timber felled by British forces increased steadily, from 17,000 tons in March 1916 to 119,000 tons in March 1918.

The number of workers used by the British Army for this work between 1915 and 1918 increased twenty-five fold. These included 57.5 per cent prisoners of war, 18 per cent British soldiers, and 18.1 per cent Chinese. But more were needed and the British government finally asked Canada for help. As before, due to submarine activity, it proved impracticable to import lumber from Canada to Britain, so in May 1916 a Canadian Forestry Corps was set up. They started work in Windsor Great Park and then in other locations, including Scotland, where many of the men found wives to take home. By the end of the war there were 17,000 Canadian forestry workers in forestry in Britain and France with attached personnel (prisoners of war, the Canadian Army Service Corps and medical personnel) which brought the total to over 33,000. The Canadian foresters tooks over five complete sawmills and gleaned large quantities of fallen timber left by the Germans in their retreat in 1917.

The total production of wood in Britain was over 257,000,000 Fcct Board Measurement (FBM), in France nearly 556,000,000 FMB, plus round material of 224,000 tons and slab-wood and fuel each of more than 604,000,000 tons. Logging in France brought demands to Royal Engineers' stores for heavy logging saws and machinery capable of dealing with logs up to 48in diameter.

Miscellaneous Supplies

Woodwork supplies included packing cases and crates, handles and helves and tent pegs. The *sheet metal* trade produced petrol cans, water bottles, camp kettles, mess and ration tins, entrenching tools and barbed wire entanglement posts. The *cutlery* trade supplied clasp knives as well as knives, forks and spoons for eating. Spoons were often tucked into the puttees for use when eating out of a communal pot. *Raffia* was used in various ways for camouflage, and although at times the supply was tight, there was always enough for government use with a little left over for civilian supplies. Prices were controlled until April 1919 and steps were then taken to release government stocks held. Even *toilet paper* was marked 'government property' on each sheet.

Staff Work

One staff officer, Colonel W.N. Nicholson, wrote of his experiences from just before mobilisation to the end of the war and beyond. To a large extent he documents a struggle against inexperience, both on his part and that of almost everyone he encountered. His first assignment was the training and accommodation of a division of Scottish territorials in Perth. His main recollection of the early days was having to sleep on his office floor, and the fact that the two ancient men assigned to help him had no experience of either war or staff work. One had what he described as a habit that led to 'a very red nose' and soon departed.

Having moved to Bedford as a complete division, the Scottish territorials had to deal with a serious shortage of transport. They were missing 150 wagons with their horses and harness, let alone lorries. Although the scales of baggage were laid down, these were largely ignored, until the bitter experiences of a series of cold wet nights taught the guilty that 'overloading wagons had its just reward' in the resultant mud.

The cumbersome staff machine creaked further when higher authority wanted to send the division to France immediately. Contrary to an optimistic report that almost all the men had volunteered, this was not true; the men stated that they had signed on for home service only and would not go abroad. It took some time to persuade them otherwise, and the division was not able to go overseas until May 1915.

Nicholson described a typical day during this pre-departure time with visits and enquiries ranging from the officer commanding the division train wanting railway sleepers to mend his depot roads; an assistant provost marshal wanting to know whether a civilian driver who had struck a special constable could be tried by court martial; a brigadier wanting permission to send his pipers to London to play at the funeral of a distinguished general and also wanting to know who would pay for this; queries on engineering work; another query from the adjutant of the division artillery on sending orders by night by cyclist; and many more of a similar type. An average morning brought about thirty of these, the afternoon slightly fewer, leaving very little time for essential correspondence before dinner. This was often at the

Bedford Club, which had generously made all the officers honorary members, leading to the complete depletion of their carefully hoarded stock of port. Another unintended result of generosity occurred at the local golf club, which welcomed the entire division as honorary members, not realising that since it was of Scottish origin, most of its members (some 17,000) were keen golfers.

Billeting

Once in France, Nicholson's work started with three months learning the rudiments of trench life, then moved on to billeting. In Flanders the standard unit was the farm. Usually built around a square, with a midden in the centre, this consisted of a single-storey house for the farmer and his family, with barns on the other three sides, one for livestock, the other two for straw and hay (the source, with the animals, of the midden). According to the season, this midden either swarmed with flies or degenerated into a swamp. Despite its primitive nature and minimal furnishings, the farmhouse with its warm kitchen was preferred by the officers to the nearby chateau (known to the other ranks as 'the chatoo').

For other ranks, a division group was usually allocated a whole village. Under French law, this was controlled by the mayor, who decided how many men could live where. The villagers made no complaint, being paid for each man accommodated plus damages. But of course there were snags, including the mistaken 'lending' of billets to allied troops, who, once installed, were almost impossible to remove. On one occasion Nicholson rashly agreed to allow what was described as 'a small party of not more than 300 French soldiers' to occupy two barns, leaving the rest of the village for the British division's artillery. This 'small party' turned out to consist of 760 soldiers and thirty-four officers, including a general and three colonels. Declaring the whole village to be 'billets de fortune', they spread out, leaving no room for the British artillery.

The ASC also had to supply quarters at home for the great influx of new recruits – 168,249 in August 1914 and 383,329 in September 1914. As existing quarters were only available for just under 175,000 men, they had to be accommodated near their homes until a reorganisation had created spaces at training barracks. The first method was to move married families out of barracks and use other barrack buildings, but this was not enough. Building large hutted camps was started but this was hindered by bad weather; other accommodation was provided in tents. By May 1915 accommodation had been found for 1,408,000 men: 262,000 in barracks, 580,000 in huts, 264,000 in tents, and 302,000 in billets and hired buildings.

They also had to find accommodation for hospitals and prisoners of war, and storage for all the necessary equipment and materiel for a large army. Amongst other places, schools and asylums were used.

BEYOND THE WESTERN FRONT

Introduction

While the Western Front was relatively close to the major manufacturing centres of Europe and was supported by extensive road and rail networks, the situation was very different elsewhere. The characteristics of the campaigns in these theatres were related to the physical features of the country and the amount and nature of the opposition encountered, so obviously supply chains had to be flexible. As the campaign tended to involve moving over large areas, they had no gun parks and normally only small-scale ammunition dumps.

A decent water supply was often difficult to obtain; in such cases, pumps were supplied by the Royal Engineers. As well as hand-operated pumps for trench drainage, heavy duty mechanical pumps were provided for water supply from boreholes, and purification equipment including sand filters. These pumps were mounted on lorries and thus could be easily moved from borehole to borehole as needed.

Expeditionary Force Canteens (EFC)

The EFC arrived in Gallipoli in August 1915, but their first canteen was promptly blown up by the enemy. Others were rapidly set up at Sylva and on the islands of Imbros and Lemnos. After the evacuation of Gallipoli, many of the troops were transferred to Salonika, where the EFC soon had thirty-five canteens. Using a fleet of some forty lorries, and ox-transport where the roads were not good enough for wheeled transport, the EFC fed the troops, staying with them as they advanced as far as Sofia, and even imported food for the Indian troops from a depot at Bombay. In Egypt, despite numerous difficulties, the EFC set up a line of canteens along the banks of the Suez canal and finally up into Palestine. Since the principal means of communication in Mesopotamia was water, the EFC set up a floating canteen on a stern-wheel steamboat. There were at least thirty-seven canteens in Mesopotamia, going up the Tigris and Euphrates from Basra to Baghdad, then spreading out to the north and south and even into Persia. They also had canteens at Murmansk and Archangel.

ASC Personnel

The ASC employed over 14,000 men in theatres away from the Western Front. This included over 2,300 bakers and 4,600 butchers. There were also

986 farriers, 504 saddlers and 732 wheelwrights, mostly in Egypt and Salonika, plus over 1,300 packers and loaders, and over 4,000 clerks.

Munitions

Other theatres did not use such enormous amounts of ammunition as the Western Front, but at these locations there were no heavy guns or howitzers and few even of medium calibre. At the end of the war there were nearly 4,000 machine guns in Egypt, these being Vickers, Lewis and Hotchkiss types, and over 80,000 grenades. In Mesopotamia there were only twenty-four guns, 16,200 rounds of ammunition for those guns, and 2,164 rounds for small arms, with 1in and 3in Stokes mortars and 2in and 6in trench mortars. Italy and Salonika had over 900 guns, with shrapnel and HE shells, and 1,400 machine guns.

*   *   *

Of the 8,700,000 men who served at some point in the First World War, 3,400,000 served in theatres other than the Western Front:

- Egypt & Palestine   1,192,500
- Mesopotamia   890,000
- Salonika   404,000
- Gallipoli   469,000
- Italy   145,760
- North Russia & Siberia   just over 10,000 British & Canadian troops
- East Africa   best figure available is 'nearly' 400,000
                           Allied troops

The British Army was also active in small numbers in several places not described in the following chapters. The medical service dealt with cases from Egypt and Gallipoli in Malta, in West Indies garrisons, Jamaica, Bermuda, Mauritius (cases from Mesopotamia) and Hong Kong, the Straits settlements and Ceylon, Togoland (where there was a German colony), the Gold Coast and Cameroon. The latter was largely bush warfare and needed a 300-strong corps of stretcher-bearers, and field ambulances. These were joint operations with the French Army, and many of the casualties were evacuated to Nigeria.

Given its location, the work in Cameroon needed better sanitation, sterilisation of water, and the destruction of insects and other vermin, including chiggers (minute insects which burrow under the skin, usually on the feet). There was much malaria and pneumonia in the wet season, and some beri-beri (vitamin B deficiency) in the French contingent, who used Cochin rice, which is over-polished and thus loses the vitamin content from its coating.

In south-west Africa, where there is a desert strip along the coast, the country is generally poorly provided with water (although Cape Town and

Johannesburg were included in this area). There were a few wells and some desalination plants, but the heavy sand made even animal transport difficult, so the railways which the Germans had destroyed when they left had to be reconstructed. Of a total of about 33,000 troops serving in the area, about 25,400 were admitted to hospital at some point.

Volunteers in Cape Town made veils to protect against flying sand; these did not keep all the sand out of the face, but did provide some comfort. Cows were sent up from Cape Town to provide fresh milk for hospitals. Eggs and chickens from Egypt, Tunis and Italy were sent to hospitals in Malta.

In South Africa some hospitals were used for casualties from East Africa and Mesopotamia, these brought in by hospital ship to Durban and Cape Town. In May 1918 there were 9,184 beds for 'white' troops and 3,207 for coloured. A total of some 60,000 cases were handled during the war. Many hospital ships returning empty to the UK took cases home. Many of the cases from East Africa were in a debilitated state from recurrent malaria, followed by anaemia and cardiac complications. They improved rapidly in South Africa due to the better climate and plentiful food, fresh fruit and vegetables. Cases of infectious diseases occurred in insignificant numbers until late September 1918, when an influenza epidemic struck. This was declared to be the most sudden, severe and malignant pestilence ever experienced in the country; there were 1,674 cases in South Africa, 3,170 in Malta and 484 in Bermuda, but there are no available figures for other locations. This was obviously what came to be known as Spanish Flu; there are no available statistics on deaths in the British Army, but there were over 313,000 cases, and an estimated 30,000–40,000 deaths.

Mail

At first, letters home had to have stamps, but within two weeks of the start of the war it was decided that letters under 4oz weight would go free. All letters home were theoretically subject to censorship by unit officers. However, green 'honour' envelopes were exempt, but might still be opened at the base post office before going to the UK. All these letters went back on the same routes as incoming mail, mostly using 'empty' transport which had brought the incoming mail. Once it reached London or other big cities, it was passed into the civil postal service and delivered in the same way as all other mail.

As British troops moved into other theatres, the Army Postal Service went with them, including to Egypt, Gallipoli, Greece, Italy, Palestine and finally, in the autumn of 1918, to North Russia and Turkey. There were some early difficulties, such as unreliable packing of mail on ships in the Mediterranean, and a lack of rail or mechanical transport in Egypt and up to Palestine. Here, pack animals did the job instead. For northern Italy, all supplies, including mail, went through France on the railways; on the east coast at Brindisi it arrived by ship. In North Russia, although Murmansk was usually ice-free all year round, Archangel was not, and horse-drawn sleighs had to be used in the winter. The trip from London to Murmansk took two and a half weeks, and from there on to Archangel a similar time, so unlike in France, where most mail was delivered in a few days, the service to North Russia took five weeks.

*   *   *

There are some statistics available on the numbers of transport vehicles sent from Britain, most of these being sent on from France (for the period 9 August 1914 to 2 March 1919):

	For Salonika, Egypt and Mesopotamia	For Italy
Guns and carriages	246	123
Limbered vehicles	21	–
Four-wheeled vehicles	81	1
Two-wheeled vehicles	635	137
Ambulance wagons	37	7
Travelling kitchens and field oven wagons	50	1
Water tanks, carts, trailers	149	2
Telegraph cable wagons	2	–
Pontoons and pontoon wagons	11	–
Motor ambulances	115	106
Motor cars and chassis	706	234
Trailers, vans, tenders	74	29
Motor store and workshop lorries	532	225
Tractors	19	24
Motorcycles	158	331
Cycle-cars (sidecars)	–	18
Bicycles	1,416	
Barrows	3,000	
Sundry vehicles	6	3
Total	7,258	1,241

Stores for the east went from Southampton to Cherbourg, then on to Taranto by train and onwards by sea.

Overseas Theatres

In overseas theatres of war, for cases which required repatriation to the UK, hospital ships were mobilised on a ratio of one per division. Early hospital ships had 250 beds, 20 of which were for officers. Later versions were larger and could carry more: 200 stretcher cases and 300 walking wounded was a typical capacity. A particular form of illness overseas was cutaneous Leish-maniasis – aka Baghdad boil, Delhi boil, Balkan sore – which was carried by sand flies. It started as an itchy red spot which developed into a large skin ulcer, usually on the face, arms or legs.

Transport Animals

Camels

Unlike in France, where there were good roads, transport in most other countries was largely confined to pack animals or local rough bullock carts. The General Service wagon was impossible to use on mountainous terrain or trackless desert. Water had to be carried in canvas bags (*chaguls*) or small portable tanks (fanatis or pakals), usually by camel, and porous earthenware jars and canvas troughs were needed in camp.

For forces in the Mediterranean, Mesopotamia and East Africa, grain for these animals was procured from the nearest theatre of supply, usually India and Egypt. In 1918, owing to the failure of the Indian crop, it became neces-sary to import maize from South Africa and barley from Algiers until the Egyptian crop matured.

In some of the other theatres horses and mules were either unsuitable or could not be obtained easily. Instead, camels and oxen were used, mostly in Egypt, Palestine and Mesopotamia and East Africa. Donkeys could only carry a small load, and thus were not so useful.

Although riding camels were available, they were not used much by the British Army. There are several breeds of baggage camel, all of which perform best in conditions like those where they were bred. They can carry from 250 to 450lb and occasionally pull carts. They generally move at approxi-mately 2 to 2½mph. They should not work for more than eight hours per day, and should ideally be allowed to graze for six hours per day and given time to ruminate. If grazing is not available, they should have about 6lb of grain or ground *gram* (chickpeas) and 40lb forage. The grain should always be mixed well with *bhoose* (chaff) to prevent it being gobbled without proper mastica-tion. Ideally all grain should be crushed. A little salt should be mixed with the feed to make it more palatable.

As far as grazing is concerned, camels like wormwood, thorn bushes, thistles and coarse prickly and saline grasses, and will fight for a leguminous plant called *rtem*. They should be supervised when grazing to ensure they do not wander off or get mixed up with another herd. After a few hours, they will begin to stand about or sit down; when this happens, the whole herd should be stopped from moving forward, when they will all sit and ruminate for a couple of hours. Herds should never be larger than sixty to eighty individuals.

Their watering needs depend on the breed, being from daily to every four days. If deprived of food and water, camels will die of exhaustion; an inexperienced handler may not recognise the symptoms of deprivation until the camel lies down and dies. Their drinking pattern is to take in a long draught, then bring their head up and stare about them for several minutes before taking another long draught. Some will do this a third time. An inexperienced handler may think they have finished and pull them away from the water, but they should be left at the water until all the group have finished drinking, since if one is led away, the others are likely to follow before they have had enough. Like horses, they should be watered before feeding, and after unloading. When watering, the nose-rope should be removed; if the camel (or another beast) puts a foot on it, he will jerk his head up and possibly damage his nose in the process.

Camels have two internal 'cisterns', one holding about 2 pints on the right side of the stomach and another holding about 1 gallon on the left. These hold a mixture of food, water and mucus. The hump is mainly adipose tissue, not a 'larder' or water store. Its size and firmness give an indication of health and it will waste away with privation.

Camels' feet are adapted to soft sand; they do not do well on muddy or slippery ground or very stony ground. When the ground is slippery, they are liable to strain their legs, or may even fall and break bones. They also get sore chest pads when parked on stony ground. In this event, a hole should be dug and filled with soft sand for the pad to rest on. Although they swim well, they cannot cross narrow ditches and need a bridge; in terrain which is likely to include such ditches, portable bridges should be carried. Consistently wet feet are not good for them. They should be kept on well-drained ground (with stones removed), with shade in the summer and wind-screens in the winter. The lines should slope away a little and a drain should be dug behind them.

It has been said that the camel's temperament is 'peculiar at times'; this translates to the bad temper of a male when in *musth* (breeding condition). The booklet on camel management issued by the Indian government remarked hopefully that all that was needed was firm handling and if this was set about in a business-like way they would rarely try to savage their attendant. But even when not in *musth*, camels still had a nasty trick of biting people on the back.

Like other working animals, camels need to be groomed regularly. They like being groomed, and doing this every day helps to develop a good relationship between the camel and his handler. In cold wet weather they may need to be covered with a fitted waterproof rug called a *jhool*.

Camels are prone to sarcoptic mange. The ground on which the sufferers have been sitting should be disinfected and no other camels allowed on it. The men handling mangy camels should not be allowed to touch other camels. Long hair should be clipped off and burned and remedies applied to the whole animal. If several camels are affected, a dip 2ft 9in deep should be dug and the camels made to sit in it with their noses held shut and the liquid dip poured over them and scrubbed in. The dip is a mixture of freshly dug lime, sulphur and liquid creosote mixed with water. The other major disease of camels is *surra*, which is transmitted by flies or ticks, usually in hot weather, at sunrise or sunset. It causes intermittent fevers, and bad cases will die quite quickly; others linger on for many months, becoming more and more debilitated.

Camel hospitals were allocated according to the number of camels with an army in the field. They were stationary units appropriately placed (ideally in *surra*-free zones). Unlike the hospitals for other animals, they did not require stables as the patients were kept in lines with mud-built feeding troughs. However, they should have wind-screens and be located where there was good shade from trees and reasonably close to good camel grazing with a water supply not used by other animals. They should be well away from culti- vated land or horse hospitals. They should be kept meticulously free of camel dung, especially close to water troughs.

Camels could be transported by train, six to a truck. There should be at least 6in of sand on the floor. They usually needed to be forced in the first time, using pulley blocks and a rope passed under the root of the tail. If they resisted, two men would take hold of the stifles of the hind legs, lift and push forward; rather than fall on its nose, the camel will step forward. Once inside, they were made to sit down until they had grown accustomed to the motion of the train, after which they could be allowed to stand. They should be fitted with nets over their noses to prevent them biting each other. After their first train ride, most camels will usually enter the trucks freely on their own.

Bactrian camels (the two-humped type) have been used for pack work in Central Asia but were rarely used by the British Army, unlike the Dromedary (the single-humped type) which was, and is, used throughout the Middle East, North Africa and northern India. Camels of either sort needed a saddle which did not touch any part of the hump. This meant careful saddle fitting for each beast. The weight was either carried in front of the hump, or on a platform mounted on pads fore and aft of the hump. As well as carrying small items packed into boxes or sacks, camels were used to carry artillery pieces: one for the gun itself, three for the gun carriage and wheels, and three more to carry the ammunition.

There were several General Service patterns of pack saddle for camels. The Egyptian Pattern Mark I was approved in 1900. This had V-shaped wooden arches connected on top by a metal rod, and at the lower edges with wooden sidebars. The front arch was 16½in high and 28in wide across the base, the back arch was 9in high and 16in wide. Across the sides of the two arches were two pairs of stretcher bars to keep the saddle arch apart, and underneath were padded panels. Rings and thongs were attached for the girth and breast straps. This saddle could be used to carry two wounded men in cacolets or one flat stretcher across the top. It included a shade for the man's head. The most recent form of approved camel pack saddle, known as the Baladi Pattern, was little different from the Mark I, and came into use just before the Second World War.

As with equines, camels were subject to sore backs from ill-fitting pack saddles, especially if they were not removed for several days. This happened on the Nile expedition of 1884–85, when many camels developed open sores, with attendant maggots.

Nets and ropes were used to attach other loads to the saddle. Camels wore a simple head-collar, steered by a rope attached under the chin – an improvement on the earlier local system of a rope through their nose.

Oxen
Oxen (aka bullocks) tended to be used for draught rather than pack purposes but were very slow, rarely moving at more than 1½mph. They can draw heavy weights uphill, but tend to lose control of their legs going down. On good roads, with a two-wheeled cart, a yoked pair of oxen can draw a load of up to 960lb. Teams of up to sixteen beasts can pull up to 5,000lb. Under packs, they can carry 150–200lb, but ideally should not be expected to carry more than the lighter load in mountainous country. They are very slow in hilly terrain.

The general rule with cattle is that they need an hour chewing the cud for every hour of grazing, ideally about six hours a day of grazing, and about eight hours' sleep. Oxen fed on corn do not need such a long digestive process, but unless in a situation where they can graze, have to carry this corn or 'long' fodder (hay or straw). The corn was either crushed or soaked. In hot countries they should not work in the heat of the day but they will not drink unless the sun is high. Ideally they should work from 2.00am to 9.00am, rest, drink and graze until 4.00pm, then work again until 9.00pm. If forced to work during the middle of the day, they just died.

Oxen are prone to the normal cattle diseases, including rinderpest, anthrax and foot and mouth disease. Rinderpest is also known as cattle plague and is so virulent that it kills 90 per cent of animals very quickly. The only sensible action on discovering it was to slaughter all affected animals and those which had been in contact with them. It can also affect sheep and goats, but horses are immune. Anthrax, although very rare in Europe, is widespread throughout tropical and sub-tropical countries. The spores which cause it can remain active in the ground for over ten years. It can also affect sheep, goats, pigs and horses. In horses, if the animal is not slaughtered quickly, it will eventually go into convulsions and die. Anthrax can also affect humans and thus is a notifiable disease. Foot and mouth disease is an acute feverish disease of cattle, sheep, goats and pigs and, in a milder form, sometimes humans. It does not affect horses.

Chapter 13

Gallipoli

This was one of the few locations outside Flanders where trenches were used extensively by both sides. The planners had not expected this, so there was a great shortage of all the items needed for trench warfare: mortars, grenades, bombs and sandbags. The grenade situation was alleviated by the efforts of a naval engineer, Major Teale, who set up a bomb factory. There were plenty of detonators, some propellant and numerous jam tins, and his team soon turned out large numbers of grenades. Major Teale also used his mining skills to extend a cave near Suvla and tunnel out a magazine some 70ft undergound. Equipped with a tramway, this was able to hold 2,500 tons.

The rest of the ordnance headquarters at Suvla consisted of five store tents and some dugouts in the cliffs, which were built of boxes of live ammunition with sandbag-covered roofs. Small stocks of only a few items were kept; when more supplies were needed, a list was sent to Mudros. As soon as ammunition began to arrive, dumps were established on the beaches at Helles and Anzac, and much of the artillery ammunition was kept in the open, hidden by bushes. These dumps were subject to shelling, but the contents were moved to better locations as soon as possible, including some 'dead ground' under the cliffs at Anzac. Elsewhere, deep trenches were dug outside the store tents to shelter the workers when shelling started.

Little was known at home about conditions at Gallipoli, as evidenced by Kitchener's decision that, as the troops were to be landed on the beach and could then walk across the peninsula, no transport would be needed. General Long pointed out the impracticability of this, as they would need a substantial amount of ammunition, not to mention their other stores, and finally Kitchener agreed to a quota of transport to accompany the troops.

The supply column was duly allocated several 3-ton lorries, but no one had been told that not only were there no suitable roads, there were no roads at all. Later, it was discovered that General Maxwell, who commanded in Egypt, had told Kitchener that there were no roads and that pack transport would be needed.

Some supplies were sent on from France, others direct from England; five ships took some 30,000 tons. Some short two-cabled ropeways were sent out to Gallipoli and ended up in Salonika.

When the mounted troops arrived in 1915 the weather in Gallipoli was extremely hot; this turned to torrential rain, followed, in late November, by a three-day blizzard. The horses lacked rugs, shelter and enough men to care for them. Inevitably they lost condition and many were transferred to Alexandria. Surface water was hard to find; a reservoir was built and several wells dug, but this water, although acceptable for horses, was not fit for troops. A steam ship carried water and mule-drawn water carts were employed. This restricted the equine population, although for them, food and fodder was plentiful and generally good. Haynets had to be used as otherwise it blew away.

One factor that was recognised about the Gallipoli pensinsula was the impossibility of establishing an ordnance depot on shore, where the Turkish opposition was strong and determined. It was therefore decided to use a floating depot instead, so the 3,000-ton steamship *Umsinga* was fitted out at Tilbury. Extra decks were added to the hold-space, allowing different types of goods to be organised in the most convenient way. However, when it was decided that two different places were to be used for landings, a second ship, *Anglo-India*, was added and some stock was transferred to her. The original intention to keep both ships off the beaches and use them as depots soon proved impossible, as the constant shifting of cargo and troops rendered them unstable and there was a risk they might capsize. Nor was it practical to unload them onto the beaches as they were under constant heavy fire.

Another larger ship, *Minnetonka*, was added to this little fleet, but it proved impossible to provide a proper depot service. In late autumn a store depot was proposed at Mudros Bay, some 40 miles from the Gallipoli peninsula. This large bay had room for over a hundred small cargo ships, but there were no plans of their holds to show exactly where items were. The only way to find specific items was to move the whole cargo to the decks; by the time this had been done several times to locate one type of supply, chaos was complete. Soon the top decks of *Minnetonka* were covered by 6–8ft of stores which remained unissued as the ferries were unable to remain alongside for long enough. As well as the general confusion, this turned out to be an invitation for theft, an invitation which was not declined by opportunists in the working parties. When the ship was finally cleared, 500,000 pairs of socks and 70 Vickers guns were found to be missing, amongst other items.

Major Man, the ordnance officer of *Minnetonka*, served on her for several months and remarked afterwards that the main thing he had learned from the experience was that a floating depot should never be used to supply a large force. If it was essential to use a floating depot for a small force, he had several suggestions. The receiving ordnance officer should be provided not only with the bill of lading for each ship but also with a detailed plan of the stowage of each hold compartment. A wide space in each hold immediately next to the shafts should be kept absolutely clear to allow some minor moving of unwanted items to find those which were wanted; the unwanted items should be returned to their previous position immediately. Each crane should be fitted with a donkey engine, large enough to lift goods out of the holds and straight over the sides to the waiting lighters, thus saving time in transferring loads from one crane to another. Finally he described the fatigue and inevitable irritation that followed from working long hours in the depths of a ship, and recommended a football as a method of relieving some of this stress.

Once it had been decided to abandon the Gallipoli campaign, evacuation began in late November. At Suvla, at dusk, the troops gathered on the beaches and embarked on the boats waiting to take them to ships offshore while the navy shelled the Turkish lines. The process took some five weeks, and guns, ammunition and clothing were sent off at the same time. The ordnance department personnel embarked on the final day.

At Anzac the process was hastier. As soon as the departure was known, whatever stocks could be issued were, and as much as possible of the rest was sent back to Mudros. But there was no time to recover everything, so the remains were either dumped in the sea or broken up; clothing was destroyed by piling it up and pouring oil over it. By 22 December they had dealt with as much as they could, and once all the troops were safely on board ships, the fleet destroyed the rest by shelling.

There was only ten days' notice given at Helles, and it was not possible to remove much of the stores, although some did go in the boats with the troops. Explosives were set to destroy both the supply dump and the magazine. They may not have been able to recover much of the stores and ammunition, but at least it didn't fall into the hands of the enemy.

By 10 January 1916 the whole of the force had been evacuated and twenty-four store ships gathered at Mudros Bay to take the remaining stores to Alexandria. It was not possible to take all the food, and the remainder was destroyed, including 1,500,000 rations of preserved meat, over 1,000,000 rations of bread and 100 tons of bacon.

Medical Care

Medical officers established themselves in dugouts in the communication trenches behind the firing lines to provide makeshift regimental aid posts. Patients who needed more care were sent to Alexandria by hospital ship; there were some 16,000 of these in the first ten days of the campaign.

Food and Drink

Water was produced by hiring a large condensing steamer and a tank steamer from Port Said. Numerous small water containers were collected to store water on the beaches and transport it inland to the troops, including tanks, oil tins and water skins. At Anzac water supplies came from Malta and Egypt, often in the form of a steamer full of Nile water, and at one especially difficult time they even had to drink the water used as ballast in ships from home.

At the end of April a shortage of food meant that the troops were told to make their emergency rations last two days instead of one, but many soldiers had already thrown their rations away to lighten the load during landing. It was another week before all the administrative staff had landed and regular supplies of food could be organised. By this time there were 86,000 men and 31,000 animals on the peninsula and 25,000 men and 14,000 animals waiting to come from Egypt. They had twelve days' immediate rations and six weeks' reserve supply.

The weather was no help. As winter approached, torrential rains followed by a blizzard caused severe damage to the piers, barges and other landing craft, while in the summer the heat brought swarms of flies which fed on the latrines, corpses and then the food. This was not always covered as it should have been, and soon there was a dysentery epidemic. The heat melted the corned beef in the tins, and there was a problem with it which caused major complaints. Ninety-six patients in the military hospital were surveyed. Eighty-eight of them said the meat was too salty, with forty-two of them commenting that it caused a dry mouth or thirst. Fifteen had thrown it away as unfit to eat, twelve said it resulted in stomach pains and thirty said it caused diarrhoea. Nine said their symptoms disappeared when they stopped eating it and three of these said the symptoms returned when they started eating it again.

This survey also covered other foods. Tickler's plum and apple jam was thought to taste of nothing but sugar and vegetables, but their marmalade was very good. The biscuit was approved, especially Huntley & Palmers' 'nice white biscuits' which were much appreciated.

One enterprising group of soldiers discovered how to catch fish easily. They threw bread into the water off a pier and then, when enough fish had gathered, they threw in a Mills bomb, which stunned the fish for long enough for a couple of men to wade in with a net and gather a good haul. This was probably done elsewhere too, as was fishing with a rod and line.

Chapter 14

Salonika

The AOC arrived at Salonika (sometimes called the Balkans) at the end of October 1915 but they lacked two essentials: an experienced senior officer and a proper plan for the department and its administration. It was not until three months later that a senior officer was appointed to command. In the meantime, as one temporary officer remarked, 'There were not enough officers or men, not enough room, not enough transport, not enough labour and not enough stationery, an important matter when any kind of storekeeping and accounting has to be established.' There was, however, no shortage of mud.

The depot was started on the Monastir road with store tents pitched on a wet night by the light of lanterns. The basic stores went in these tents, but the ammunition had to be kept in the open under tarpaulins. At a mere 120yd by 80yd, this site was soon shown to be too small and another of the same size was set up 400yd further along the road. A visiting general from Alexandria decreed that a better site should be utilised. This was on a bare hillside, some of it recently ploughed, above a road which rapidly turned into a river with the winter rains. A start was made on the slow process of moving all the stores to the third site, but before this could be completed, new stores began to flood in. Not only was there no proper place to put them, but there were very few AOC men to handle them. They tended to be dumped in any space that the dumpers deemed convenient; much of the supplies ended up stacked in the streets close to the docks. Finally, in January 1916, it was decided to make an ammunition depot at the docks, and twenty-six existing stone buildings were taken over for this.

As if the rains had not caused enough havoc, at the end of November a blizzard raged for three days. Then, in the middle of December, just at the point when numerous tents were being pitched at the third site, a storm blew them down, many of the tents disappearing for ever in the mud. The road from the docks was so bad that many lorries bogged down and had to be dug out, and the roads in the depot were no better. It took three months to get decent surfaces on the main roads, partly due to the shortage of labour.

Local labourers were not much use, being 'at their best capable of a certain sullen steadiness', but in the opinion of one officer they could 'do nothing quickly'. Their weakness for pilfering was ineradicable, but they were not the only culprits, this officer continuing, 'units believed that once on active service there was a community of goods … small items, especially of clothing, continually vanished'.

To make things worse, stores and troops were being landed together, and often the store ships had to retire into the harbour to make room for the troopships. On one occasion the store ship *Stork* had unloaded the tentage she carried but not the tent poles, which were still at the bottom of the hold when she had to back off. The weather turned bad and some troops had no option but to cut down trees to make their own tent poles. Once the first awful winter was over, matters improved. Good roads were made, proper buildings replaced tents and tarpaulin-covered stacks of stores, and at last it was possible to control theft, if not stop it altogether.

As soon as they arrived, the AOC personnel asked for field bakeries, lorries, butcheries and several depot units of supplies from Egypt. By the end of the month three ships had brought large quantities of rations, frozen meat and forage. Before the Greek government banned further purchases, they managed to obtain hay, oats, potatoes and wood for fuel locally. The Greek government had itself entered the war in October and in the process of mobilising was buying up all the easily available wagons and draught animals. All the AOC could find were some small dock carts and a few half-starved ponies, and even these were liable to seizure if not guarded. The Greek government also banned the sale of petrol to the British, and put guards on the Standard Oil Company premises, which had the only substantial stocks. However, these were next to a British depot and supplies were pushed over the wall out of sight of the sentries.

One very useful task carried out by the ordnance department at Salonika was converting waste fat salvage into soap, either soft or hard soap, or dubbin, producing 1,500 tons in under twenty-one months. This activity was then extended into manufacturing glycerin.

Towards the end of January 1917 the troopship *Norseman* was torpedoed in the Gulf of Salonika but its crew managed to beach it, saving all the personnel and half the 1,000 mules on board. This landing of troops in this unhospitable country in winter caused great hardship, as they lacked tents, transport vehicles and even transport animals. There were several heavy snowfalls and a gale force wind; many of the men had no outer wear besides goatskin coats. Proper warm clothes did not arrive until March. Summer dress of shirts and shorts arrived in the middle of July for all but mounted men.

Food and Drink

Despite the unhelpful attitude of the Greek government, some local supplies of potatoes, eggs, tomatoes and even mutton, as well as hay and oats for the horses, plus wood for fuel, were purchased locally. There were also black-berries to be picked in the autumn, and hares and partridges for hunters.

In the wet and stormy weather, baking bread proved impossible with the Aldershot ovens as the sods which formed the covering were washed away. Two field bakeries were established in the suburbs of the city, with 250 men using twenty-eight Perkins ovens. These produced up to 97,000 loaves a day, some of which went by train to northern Greece. Soon after the troops arrived, 120 lorries and ten depots' worth of supplies arrived from Egypt, followed by three shiploads of emergency rations, and 900 tons of frozen meat and forage.

On 18 August 1917 a serious fire broke out and destroyed about a square mile of the town. It did not actually affect the ASC premises, but they had received two new fire engines a few days previously, and used these to fight the flames. They also took the lion's share of the evacuation of the townspeople, transporting some 80,000 homeless people.

Chapter 15

Egypt

In February 1915, when the attack on the Dardanelles was planned, it was at first suggested that the island of Lemnos would make a good base. However, there was no pier for ships, and it was finally decided to use Alexandria – a good decision as it became a good and large clearing house for all supply and medical services for Palestine, Salonika, and Mesopotamia, and provided some of what was needed in East Africa, the Persian Gulf and India.

Alexandria had a fine harbour and docks; its industrial base, much of which was already working in government service, was able to provide many useful supplies locally, thus saving much time and expense in shipping. Gun fittings were produced, and machine guns, complete except for barrels and barrel casings, were made by the railway workshops. The engineering workshops turned out wagon parts, desert ambulances, water tanks and pumping machinery. Other workshops made pack saddles, water tanks, desert ambulance carts and various textile-based items including uniforms.

A small tented ordnance depot was set up in March 1915, at first holding only a small amount of clothing and small arms ammunition. There were already some small depots serving the British Army of Occupation in Alexandria and Cairo, but despite appeals for assistance they were unable to provide much from the stores needed for the force defending the Suez Canal from the Turks. Ships from home were despatched and over a two-month period some seventy store ships arrived at Alexandria.

Much of the material from the engineers' siege parks was transferred there from France, as was a complete kit for a narrow gauge railway, which was extremely useful in the defence of the canal zone. A number of locomotives were also sent for Egypt.

From 1917 onwards, as a result of losses at sea from submarine attacks, supplies and troop reinforcements sailed from Taranto, the cargo and passengers having crossed from Cherbourg by train. This worked well for troops, but less so for stores. Quite apart from the possibility of store trains being sidetracked to make way for troop trains, the overland journey took much longer than the sea-route. Nor was this route immune from submarine attacks, as the harbour at Alexandria was a favourite hunting ground for submarines. Towards the end of 1917 two troopships were sunk, fortunately near the shore so that most of the men aboard were rescued.

The expanded activity required more ammunition and stocks to be moved up the line to advanced magazines at Rafa and El Arish. Purpose-built of timber and sandbags, these magazines were separated into splinter-proof bays which also allowed heat-reducing air-flow around the ammunition. Gun repair workshops were added, with other light workshops, including one for tin-smiths who repaired the smaller portable water tanks.

In 1918 it became necessary to reinforce the armies in France, and several British divisions were sent there from Palestine, to be replaced by units from India. Several of these arrived without rifles or camp equipment which all had to be supplied, as did the varied foodstuffs required by personnel of different religions.

Land transport in Egypt was mainly by camel. Based near Cairo, the Camel Transport Corps had thousands of camels, many coming from the Sudan, Somaliland and Algeria. These carried the small water tanks known as *fanatis*, plus ammunition, stones and tools for road-making. In Palestine there were two donkey transport companies in the Judaean Hills, each with some 2,000 animals, as well as 74,800 horses and 39,000 mules.

In September 1918, in support of a fighting force of 466,750 men and 159,000 animals, the ASC had 1,601 lorries, 1,467 vans and lorries, 530 ambulances, 1,487 motorcycles and 258 tractors, with 1,094 officers and 17,817 other ranks, plus 2,725 Indians and 32,744 Egyptians.

The Asiatic Petroleum Company supplied Egypt and Salonika with petrol. This was shipped to Alexandria and canned for use in the various Middle Eastern theatres and Mesopotamia, totalling 2,000,000 gallons per month.

The traditional form of transport in Egypt was on the Nile, and this continued. Between March 1917 and October 1918 over 37,000 passengers were carried, and the fleet of small vessels consisted of as many as 82 tugs, 17 steam barges, 421 lighters, 16 steamers and some 1,712 native craft.

Water

One thing which had to be provided was water, particularly where existing supply points could not be relied on for quality or quantity. Providing water, if it was needed on a larger scale than could be transported in tanks, was the responsibility of the Royal Engineers, who created pipelines, wells, pumps and filtration plants. Their work during the campaigns in Egypt and Palestine was fairly typical of what they had to do elsewhere.

Historically, the Nile had provided much of the water in Egypt; this was acceptable to the locals, but certainly not for the British Army. The water was contaminated with sewage, partly due to the *fellaheen* interpreting 'wash after defecating' as meaning 'it's easier to do this if you stand in waist-high water to defecate'. Not only did this spread intestinal diseases like cholera, it also caused bilharzia, a disease resulting from parasitic worms which have two larval stages, one in water snails, including those in the Nile, and the other in humans. As a result, the only safe water for washing and drinking was pumped up from wells at least 150ft deep. Although there were already waterworks at the main towns (Alexandria, Cairo, Port Said and Suez), British troops tended to be based away from the irrigated (and thus mosquito-ridden) land. Water for these camps had not only to be piped and pumped in, but stored in tank farms, balloon tanks and purpose-built concrete reservoirs. In some areas, where no pure water was to be found, the Royal Engineers built and operated coal-driven condensers. The engineers working on the water supplies accompanied, and sometimes preceded, the other troops on the route from Egypt to Jerusalem. (The other side of this picture was the disposal of waste water. This was not as easy as the sandy terrain might indicate. Soakaway pits soon made the area around them waterlogged, and proper drainage had to be created.)

It was considered essential to protect the Suez Canal, partly for its importance as a route to India and the Far East and partly as a 'natural' obstacle between the Turks and Egypt. In November 1916 a cable was received from the COG force in Egypt:

> The defence of the Canal must be taken up seriously and in depth. In anticipation, stores and materials for water supply and roads, for trenches for either forward line trenches or posts, as may be decided after study of problem [sic], should be ordered. The work should not be delayed for want of material.

Following this order required some assumptions to be made, as no solid information on numbers of troops was available, and the line of defence had not been decided. The available water on any of the possible lines was clearly going to be insufficient, so some test bores for wells were sunk but these, even when 300ft deep, produced nothing but salt water. Attention then turned to the area around the existing 'Sweet Water Canal' (that is, not salty), and the Cairo Water Works Company volunteered to design and construct mechanical filters and settling tanks. The Jewel Filter Company, which owned the patents to some of the filter parts, generously waived their right to royalties.

Contracts were placed for constructing concrete reservoirs, all the available pumps and pumping engines were purchased, and orders were cabled to England for more. The same happened with steel piping, and 280 miles of pipe was ordered, with tanks for water storage. By July 1916 new filter plants capable of producing some 1,000,000 gallons per day, and new concrete reservoirs capable of holding 1,200,000 gallons had been built. Other reservoirs made of iron, wood and canvas storage tanks had also been built. Once El Arish was occupied in December 1916, this pipeline was no longer needed;

it was dismantled during 1917 and the piping and machinery salvaged for use elsewhere.

Food and Drink

There were plenty of sheep available for fresh meat, but other provisions had to be brought in by the Camel Transport Corps. In 1918 the Sudanese Ministry of the Interior gave the Expeditionary Force 30,000 tons of wheat, 30,000 tons of barley, 12,000 tons of beans, and 6,000 tons of lentils, together with 275,000 tons of tibben (a type of soft chopped barley straw) and 25,000 tons of millet. Several large industries were set up, such as the pressing of straw into bales for easier pack transport, plus food industries including the manufacture of jam and biscuits. Egypt was a good source of supply for sugar, potatoes and fresh vegetables. A large fishing fleet was organised at Lake Mazala and fish curing works were set up at Port Said and Qantara, where fish surplus to hospital needs was dried or smoked.

A later development at Kantara was a remount facility which covered some 640 acres and could handle over 8,000 animals at a time. The canal provided access to ocean-going ships, the railway and a network of newly laid good roads, allowing development of an infrastructure of depots, camps, canteens, administrative offices, hospitals and small factories. The ordnance personnel at the depot increased steadily to 3,000, until military activity moved north to concentrate on Palestine.

Medical Care in Egypt

The headquarters of the RAMC was in the Citadel of Cairo, where there were 17 officers and 120 other ranks. There were two hospitals, one at the Citadel and the other at Ras-el-Tin near Alexandria. Three field ambulances arrived in September 1914, and when numerous Indian troops arrived to guard the Suez Canal, so the hospitals were expanded; the New Zealand Imperial Force arrived next, followed at the end of the year by the Australian Imperial Force, which brought five complete units of the Australian Army Medical Corps. These were soon occupied by numerous cases of measles, mumps and intestinal disorders, many of the patients coming from the Australian units and other overcrowded camps.

Despite two more complete hospitals being set up in Alexandria, all beds there were soon filled and the overflow patients were sent on to Cairo. Elsewhere hospitals were expanded and additional camps and depots were set up for the convalescent. At the beginning of 1915 the Director of Medical Services in Egypt had 2,000 beds, by May there were 13,500, and eventually there were over 36,000. The home authorities sent out a good supply of stores, equipment and medical personnel as soon as they were notified by cable of the need. There were a few female nurses and nursing sisters at the start of the Gallipoli campaign but more soon followed, including some from Australia and New Zealand, as well as Queen Alexandra's Imperial Military Nursing Service.

The Egyptian state railway provided and equipped six hospital trains to move patients between the great towns; these could carry 100 lying down or 150 sitting. Hospital ships carried patients from Gallipoli and the other Mediterranean theatres to Egypt and then took them on to their country of origin. All the hospitals and medical depots except those on the Indian line were staffed by RAMC and Alexander Colonial Nursing Services personnel.

A new system of store depots was set up for medical stores, each being supplied directly from England, and a single main medical depot for the armies in the Near East was established at Alexandria. This depot had considerable expertise at anticipating what would be needed and getting it. This included dressings and appliances, many kinds of drugs and medicinal preparations, instruments for operating theatres, equipment for x-ray rooms, laboratories and dental departments. The depot and its contents arrived in the spring of 1915 and established itself in a shed at the docks, and immediately began working at high pressure, sending wound dressings to Gallipoli. It soon outgrew its original premises and took over several large cotton warehouses, eventually having 85,000 square feet of floor space. As well as basic supply work, personnel also refitted and refilled mechanical and surgical panniers, field haversacks, fracture boxes, water-testing cases and other items of field medical equipment. A complete electro-plating outfit was installed and there was an expert cutler who renovated surgical instruments which had been returned as unserviceable.

Field ambulances in Egypt consisted of six basic general service wagons, four more with limbers, three water carts, one Maltese cart and over a hundred horses and mules. The men staffing these units had to understand how to get the best not only from equines, but also from camels, and learned a smattering of the local language to direct the camel men.

In western Egypt malaria, enteric fever, smallpox, dysentery, typhoid and the plague were all indigenous. It was soon realised that the health of British troops in the trying heat of summer could be improved by providing a high standard of comfort in the permanent camps. All troops were housed in double-skinned tents. They were not allowed to eat in the sleeping quarters, and mess tents made of a light wooden framework and grass matting were provided. This type of tent was also used for fly-proof larders and cookhouses, and for resting in the hottest part of the day. Similar shelters were built for the stables so men did not have to groom their animals in the sun. All camps were located away from agricultural areas as this tended to put unpleasant and potentially infectious dust in the air.

Avoiding contamination of food was a continual process, especially with soft perishable foodstuffs like fresh meat, bacon and bread. Fly-proof larders were used, but these were not necessarily sand-proof, which tended to make the food gritty to eat.

Bilharzia germs lurked in all open water sources; mere skin contact was enough to transmit it to British troops who had to be prevented from bathing in the rivers and canals. All well water had to be chlorinated.

During the move into the Sinai desert in 1916–17, they took two complete hospital trains, which took five to eight hours to reach Kantara, where a fleet of motor ambulances took patients either to the steamers on the Suez canal, or to stations of the Egyptian state railway where well-appointed ambulance trains took them to the base hospital.

At El Arish the town was in a filthy state, with overflowing latrine pits and excrement lying in the streets; even the nearby date plantations swarmed with flies. Smallpox was rife in the population and cholera was suspected. The RAMC set about cleaning up the town; proper latrines were established and the locals were compelled to use them on pain of severe penalties, then a house-to-house tour was organised with a local doctor acting as interpreter. Each house was thoroughly cleaned, sprayed with germicide, and all rubbish consigned to the nearest incinerator. Fly-papers were distributed and all moist places and stagnant pools were given a surface film of petrol to kill the larvae of mosquitoes and the culex gnat which carries dengue fever. The larvae of these flying pests hang just below the surface of the water, breathing through a tube, and the film of petrol prevented them breathing. In the deeper pools larvae-eating fish were installed. By the end of 1916 it had become rare to see a mosquito and cases of malaria had reduced almost to zero.

The town was systematically searched for cases of smallpox and other infectious diseases. These were taken to an isolation hospital and their clothing destroyed. It was then decided to vaccinate the whole population; inevitably they missed some, but of the estimated 3,700-strong population, they did manage to vaccinate 3,000. All this was done before the railway reached El Arish, so everything had to be brought in on camels.

The British troops then suffered an outbreak of scabies (an itchy condition caused by tiny mites burrowing beneath the skin). Dealing with this was helped by finding a steam disinfector left behind by the Turks. The RAMC had their own, but it was stuck at the railhead.

Sanitation work and pest destruction was necessary in the camps. The main work of the sanitary sections, who were based at Kantara, was supervising water treatment systems, disposing of excreta and other camp refuse, prevention of illness through the destruction of insect pests, and disinfecting against other forms of disease carrier.

Large filtering works were established on the west side of the Suez Canal, using water from the Sweet Water Canal. This water was full of germs and the parasitic larvae of bilharzia, and thus had to be sterilised with acid sodium sulphate as well as filtered. Once delivered to the end of the pipe-line it had to be carried onward by camels, each carrying two water tanks. Great care had to be exercised to prevent contamination of this water; the tanks were filled by hose but, unless closely supervised, these tended to be just dropped on the contaminated sand. The troops' water bottles had to be regularly sterilised.

They built better box latrines and sprayed them regularly with LeFroy's Fluid to keep flies off. Otherwise buckets filled with creosol and fitted with a hinged ring-seat top were used. When full, these were removed and replaced with an empty bucket by native latrine-duty men. Urine was dealt with by digging a pit and filling it with drainage material and light sheet-iron 'trumpets' which could be removed and fitted into each other when the unit moved, at which point the pit was filled in. The same system was used for waste cook-house water. However, this water was full of grease, so grease traps had to be incorporated; the easiest method was to make a frame of wire-netting filled with hay to collect the grease.

Lice, fleas and other bugs were not only carriers of disease but also pre-vented sleep from their itchy bites. Regular body searches were carried out, and all clothing and blankets were passed through the steam disinfectors as often as possible, but success was only relative.

By taking all possible measures to combat infectious diseases in the desert camps, the British suffered only thirty cases of cholera, resulting in seven deaths. The disease was known to be raging in Syria where the Turkish Army had its base. Almost the whole Allied Army was inoculated against it, as were the camel-men and labourers.

Drinking the local well and spring water was forbidden, except where there was no access to official supplies, but sterilisation tablets were issued for water bottles. All cases of diarrhoea, no matter how minor, were regarded as suspi-cious and the affected men were immediately isolated and closely watched, and stool samples sent to the nearest laboratory for examination. Despite dif-ficulties in teaching locals about hygiene and sanitation, the message finally got through by repetition and there were no cases of cholera among the Egyptian labourers on the Sinai peninsula.

There were other widespread diseases: epidemic jaundice on the Darda-nelles, enteric fever, dysentery, diphtheria and plague elsewhere. Plague was always present in Egypt and India, and the period from April to the end of July was even known as the plague 'season'. The first cases of plague were found at the end of April 1917, all in the Indian troops and Egyptian Labour Corps. Investigations showed it had come in on rats from the ships bringing food from India, and a grand blitz on rats followed. A Central Military

Bacteriological Laboratory was established at Alexandria. This also acted as a training college for bacteriological medical officers and laboratory assistants. From September 1915 to the end of December 1916 over 18,000 specimens were examined. Travelling field laboratories moved with the army; there were a number of these on the line from Kantara to the front. They were housed in light huts which came in sections made of wooden frames with canvas stretched over them.

In the desert, it was difficult to clean one's teeth properly, and many soldiers' teeth wore badly on the hard tack rations and sand; this prevented proper mastication and sickness followed. Some thirty dental surgeons were attached to the field ambulances. Their main function was dealing with cases that could be corrected quickly. Necessary extractions were done on the spot, while other cases were sent on to base depots, including those needing dentures. Dental surgeons at the base hospitals also had to deal with jaws wounded by shell or shot.

Hospitals were all equipped with mosquito nets and fans (even if these were just hand fans), an x-ray room, operating theatres, clinical laboratories, dispensaries and a lavage room for the inevitable VD cases (some 10 per cent of soldiers).

The Egyptian Labour Corps and the Camel Transport Corps were cared for by a separate department of the RAMC in a special hospital with twenty medical officers, sixty-five RAMC orderlies, sixty native doctors and 400 native orderlies. Many patients had 'relapsing fever' which was carried by ticks and small body lice; others had eye problems (probably carried by wind-blown sand), skin diseases and injuries from accidents and camel bites, which were very common and often turned septic. Most of the 'beds' in these hospitals were on the ground, with the patients keeping the area round their bed clean if they were able.

They were all given milk at 6.00am, with a breakfast of dates, lentils and bread; at midday they were given just tea and milk, then at 4.00pm they had dinner of rice, a small amount of meat, with onions and other vegetables, and bread. They had more milk at 8.00pm. If they were able, they had their meals in the open air, the food being served in large bowls shared by all, eating with their fingers. Helpless patients had food taken to them in bed. To the great delight of those who were able, there was a 3.00pm bathe in the canal. The other big event of the day was the 5.00pm discharge parade, when those discharged could go home.

Chapter 16

Palestine

The campaign for Palestine was in three parts: on and around the Suez Canal, up into the Sinai Peninsula, and then further north into Palestine itself and Syria.

In 1915 the main depots for the British Army of Occupation in Egypt were at Alexandria and Cairo, with Alexandria serving as a regional depot for all British forces at the eastern end of the Mediterranean. At first defensive, their activities soon turned to offence. The autumn of 1917 saw an expansion of activity, and this, together with the longer line of communication created by the move to the north, led to an equal expansion of ordnance department personnel to serve the expanded fighting force. By this time there were some 249,000 British soldiers in theatre, with 18,000 Indian troops and 80,000 Egyptians.

Food and Drink

In 1917, when General Allenby arrived, his regiments were fed on dried fruit and potatoes from Cyprus and Sudan, as well as the usual corned beef, biscuits, jam and tea. In the area around Jaffa, fruit and the local unleavened bread could be bought.

Elsewhere, especially in Palestine, obtaining water whilst on the march was difficult. In this dry terrain water was scarce and the horses were only watered three times a day instead of the recommended four. This was then reduced to twice a day, although it was found that they drank more overall on this regime than with more frequent watering. During the period from May to October 1917 it was only possible to water once a day, and later this was reduced to once every thirty-six hours. One officer reported that he kept a biscuit tin of water handy and wiped his horses' mouths and nostrils with a wet cloth; another discovered that horses who would not eat dry food when exhausted would accept small balls of moistened grain if fed by hand.

The Desert Mounted Corps commonly made marches of up to 60 miles in a day in waterless desert terrain, often at temperatures of over 100° Fahrenheit. Few wells were available, and many of those were often 150ft deep and water could only be obtained by letting down buckets on lengths of telegraph wire. It took up to an hour to water each troop of thirty horses, which meant that instead of watering four times a day, as was usual, they could only manage it once a day.

In Palestine in 1917 much work was done on railways and laying water pipes from Egypt. New wells were dug and pumping equipment installed. In April 1917 a bridge to carry all sorts of traffic across the Jordan was requested. After the details were settled by telegraph, the bridge arrived in Alexandria at the beginning of July. After the capture of Jerusalem in 1918, large amounts of building stores including cement and workshop machinery were required.

During the second half of 1916, once the advance to the north around the edge of the Sinai Peninsula to Jerusalem had begun, several advance ordnance depots were opened on the east bank of the canal, at Suez, Ferry Post (Ismailia), Port Said and Tel-el-Kebir. Later a large depot was established at Kantara (between Ismailia and Port Said). In the early days this depot was supplied from Alexandria by rail, stores being off-loaded on the western bank of the canal and transferred by motor lorries or horse-drawn wagons. This was not only cumbersome but also a strain on the resources of the Egyptian state railways, so this method was gradually replaced by water transport. This required the building of wharfs and extended railway sidings into the depot. This arrangement was completed by late autumn.

The depot was at the starting point of the desert railway and soon grew from a bare patch of sand into 65 acres of highly organised depot, equivalent to a small city of some 100,000 people. There had been a small railhead depot at El Arish; this was enlarged to an advance depot, holding a month's stock of the bulk items which were needed most urgently during operations. This depot was closed at the end of summer and most of its personnel went to the terminus of the light railway at Der-el-Belah. Supplies which had been sent to troops via El Arish then went direct from Kantara.

About this time, an order was issued that spare pumps should be carried and used to replace those worn out by the pervasive sand. Pumps were not to be repaired, nor replacement parts carried, as these tended to be lost, whereas it was difficult to lose a whole pump.

Wherever possible, mechanical pumps were replaced by the local *shadoof*. This consists of a long pole with a bucket attached at one end and a counterweight at the other. The bucket was lowered into the well, and when full the weight was allowed to draw it out. Unlike buckets on ropes, this one was lifted straight up and did not bang on the sides of the well and spill its contents. Other types of local water 'pumps' were the *churra*, where a rope passed from the bucket through a series of pulleys to a donkey yoke, the bucket being lifted as the donkey walked away from the well; and the *saqqia*, which consisted of a waterwheel turned by a geared wheel and a donkey.

The pipes came in fairly short lengths, each piece with 'male' and 'female' screw fittings at the ends; to achieve the length needed, they had to be screwed together. The native labourers, although willing, were not used to this concept and had to be constantly supervised. When the task started, each gang could only screw together fifteen lengths of pipe in a day, but experience (and piecework rates) soon increased this to forty.

The whole operation was quite complex. Firstly a party of seven officers and fifty labourers had to locate and mark the route. The pipeline was meant to follow the railways, but it could not be bent to make the same curves, and had to take its own line. Nor could it cope with sharp changes of gradient, so the ground had to be modified with cuttings and banks. A second work group of fourteen officers with 1,500 labourers followed the first to modify and prepare the surface for the pipes. Labour gangs travelled on the delivery trains to load the pipes at Kantara and unload them where needed. Where the pipeline route was close to the railway line, single pipes were rolled off the train as it moved along. Elsewhere they were unloaded in bulk and carried to the laying gangs by tractor and then by labourers. Only strong men could be used as each length of pipe weighed half a ton.

The screwing gangs (three European foremen and 250 Egyptian artificers and labourers divided into twelve gangs) started screwing in the middle of a section and moved away from each other until they met up with another gang. Special expansion joints were used every 3km. Once the pipes were connected and laid in place, other parties of labourers covered them with sand to avoid damage from sharp changes of temperature. In some places the wind blew away the covering and even what lay under the pipes; to counteract this, camel scrub was planted beside the pipeline.

While the pipeline was under construction, there was little water available on the line of march between Romani and El Arish, and supplies of filtered water were brought up by train.

Moving up from El Arish to Gaza there were several good wells en route, and those at Gaza were also good, but it was still thought necessary to extend the pipeline. Local water tanks (*fantasse*) were filled at specially fitted sites and carried to the troops on camels. One particularly useful area of ground water was the Wadi Guzze. An Australian engineer officer with water-divining skills found places where the water could be reached at little more than 13ft deep. As well as water for the troops, 200 wooden troughs were erected for horses and other animals.

Once in Palestine, the Royal Engineers personnel found themselves in a different kind of terrain. Away from the coast, where sand and dunes predominate, the Judaean Hills consist of thick strata of limestone and sandstone. In the lower hills there were a few springs, but most of the rain which fell in the winter months quickly soaked through the porous limestone and could only be reached by boring into the underlying sand.

After capturing Beersheba and Gaza in November 1917, the troops moved on towards Jerusalem. Water here was also in short supply, for both men and horses. Springs and well pumps managed to solve that problem, but when the Allied troops reached Jerusalem in January 1918, they faced another. The water for the town came from rain water collected in reservoirs and cisterns, and sets of springs outside the town. None of this was pure enough to drink and one of the springs had been polluted by sewage from the town.

This was not a new problem. In 1908 a French engineer, M. Franghia, had measured the output from the springs over a two-month period in autumn. From these measurements he had produced a plan for a water supply, and this plan was made available to the Royal Engineers. Unfortunately, although the plan anticipated a yield of 380,000 gallon per day, the rains were less prolific in 1918 and additional reservoir capacity had to be organised, with pumps and pipes from the nearby deep valleys.

The actions of the fighting troops took them far from the southern deserts to the bitterly cold mountains of Judaea, where the foothills were extremely wet with torrential rains and swampy ground. Winter clothing was urgently needed, as were boots, which soon wore out in the wet and rocky country.

The route there from Alexandria was a standard gauge railway built by the Royal Engineers just inland from the coast, via El Arish to Gaza, then on up to Ludd on the coast north-west of Jerusalem. Wire netting was laid to stabilise the track, and horses were forbidden to use it for fear of damaging it.

The advance northwards was rapid; by December, Jaffa, Gaza and Beersheba had fallen to the British, and finally the Turks in Jerusalem surrendered. With the exception of the railway station, the Turks left Jerusalem in a state of disrepair and its inhabitants near starvation. The work of the ordnance department, as well as taking over some factories, included providing food for the Syria and Palestine relief organisation to distribute free to the population. This helped provide work for those who were able, and the improving health of the population made more people fit and able to work.

Chasing the Turkish Army eastwards, many British troops were caught in the Judaean foothills and mountains by bad weather. One division had left all its winter clothing behind; clad in the khaki drill uniforms they had worn in the desert, the men moving across the bitterly cold mountains suffered through a series of storms which turned the foothills into swamps. The advance had moved more rapidly than railway lines could be laid and it was some time before winter clothing got to them. Eventually this line reached Ludd, and an extensive depot was established there.

Chapter 17

Mesopotamia

Then, as now, the main concern over Mesopotamia was oil production and the protection of the oil pipeline which ran to Abadan on the Persian Gulf. This was, at first, undertaken by the Indian Army but after the Germans announced their intention to build a railway line from Constantinople to Baghdad and Basra, British troops were sent. There were some fears that the Germans might incite the Arab tribes to revolt, but the real danger was that from Basra it would be worryingly easy for the Germans and the Turks to reach the British sea route to India and further east.

Mesopotamia consists of a fertile strip of land along and between the two main rivers (the Tigris and Euphrates). Replenished each year in the annual floods like those of the Nile, its alluvial soil was the richest growing land in the Middle East. The rest of the country was desert and that, combined with the ferociously hot summers (with temperatures up to 130 °Fahrenheit in the shade), meant there was an ongoing shortage of good drinking water. Apart from a few palm trees along the river banks, there were no trees. This, with the monotonous wastes of sun-baked mud, was extremely depressing.

It was almost impossible to undertake any strenuous activity in the heat; the only clothing that could be tolerated was an open-necked shirt and khaki shorts with a sun-helmet and perhaps a parasol when out-of-doors. In the winter, there could be 10 degrees of frost, and thick underclothing, service dress uniform, overcoats and blankets at night were needed. This involved extra work for depot workers who had to handle the twice-yearly change over, followed by disinfecting, washing and repairing the returned clothing before sending it back it to store.

The ferocious climate included strong winds and dust storms from the desert between April and mid-October. General Maude, who took over as Commander-in-Chief in August 1916, wrote that autumn was the best time for active operations.

The British force arrived in Mesopotamia in late 1914; the first town of any significance was Basra, a few miles inland from the Persian Gulf, and they took this three weeks after their arrival, occupying the nearby oilfields. Before they could move on towards Baghdad, they had to accumulate stores and get to grips with the transport situation. There was only one feasible way to move north at that time: on the rivers. The Euphrates was navigable only by very small craft, but the Tigris was navigable by larger craft as far as Baghdad, although on the shallower reaches barges had to be used.

The river at Basra was deep enough to take sea-going vessels, and it had a port, of sorts. This was undeveloped and had no wharves when the British arrived. Ships had to be unloaded into lighters and from them into barges which had to be towed further up the Tigris. Labour was scarce and bad, and it took anything up to twenty days to unload a ship. The town of Basra had no street lighting and only 2 miles of road. The town was subject to flooding in the wet months (March, July and December) when strong winds combined with a high river and spring tide.

Supplies they did manage to unload at Basra could only be moved north slowly due to inadequate river transport. In November 1914, when the British arrived, there were only three steamers, one of which needed new engines. There were also four lighters of 60 tons, one of 80 tons, two of 110 tons and ten of 200 tons. The two rivers were shallow, and had sharp bends and concealed shoals. Flooding on the river in the wet months produced a 5-knot current against which the river steamers had to battle. In summer the river's depth fell to 5ft.

River transport gradually increased. By the end of 1917 there were 1,215 vessels, including 521 barges, 425 motor boats and 189 paddle-steamers, plus motor barges, hospital ships and other miscellaneous small vessels. The Inland Water Transport department took over during this time, employing 17,000 people, running the transport fleet, constructing dockyards, slipways and workshops.

By the end of the war Maude's successor Sir William Marshall had one of the largest river fleets in the world: 419 river steamers, 27 hospital steamers, 774 barges and 414 motor boats. They also had nine dredgers. This inland transport carried a daily average of 3,700 tons of supplies from Basra to Mosul, nearly 800 miles upstream. Maude reckoned that for four infantry divisions he needed 500 tons of transport per day for rations, forage and fuel, with another 100 tons per day for mail, canteen supplies, ordnance and Royal Engineers' stores. They also carried nearly 227,000 personnel (this figure included inbound troops, sick and wounded, leave men, camp followers, refugees and prisoners of war). In addition, they carried 20,272 animals, but the *Statistics* do not define these, and they could have been a mixture of riding or pack animals, and meat on the hoof.

Roads were almost non-existent and in the rainy season it became cold and the whole country became an impassable morass, while in the summer dust and the lack of potable water away from the main roads made travel extremely difficult.

The only railway was a 70-mile stretch north of Baghdad. The Royal Engineers under the Mesopotamia Command built railways, adding 155 miles of

4ft 8½in standard gauge, 421 miles of metre gauge and 200 miles of temporary light gauge (2ft 6in). The rails came from the Tata steelworks at Bombay, and the teakwood needed for the metre gauge lines came from Mysore. Other timber came from Cochin. All of this steel, wood and coal for the locomotives was brought in by sea. The labour for building these railways was also from India. Indeed, much of the army's requirements came from India, and there was a monthly ship from England with items not available in India, including some hospital comforts.

A high proportion of the British success in Mesopotamia was due to the efforts put into developing the country's infrastructure. Seven wharves were built at Basra and the amounts of cargo unloaded rose from 43,000 tons in the spring of 1916 to 132,000 in January 1918. As well as developing the port facilities and the town of Basra, they also built earthern embankments to alleviate flooding in the town and the surrounding countryside. Eight pumping stations with automatic chlorination and sedimentation tanks were built for drinking water with a capacity of 320,000 gallons per day. Water heaters and small ice plants were provided for hospitals, as well as portable huts and small bridges with 60ft spans, and several small power stations for lighting. The power plants and ice plants soon proved insufficient and in the autumn of 1916 a 1,000kw central power station was requested for Basra. This would provide current throughout the port, 7,000 fans in hospitals and aid the manufacture of 20 tons of ice per day. Some plant manufactured in Britain for private concerns in India was diverted, and with some emergency work carried out when the first consignment of boilers was lost to enemy action en route, the central power station was in operation by April 1917.

Some 40 miles of road was laid, including bridges over the creeks which ran into the main river. This allowed some motorised transport to operate alongside the columns of mules and camels delivering supplies from the depot to the troops.

Depots

A high proportion of the troops in Mesopotamia at the beginning of the campaign were from the Indian Army, which handled its own supplies (although not very well by British standards). It tried to provide supplies as it would have done in a peacetime situation, which soon proved inadequate. Eventually, in late 1916, a few months after Stanley Maude had been appointed Commander-in-Chief, the War Office took over the supply situation and sent out Major General Hugh Perry to take charge of ordnance services.

The base depot was at Basra, where the director of the Indian Ordnance Services had his office. He had only two administrative officers and four executive officers under him. There were two advanced depots, run by no more than four officers, and three very small depots, the whole operated by sixty-seven warrant officers with a few Indian clerks and some lascars. There were also two supposedly mobile workshops which in fact did not move. On his arrival Perry found that there was no proper organisation to receive, check, store and cover the supplies when they did arrive. There was no roofed storage or accommodation for the personnel, and a general lassitude prevailed. Concerned about the small number of personnel available to run the depot facilities, Perry cabled home requesting more officers, two ordnance companies and more mobile workshops. He also asked India to provide two more ordnance companies, comprising 100 British and 40 native clerks, 500 lascars and some Indian artificers. He also asked India for more officers, and these were promised but never provided. Perry then moved the whole depot to a new site on the river bank. Wharves and sheds were built, with large comfortable officers' quarters and an officers' mess which were much admired by other officers.

Until the supply situation at Basra was taken over by the AOC, it had been handled by the Indian Army, but when the AOC made a stocktake they found serious discrepancies in what they were meant to have taken over. The Indian system was based on what they had sent and what was meant to be in stock in Mesopotamia, but at the same time they had to send a daily cable on the number of days' supplies held on each front. These two reports could not be reconciled and it led to considerable confusion and worry at the War Office. Although the AOC and the Indian Supply and Transport Corps were theoretically working together, all requests had to go through the directorate at Simla, where the AOC had no representative.

So two senior AOC officers were sent to India, one to act as liaison between General Headquarters in India and the War Office, and the other to keep the War Office informed of the state of supplies held at the base ports in India, the schedule of proposed shipments and what was awaited from the sources of origin. This helped clarify the situation and reduced the strain on the base at Basra. However, AOC efforts were complicated by continual increases in the number of troops.

When the British finally took Baghdad, Perry found the depot, situated in the Citadel, in a state of complete chaos. The first storehouse he investigated contained a collection of arms ranging from old Arab swords to revolvers, automatic pistols and rifles. 'The rest of the space', he wrote, 'was occupied by fleas. These were fairly plentiful all over the Citadel, but in no place did they swarm quite so badly as in this room.' The second store had been burnt out and its floor was covered with a layer of melted lead. Pulled off in sheets, this was seized on with delight by the Royal Engineers' bridging division, who used it for foundations. Elsewhere they found thousands of ancient muzzle-loading flintlocks; with very long barrels and large bores, these had fine inlay work on the stocks.

There were workshops too; the Turks had done their best to render the machinery unusable but their best had not been good enough. The machine tools, although damaged, were not beyond repair. They were old-fashioned but usable and were added to the British repair equipment.

One major task which the depots did not have to perform, owing to the enterprise and hard work of a Punjabi gentlemen and his family, was repairing tents. Bhoota Singh ran a large firm and raised several tent repair teams, managed by his sons and staffed by his employees. These teams worked at the main depots and in groups which moved from camp to camp repairing tents on the spot.

Another successful repair operation was that for boots. The extreme dry heat rapidly dried out the leather if boots were left unworn for as little as forty-eight hours. The men were reluctant to surrender a comfortable pair for long enough for repairs to be made, so by the time they did hand them over they were too far gone for repair at all. The solution was to send boot repair gangs around the regiments; while each pair of boots was being repaired, its owner was loaned a soft pair until his own were ready.

One last depot was established towards the end of the war at Mosul (now al Mawsil) but this was more for collecting redundant and salvaged items than for issuing materiel to the troops. These salvaged items were passed back down to Baghdad or Basra, at each of which large areas of the desert were enclosed for their reception. Each consisted of two parts; one part received equipment which was roughly checked before being passed to the storage section, where it was examined more closely, cleaned and packed before stacking for final disposal. This work was mostly carried out by prisoners of war.

This all took some time, to the disgruntlement of the AOC staff who had to stay in the country to deal with it. India took most of the guns and ammunition to fight Afghan insurgents on their borders. The rest was sold off through a newly reinforced disposals board.

There was a fear that ammunition might run short, so a new depot was built near Basra, sufficiently isolated to reduce any threat of accidents to the town, and specially constructed to resist the heat and damp which caused the ammunition to deteriorate rapidly. Prior to this the ammunition had been stacked outside in the sun and high explosive shells had sweated; as a result, fused howitzer shells had to be re-fused just as operations were building up. Much of the stock of Mills bombs was found to be unusable as the ammonal fillings had crystallised.

Another difficulty which had to be resolved was that the troops from India had an old type of rifle, while troops from France and Egypt had the latest types. In some divisions both were in use and, as the two types used different cartridges, ammunition supply was unnecessarily complex until rearmament was completed and all the troops had the new type of rifle.

In 1919 the task of disposing of unwanted guns and ammunition was handed over to the Indian Army. Very little of it was deemed serviceable and the rest was moved to great dumps in the desert and exploded.

Medical Care

The medical situation in Mesopotamia was much the same as in Egypt: the almost complete lack of cleanliness and sanitation among the population led to cholera; there was also bubonic plague, and various skin and eye diseases. Heat stroke was also common. Great swarms of flies and mosquitoes spread malaria, typhoid and cholera. Sand-flies carried leishmaniasis, and bites caused what were known as 'Baghdad boils'. This affliction started as a small red spot, which became itchy and then developed into a large open sore, usually on the face, arms or legs. There was little that could be done to treat it, but it often spontaneously cured itself. Heat stroke and fever were common.

By May 1916 the medical situation was improving, with a hospital ship evacuating the sick and wounded. There had been a second hospital ship but it sank en route to Basra. Cholera vaccine was obtained, but many other items for the sick and wounded were lacking, including stretchers, some medicines and blankets.

By November 1918 the sick and convalescents numbered 278 British officers, 47 Indian officers, 5,580 British soldiers and 3,740 sepoys and sowars. Throughout this campaign nearly 15,000 men were killed in action or died of wounds and 13,000 died of disease; 51,000 were wounded and 13,000 taken prisoner or reported as missing.

Animals

Without decent roads or railways, stores had to be taken from the river ports by animal transport. Even in the fertile areas, there was little grass, and hay had to be imported, as was corn feed. Despite this, almost 84,000 animals were brought in, mostly from India, this number consisting of over 36,000 horses, 44,800 mules and 3,362 donkeys.

Such animal transport as there was mostly consisted of camels, but in some places in the rainy months they might sink up to their girths in the mud and have to be abandoned. Over the period from August 1917 to August 1919, there were 2,952 camels in 1917, 4,713 in 1918 and 808 in 1919.

In September 1917 the attack on the Turkish garrison of Ramadi used ten Fiat and 350 Ford vans. More Fords were required, and as these were not available elsewhere, over 3,000 Model-Ts were bought from America. Light-weight and easy to maintain, they were ideal for the desert and other poor surfaces.

Food and Drink

Away from the rivers, water had to be brought in. There was little food available, and the local meat was likely to be infested with maggots; oxen and horses and mules had to be slaughtered for their meat.

The main supply port was Basra; one monthly ship from England brought hospital supplies and provisions not available in India: preserved meat, bacon, jam and acceptable biscuit. At first the biscuit was obtained from two Indian factories, the Hindu Biscuit Factory at Delhi and the Great Eastern Hotel Company at Calcutta, but these biscuits proved unpopular, so supplies had to be ordered from home, and also from Egypt and finally Australia. Australia was also approached for supplies of condensed and sterilised milk for hospital patients. Fresh fruit and vegetables were also in short supply, except for locally grown dates. After the Turks had been driven from Baghdad, irrigation pumps were requested for irrigation schemes in the Tigris and Euphrates valleys, followed at the end of the year by requests for agricultural machinery: ploughs, harrows, rollers, corn-crushers and hay-balers.

Administration of army supplies had been dealt with by the Indian Army, and this was, to say the least, chaotic. There was no proper system to check supplies in when they arrived and they tended to be dumped in random mixed heaps of food, forage, medical supplies and everything else. This made stocktaking and onward shipping difficult. The British administrators sent an emergency cable to Britain for sheds, and moved the forage store further upriver where the river was deep enough for ocean-going ships to tie up. A frozen meat ship was sent from home to hold supplies, and after a few months the troops were getting regular supplies. Some marshland was drained to allow for expansion and finally the depot was laid out to accommodate railways sidings.

Under the Indian system, there were no fewer than forty substitute items which could be requested as required. There was a generous issue of condensed milk and tinned fruit, but there were early indications of a scurvy problem, which was 'dealt with' by an issue of Marmite, peas and lentils. This is strange, as it had been known for over a hundred years that citrus fruit was the answer to scurvy, both as a cure and as a preventative, and they should have been aware that Marmite, peas and lentils were ineffective – but perhaps what was well known to the Royal Navy was not known in India.

When they did a stocktake, they found what they thought was fraud, but it turned out that this was due to two different accounting systems. One, sent to the British government by the Indian government, listed what they had sent, and thus believed to be in stock in Mesopotamia; the other was a daily report of the number of days' supply in each location. The two reports, not surprisingly, did not reconcile. It turned out that although the British and Indian staff were working together in Mesopotamia, there was no British representative at the directorate in Simla. To ease this problem, two senior officers were sent out, one to liaise between the War Office and General Head-quarters in India, and the other to send back regular reports to the War Office of supplies held at the Indian ports, with a schedule of supplies going out and those coming in from their point of origin.

In addition, some 250 acres were turned into a vegetable farm; this was later increased to 3,500 acres. Dairies and chicken farms were started, and additional ploughs and ploughing oxen were sent from overseas, with irrigation pumps and stocks of seeds. Purchase officers were sent throughout Persia to buy sheep to meet the requirement for 70,000 per month. In preparation for the coming summer, soda water machines were installed with a corps of mechanics to work them. They also arranged to make and distribute ice.

By June 1917 apples, apricots, tomatoes and cucumbers, plus soda water and ice, were issued on top of the usual rations, and hospitals were getting plenty of butter, milk and chickens. This was fortunate as the Tigris was lower than normal that year, making navigation difficult.

Chapter 18

East Africa

This campaign covered the territory from Uganda in the north to the River Zambesi in the south, and from Rhodesia (now Zimbabwe) to the Indian Ocean, some 470 miles long and 700 miles wide. A 30-mile strip along the coast is low-lying, then it rises to a high plateau. Along the coast it rains from November to May, the heaviest rains falling in April when rivers flood for miles either side of their banks, creating swamps further out. It is drier and cooler from June to October. In the wet season the 'red' soil will allow the passage of light traffic on upland roads, but when it is dry the red soil is soon ground to sand by wheeled traffic and needs to be fixed in place with wire netting or plaited plantain leaves. At the same time everything else dries up and turns to desert. Elsewhere there is 'black' soil which quickly becomes impassable bog. This meant the army needed to be able to switch from one type of transport to another, not just according to the season but also according to the location of operations; as one officer remarked, 'resourcefulness has to be cultivated'.

The highland climate, around Nairobi, was generally healthy, but much of the fighting took place on the lower areas which, especially in the rainy seasons (October and November, and March to April), brought plagues of mosquitoes and other disease-carrying insects.

The first force of about 6,000 men came from India, but it was soon realised that many more would be needed and six months' worth of supplies were ordered for 20,000–24,000 white troops, the same number of coloured troops, plus 4,400 white mounted troops. Among the first difficulties which occurred was a shortage of tents; these had to come from India, and although they were expected to be available by the end of the year, this was not certain.

Depots

Colonel R.K. Scott was appointed head of ordnance services, arriving with his staff at Mombasa in February 1916. There he found that the Indian Ordnance Service was running the operation; at its head was Colonel Foote, many years Scott's senior. Apart from this, Scott found himself in a difficult position, brought about by the attitude of the Indian heads of services, who showed very plainly that they did not like it. This was not surprising, but they were unnecessarily aggressive about it. What they disliked as much as losing their places was being brought under British ways of working in place of Indian. With the exception of these departmental officers, however, everyone seemed pleased with the change; glad that, at last, there was a chance of something being done, and that there was a staff in the country to cope with the work. The final solution was to leave the Indian regime in place for a few weeks while the department was reorganised, until the home system was ready to take over in March 1916.

The troops were a mixed force of British, South African, Indian, some Nigerians and some other locals, including the Kavirondas (known locally as 'the skin brigade' because their uniform was non-existent and they fought naked). Five types of rations were needed: European, Indian, West African, East African and Chinese, with all the usual religious taboos to be dealt with.

From September 1916 Dar es Salaam was the main base depot, run by seven officers and 150 others. It included an ammunition depot about a mile from the other site. There were four other main depots, at Kilindini, Voi, Nairobi and Entebbe, and four advanced depots at Mbuyuni, Kajaido, Kisumu and Simba. Later in the campaign a further eleven depots were opened. This seems like a lot, but most of them were only open for a few months, and they were widely spaced in a country where there were few roads or railways and most of the supplies had to be carried in by porters.

The British ordnance department had to deal with eight East African governments and five London ministries. The force cobbled together by the British government had numerous different requirements and was spread over a 1,500-mile front. In November 1914 there was no real ordnance or supply system in place, and regular British soldiers arrived to find to their horror that they had to buy much of what they needed locally at vastly inflated prices. It took more than sixteen months to get the supply system more or less sorted out. Problems included different guns on the Lake Victoria steamers and .303 bullets which dropped out of the rifles if they were pointed downwards. By the middle of 1916 the ASC had taken over, including ordnance supplies, and the situation soon improved.

Long lines of communication hampered the delivery of supplies: supplies went from Durban to Baira by sea, then were transferred to smaller steamers to Chinde (80 miles), then to river boats on the Zambesi to Chiromu, via railway to Blantyre, then overland to Lake Nyasa for a 200-mile section by lake steamers. An alternative route was from Cape Town by rail to Livingstone (700 miles), then by carrier and canoe for another 700 miles through Northern Rhodesia (now Zambia) to Fife, then another 200 miles by porter through thick bush and over mountains. In March 1916 there were some 41,000 porters, but by June 1917, after a major search by the Directorate of Military Labour, the number had increased to 168,000, which meant additional packing cases and other items had to be provided. An attempt was made to use improvised wheelbarrows, but it failed as the native porters could not learn how to get them round bends and stay upright. All this led to the conclusion that sometimes the old ways are the best, and they reverted to human porters.

The porters had to be supplied with khaki shorts. Their usual wear was a short jumper which shrank and rode up, exposing parts which the local missionaries and nursing sisters did not want to see. The other personal equipment carried by the porters included a blanket, a haversack, a water bottle and a *panga* (machete). They had to be paid by barter, money being pointless as there was nothing to spend it on. Fabric for women's clothing was a popular form of payment.

In the few places where mechanical transport could be used, tracked vehicles were needed, as the mimosa bushes which grew everywhere had vicious thorns that could punctured rubber tyres. At best, other transport consisted of ox-wagons and pack mules, but once the fighting force began to move, the lines of communication were extended and more transport was needed. Wagons and ox-harness were made at Nairobi and sent to Kisumu, but had to be scrapped as all the oxen (some 28,000) died from trypanosomiasis (carried by the tsetse fly). More wagons were called for elsewhere, especially in South Africa, along with additional ox-yokes, trek-chains and other items which had to be carried on the wagons for replacements when the appalling roads caused breakages. After the oxen died, the wagons had to be converted for mules to pull, but they too died from the attentions of the tsetse fly. Donkeys, which seemed a little more resistant to the tsetse flies, were brought into use and orders were received for 5,000 sets of donkey pack-saddles.

The only materials available were jute sacking with raw cotton for stuffing, and there was no agreement on the correct pattern. Sewing machines were acquired, but they lacked needles until the ever-resourceful ordnance factories made needles from umbrella spokes, but by the time the pack-saddles were ready the donkeys had died as well.

In all, between September and November 1916 some 10,000 horses, 11,000 oxen and 2,500 donkeys died in the field. The total losses at the end of 1918 were 31,000 horses, 33,000 mules and 34,000 donkeys. Part of this was exacerbated by the German General von Lettow-Vorbeck, who deliberately chose lines of retreat through tsetse-infested areas. The only time when camels were used was in the year to 31 August 1918, when there were 1,601.

Food and Drink

Human porters could carry only 60lb each, moving in long lines from stage to stage, but much of what they carried was food for themselves, so it wasn't long before that was all they carried and the troops went hungry. In Rhodesia the carriers breakfasted on mealie-meal, peanuts, dates and potatoes. The mealie-meal (i.e. ground maize) was cooked a little, then rolled into a ball in the hands and eaten after being dipped in a bowl of *ghee* (melted butter).

It was not long before rations became short, a problem exacerbated by the dietary requirements for soldiers of different religions. As well as Europeans, there were Chinese, Indians, and East and West Africans. Flour was short, leaving only biscuit and maize meal, and vegetarian Indians suffered from a shortage of *ghee*. British troops only received the basics: tinned meat, biscuit and a little cheese, which soon deteriorated in the hot weather. Game birds and animals could be hunted, and in a few places there was local fruit such as pawpaws. One group of soldiers lived for two weeks on the meat of hippopotami shot on the banks of the river Mgeta.

Medical Care

In addition to the attacks by flies during the day, there was considerable difficulty over mosquito nets. Obtaining these was easy enough, once the shape and mesh size had been decided, but the medical authorities kept changing the specifications. A British expert on malaria was sent out; he insisted that only nets to his own design should be used, and that the existing stock of over 300,000 nets should be scrapped. However, the local Director of Medical Services intervened, suggesting that the 'expert' should go to investigate malaria at Morongoro,where the situation was at its worst. Within three days he had succumbed to malaria himself and had to be evacuated to South Africa. His successor took what was described as 'a more reasonable view of the matter'.

The financial cost to the Allies of war in sub-Saharan Africa was immense: unofficially estimated at more than £70m. The butcher's bill was equally colossal: over 45,000 soldiers and carriers in Africa, plus British Imperial combatants and support units (officially 11,189 of the 126,972). Much of this toll was attributed to poor medical provision. There was also Spanish flu there from October 1918, affecting Germans as well as British and natives. Such numbers as are available state that there were probably some 200,000 deaths in East Africa. Sick and wounded were evacuated by hospital ship from Dar-es-Salaam to South Africa.

After the German surrender in Rhodesia in September 1918, the ordnance depots turned their attention to dealing with unused stock. This was collected at Dar-es-Salaam, then dispersed from there. Much of it had originated in India, and went back there; the rest was sent to Durban for disposal by the South African government.

Chapter 19

Italy

Communist Italy joined the war in May 1915, seized positions on the Austrian frontier, then spread eastwards and south to the Adriatic. In 1917 it was decided that Trieste should be taken from the Italians, and sixteen artillery batteries of 6in howitzers were sent to do the job, with half a company of ordnance corps. Headquarters was at Gradisca, and an ordnance workshop was set up nearby, with the ordnance depot 9 miles to the north. As the force was entirely artillery, the depot was mainly for ammunition. Each artillery battery had its own ammunition dumps. Replacement ammunition was sent direct from England via Havre and rail. Delays meant nothing arrived until 12 May, the day the bombardment was scheduled to start, and new supplies arrived just as the stock brought with the guns ran out. By the time the operation was completed, there was plenty of ammunition in stock.

In August, a fresh push to Trieste was planned and six more batteries were sent, bringing the total to sixty-four guns. The assault was then postponed until October 1917, and these batteries finally came into action when German troops joined the communist Italians. They soon breached the Allied lines and there was a general retreat to the river Tagliamento. Panic ensued and the retreat turned into a rout. After having used all their ammunition, the British batteries joined the retreat to rendezvous at Treviso; the ordnance depots could do no more than save what they could of their stocks and try to join them. The lorries normally used had disappeared and the trains were full of troops and civilians. Appeals to Italian headquarters for transport were mostly unsuccessful, except for two lorries which were used to remove the reserve howitzers. The workshop at Godisca and the depot at Palamova both had to be abandoned and the personnel sent to Trieste. They had to go on foot, although many of them were already in poor health and unfit for further exertion. Torrential rain began and the depot workers had to have frequent rests to recover a little before they could carry on.

After this initial defeat, it was decided that the enemy should be prevented from reaching the fertile Italian plains south of the Alps by sending a joint British/French expeditionary force. The move to Italy started in late October 1917. This was expected to be a temporary measure, with its maintenance treated as a detached part of the main force in France, so supplies were not sent directly and some restrictions were applied. No more than one month's stores were to be held at any one time, and repairs were not to be started if they could be sent to France. This turned out to be a matter of hope over experience, the least of this being the need to maintain larger stocks. It took stocks longer to come from France than expected, due to lack of available capacity on the railways; also, goods trains were given lower priority than those carrying troops and civilians and were frequently shunted on to side-tracks. Nor was it practicable to use these overused lines to send repairable items to France (and back) when local firms could do the work. Several contracts were made with firms in Milan for cleaning and disinfecting textiles, and a large workshop was built at the base to make wooden tent floors. It was not long before the supply system in Italy was self-supporting, as it was elsewhere.

There were two railway routes into Italy. The distance from the British positions on the front in France was a minimum 800 miles by the shortest rail route via Modane and the Mont Cenis tunnel to Bussileno, or almost 1,200 miles via Etaples, the Rhone valley and Ventimiglia. The former's capacity was twenty trains per day and it was already carrying sixteen. The latter route carried twenty-one trains over an electrified section, or a maximum thirty otherwise. The possibility of going by road was limited by the upkeep of the roads for heavy traffic and the closing of the passes in winter when they were blocked by snow.

In the high Alps there were numerous difficulties, not least getting there. There were rack and pinion railways, or the Teleferica (a chain of cradles slung from a high rope) which was used to supply troops at high altitudes, mule tracks or motor car. The roads zigzagged all the way but did get to the high plateau in the end.

There were railheads at Asiago and Villarverla. Horse- or mule-drawn wagons were used to take supplies from the railheads to the units, and the Italians supplied twenty-seven small (30cwt) Fiat lorries for the purpose.

For operations in the mountains, 6in mortars were considered the ideal weapon, as their trajectory enabled them to reach reverse slopes and deep ravines. Wheeled transport could not be used, so they had to be moved by pack transport, and at 170lb they were too heavy for a single animal. The solution was to cut the mortar tube in half for carrying and then fit it back together with a gas-tight collar; the bed made a third load. In some cases soldiers had to carry what they could. Most preferred to use canvas bags or buckets or multi-pocketed waistcoats, while Canadian troops used Alaskan packs and tumplines.

Winter clothing had to be provided for troops operating in the mountains; this included fur coats, fur-lined trench slippers and sleeping bags. Other necessary equipment included skis, snow-shoes, ice-crampons, alpen-stocks, ice-axes and splinter-proof goggles for protection from rock splinters, non-freezing oils, and heavily nailed boots. Special mule shoes were also needed. When the force moved to cross the Piave river, bridging material was called for together with long waders and several thousand life-jackets.

During preparations for specific attacks, special battle stores were sent, including wire cutters, flares and daylight signals for aircraft, and smoke candles for use if the wind was right. But even the supply of these simple items could be fraught with difficulty. Forbes told of being called to see the Quartermaster General, who had been visited by a general worried that he had no flares of a certain colour. A Royal Flying Corps officer was sent to the Ministry of Munitions in London, where the official who dealt with such supplies was not aware of any problem. He promised to investigate and provide an answer the next day, but by the time the RFC officer called back the official had been conscripted. A visit to the War Office and emphasis on the importance of the matter justified his release. He found that the chemical needed to produce that particular colour had been misused and there was no more available. There were plenty of flares in other colours, but the lack of this one meant accurate information was not available to the attacking force.

Depots

There were few problems over food in Italy. There was a large railway station at Aquata, 20 miles north of Genoa, with sidings and store sheds. More were built and it was soon considered a 'model' AOC depot. Up to 10,000 tons of stores could be landed there each day. Soon after this, a second store was set up at Granezza, where 40,000 rations of preserved meat were kept as a reserve. This store also held 10,000 animal rations. There were two field bakeries and two field butcheries. Groceries came by rail from Rouen, vegetables and fruit were bought locally. Flour and preserved meat came in by sea.

At Genoa a transit depot was established with a small staff to receive goods by sea and pass them to Arquata. Ammunition was at first just dumped on the side of the railway line at Ovada, 15 miles east of Arquata. A proper ammunition depot was built at Rivalto Scrivia with some haste; there it could be guarded against attacks from anarchists who specialised in destroying trains and ammunition dumps.

The depot was laid out with four grocery hangars, each of two blocks with railway lines running on both sides of each. Each block was the length of three railway trucks, the right number for a division. A small carpenter's shop was provided to repair any damaged cases, and two aeroplane hangars were made available for repacking certain items and for storing perishables. All the stock, where its shape permitted, was built into two stacks with a tally board to keep track of the contents. The forage was also laid out in stacks, well separated to avoid fire spreading. These stacks alternated between hay and oats to facilitate loading. The stacks were made on top of wooden dunnage to avoid dampness creeping upwards, and covered with tarpaulins. There were three baling machines to cope with the inevitable loose hay. A full complement of hydrants and hoses, with fire buckets and extinguishers, was also provided.

However, the problem with the depots at Arquata and Rivalto Scrivia was that they were on the wrong side of the country, in the north-west, while British troops were over 250 miles away in the north-east. So a further depot was set up at Padua, with a workshop and gun park. As well as defending that line of communication, the Italian Expeditionary Force had responsibility for the 1,000 miles to Taranto, creating rest camps and halting places, and building temporary depots at Taranto for items going to Alexandria and the Middle East.

There were some problems with petrol supply. This, and the necessary grease, came from Rouen to Genoa by sea, and was then stored in stacks on brick or shingle platforms; carbide and paraffin in solid form had to be covered. A special shed was made for repairing all leaking containers, and a barbed wire fence was erected around the whole and patrolled by guards. Bagged coal was used to build coal stores: the bags were emptied and then used to build 'walls' which were then filled with loose coal that could be bagged as needed. In fact, they used little coal in Italy: only some 8,000 tons were sent from England and, even when they lent some to the Italian railways, it lasted for the whole campaign.

The maximum strength of the ASC in Italy was 275 officers, with 4,180 other ranks for mechanised transport, 2,120 for horse transport, 900 supply personnel and 1,534 vehicles. When operations started in Italy, large amounts of mechanised transport was sent overland from France, but the wear and tear of the long journey rendered these lorries nearly useless. In addition, the Italian roads were not suitable for the heavy lorries from France, so instead Fiat cars and lorries were purchased instead.

Chapter 20

North Russia

British involvement in Russia did not start until September 1918, when the Allied Peace Council in Paris decided that the fight against Bolshevism should continue. Britain sent munitions and other supplies to equip the 'white' Russian army, but much of this was wasted by a combination of corrupt Russian officers and disheartened conscripted peasants.

In August 1818 a military and supply mission was sent to Vladivostok, its personnel consisting of five officers and sixty-eight other ranks. Seventy-nine store ships arrived there in the twelve months from October, carrying 97,000 tons of arms, ammunition, clothing and other stores. Large amounts of Russian equipment and clothing were taken over, and fur clothing and under-clothes were bought on the spot. Everything needed to equip an army of 200,000 men was provided, including rifles, machine guns, artillery, wireless, signal and telegraph equipment, transport wagons with harness and saddlery, plus 346,000 rounds of rifle ammunition, 210,000 sets of clothing, 400,000 sets of Russian underclothing, 300,000 pairs of boots, 435,000 blankets, 725,000 field dressings, 1,000,000 hand grenades, 44,000 sets of harness and saddlery, and 1,200,000 pairs of horseshoes.

On the western side of Russia, in the Baltic, British activity consisted of supplying loyalist Russian troops, with one depot at Revel and another at Riga. These two depots dispersed over 100,000 sets of equipment and clothing, with rifles, machine guns and artillery pieces ranging from 18-pounders to 6in howitzers, with ammunition for all of them.

A more ambitious expeditionary force was sent to North Russia from Newcastle in June 1918. Based at Archangel, on the northern coast, it was expected that the ordnance corps would simply be instructing and training the Russians in the use of the special clothing and equipment, so the Archangel corps consisted of a colonel, three other officers and twenty NCOs. The corps for Murmansk consisted of a lieutenant colonel, one other officer and eleven other ranks. They had no stores at first, but after a while they started giving surplus food to the locals in the interests of good relations, then it was decided that the whole of the local population (some 100,000) should be fed and special food ships were sent in. Their contents included lime juice.

Ice-breaker services were erratic so convoys of 300–400 pony sleighs were used to send provisions and other stores overland to Archangel. The only problem they encountered was with supplies of frozen meat. This was delivered from the cold-storage ships to ice-houses on land, but these failed in April from a combination of structural defects and a rapid thaw in that month. A mobile supply train consisting of bakery wagons and supply stores with mules allowed these essentials to follow the advancing troops.

A farm was established at Lumbuhzi and produced a satisfactory amount of cabbages, potatoes, peas, lettuce, and mustard and cress. There was also an attempt to establish a fishery on the Kem river, but after a particularly poor fishing season this was abandoned.

The conditions of the area made travel and transport of stores very difficult. In summer goods could be sent up river, but in winter the rivers soon became ice-bound and sleighs, the only alternative, were too small to be useful. This expedition was short-lived. Loyalist troops failed to materialise and the 'Reds' increased in number. The Russian officials at the bases in Siberia were described by one British officer as 'incompetent and apathetic, if not actually obstructive; and were apt to look on our stores as a useful means of getting anything they fancied for themselves'. One example of this came from the ordnance store at Kurgan, in the form of an indent for the supply of sundry stores for officers and civil employees. Among the items asked for were 350 cigars, 58lb candy, five dozen ladies' stockings, 30yd of fabric for ladies' dresses, 85 tablets of scented soap, plus 38 bottles of eau-de-Cologne and 29 bottles of scent. When this was discovered, the two signers of this indent were removed from their posts and returned to their regiments; the counter-signing military clerk was removed from his post, and ordered to be conscripted if of military age, otherwise he was to be dismissed the service.

Distribution of winter clothing started in October: blouses, hoods and trousers of a pale Burberry fabric, sheepskin-lined coats, fur caps, mufflers, sweaters, mittens with gauntlet cuffs, moccasins to wear with snow-shoes, thick stockings and socks, snow-goggles and boots with no iron in their construction (iron components transmitted body heat down and out, chilling the wearer). Unfortunately these boots were produced with a smooth leather sole; this made walking on snow difficult and running impossible. Wearers ended up nailing leather or felt strips to the soles.

By November 1919 it was realised that the Bolshevics held such mastery over the country that it was doing more harm than good to continue sending supplies to be looted en route or diverted on arrival. The mission was duly withdrawn.

Another mission was sent to Novorossisk on the Black Sea, intended to provide advice and training on British equipment; it soon found itself running a supply depot. Willing workers for this were almost non-existent; the only enthusiasm was for working with (and stealing) clothing and boots. Guards were posted but were useless; they would not arrest thieves for fear of being murdered. When store ships were unloaded, the goods had to be dumped on the quays to speed ship turnaround times and the local inhabitants looted them wholesale. Such goods as did reach the storehouses were treated in ways that seem incomprehensible. For instance, horseshoes were neatly packed in sets (two front and two hind) with a tin of the right number of nails; when an ordnance officer went to see why there was a delay in issuing them, he found the packing cases had been smashed and the shoes piled up in a heap, then tied in bundles of ten; the nails had been emptied out of their tins and tied in bundles of fifty. Much the same happened with gun components, harness and saddlery.

After a year of this, plus the loss of 4,000 tons of ammunition after an explosion on one quay, the British government realised the futility of the exercise, the mission was disbanded and the staff returned home in June 1920.

Transport

In addition to pony sleighs, other methods of animal transport were tried. Reindeer were not very bright. One officer reported that on coming to a cross-roads, they might understand what was wanted by a jerk of the rein, but otherwise they had to be stopped and forcibly turned into the desired road.

Dog sleighs were used on a small scale, but it took as many as eight dogs to draw one sleigh. They were, however, very useful for dragging light trench mortars or the wounded on stretchers. Canadian dogs (Huskies, Malamutes and Siwash) were brought from Canada with their drivers. They were easy to handle when in harness, but not otherwise. They ate a diet of fresh fish, with cornmeal and seal oil. If the sleighs (the long and narrow 'Shackleton' type) were properly loaded, they could carry up to 800lb.

For the expedition to the Murman coast, the department arranged for the supply of 4,000 pairs of skis, 10,000 pairs of snow shoes and 550 sledges.

Appendix

Weights and Measures

As I find it cumbersome, I have not included conversions from imperial to metric in the text. For those younger readers who are not familiar with the imperial system:

1 mile	= 1.609 kilometres
1 yard	= 0.9144 metres
1 foot	= 0.305 metres
1 inch	= 25.4 millimetres
1 acre	= 2.5 hectares
1 ton*	= 2,240lb or 1,016 kilograms
1lb (avoirdupois)	= 16 ounces (oz) or 454 grams
1 ounce	= 28.34 grams
1 knot	= 1.15mph (used as a measurement of speed, or as maritime people like to say 'a little longer and a lot wetter than a land mile')
1 gallon	= 4.546 litres
1 pint	= 0.5682 litres

*Not to be confused with the metric measure of 1 tonne, which is 1,000 kilograms.

Bibliography

General

The Official History of the Ministry of Munitions, Vol III (Repr. 2009).
Statistics of the Military Effort of the British Empire during the Great War, 1914–1920 (London, 1922).
History of the Great War based on Original Documents (multi-volumed).
A. Forbes, *A History of the Army Ordnance Service, Vol. III: The Great War* (London, 1929).

Chapter 1: Money, Contracts and Control

TNA WO 33, Director of contracts.
TNA RMS/1440, Price of contracts.

Chapter 2: Supply Depots

Lieutenant-Colonel Beadon, *Report on Base Supply Depots and the Working of Supply Distribution on the Line of Communication* (Undated).
W.N. Nicholson, *Behind the Lines: An account of administrative staffwork in the British Army 1914–1918* (London, 1939).
Instructions for Officers Commanding Army Service Corps Units in the field (1917).

Chapter 3: Horses

Janet Macdonald, *Horses in the British Army* (Barnsley, 2017).
Manual of Horse and Stable Management (London, 1904).
Catechism of Animal Management (Undated).
Remount Manual (1906).
Notes on March Discipline, Entraining, Slinging and Care of Animals at Sea (Aldershot, undated).
Patent application no. 17805, for New or Improved apparatus for use in Instructing Persons in the Art of Farriery (1915).

Chapter 4: Animal Transport

Regulations for the use of the Provost Marshal's Branch (Undated).
Janet Macdonald, *Horses in the British Army* (Barnsley, 2017).
Harness in use in the Army Service Corps (Aldershot, 1917).

Chapter 5: Mechanised Transport

G.J. Robbins, J.B. Atkinson, *The London B-type Motor Omnibus* (Hong Kong, 1971).
A.M. Beatson, *The Motor Bus in War: being the impressions of an ASC officer during two and a half years at the front* (London, 1918).
March Discipline and Traffic Control (AP&SS, 1918).
Second Army Traffic Orders (AP&SS, 1917).
System to ensure proper gaps being maintained … in MT columns.
Extracts from circular memoranda issued to officers commanding Army Service Corps transport units in the field (HMSO, 1915).

FO Precautions to be taken for the prevention of damage by frost to mechanical transport vehicles (AP&SS, undated).
Regulations for the use of the Provost Marshal's Branch (Undated).
FO Drivers' orders. Army Service Corps mechanical transport units in the field (Undated).
Notes on supply and transport (HMSO, 1915).
[Instructions on] The Impressment of vehicles (Undated).
First Base Mechanical Transport Depot (Southern) Stores Branch. Procedures.
M.T. Vehicles – marking of.
Vehicles in use with the Army Service Corps 1914–1918.
Instructions for Officers Commanding Army Service Corps Units in the field (1917).

Chapter 6: Railways, Inland Water Transport and Docks

Mark Whitmore, *Transport and Supply during the First World War.*
J.A.B. Hamilton, *Britain's Railways in WW1* (London, 1967).
Bob Butcher, 'Other Administrative Services on the Western Front', in *Stand To!* (Western Front Association, no. 101).
Ian Malcolm Brown, *British Logistics on the Western Front 1914–1919* (1998).
Ken Gibbs, *The Carriage and Wagon Works of the Great Western Railway at Swindon* (Stroud, 2016).

Chapter 7: Munitions

R.J.Q. Adams, *Arms and the Wizard: Lloyd George and the Ministry of Munitions 1915–1916* (London, 1978).
History of the Ministry of Munitions, Vols XI, XII (Reprinted 2009).
Ian Malcolm Brown, *British Logistics on the Western Front 1914–1919* (1998).
Paul Strong and Sanders Marbles, *Artillery in the Great War* (Barnsley, 2011).
British Artillery and Weapons 1914–1918 (London, 1972).
Anthony Saunders, *Weapons of the Trench War.*

Chapter 8: Engineering

Edward Wells, *Mailshot* (1982).
The Work of the Royal Engineers in the European War, 1914–19, several volumes (Chatham, 1921).
TNA ROD, Railway operating division of the Royal Engineers.

Chapter 9: Food and Drink

Rachel Duffett, *The Stomach for Fighting: Food and the soldiers of the great war* (Manchester, 2015).
History of the RASC.
Janet Macdonald, *From Boiled Beef to Chicken Tikka: 500 years of feeding the British Army* (Barnsley, 2014).
Bob Butcher, 'Supplies on the Western Front', in *Stand To!* (Western Front Association, no. 99).

Chapter 10: Uniforms and Other Supplies

W.N. Nicholson, *Behind the Lines: An account of administrative staffwork in the British Army 1914–1918* (London, 1939).
Jane Tynan, *Men in Khaki* (London, 2004).
Instructions for Officers Commanding Army Service Corps Units in the field (1917).
TNA WO 32/5521, strike by bootmakers.

Chapter 11: Medicine

W.G. Macpherson, *The Medical Services on the Western Front*, 3 vols (London, 1922–1924).
T.J. Mitchell, *Casualties and Medical Statistics of the Great War* (London, 1931).

J.E. Edmonds, *Military Operations France and Belgium*, numerous volumes (London, 1932).
TNA MH106, Hospital admissions.

Chapter 12: Other Supply Activities

W.N. Nicholson, *Behind the Lines: An account of administrative staffwork in the British Army 1914–1918* (London, 1939).
Bob Butcher, 'Other Administrative Services on the Western Front', in *Stand To!* (Western Front Association, no. 101).
TNA DSIR 26/366, Cardboard instead of tin packaging, dept scientific & industrial research.
TNA NWM 7/535, Price of jute goods.

Chapter 13: Gallipoli

Peter Hart, *Gallipoli* (Oxford, 2013).
Alan Moorehead, *Gallipoli* (London, 2015).
L.A. Carlyon, *Gallipoli* (London, 2003).

Chapter 14: Salonika

D. Jordan, *The Balkans, Italy and Africa* (London, 2012).

Chapter 15: Egypt

'RAMC Sergeant-Major', *With the RAMC in Egypt* (1917).
TNA WO 158/608, Water supply Egypt & Palestine.

Chapter 16: Palestine

Christian Wolmer, *Engines of War* (London, 2010).
Edmund Carver, *The Long Road to Baghdad* (London, 1919).
Report of the Commission appointed by Act of Parliament to enquire into the Operation of War in Mesopotamia (London, 1917).

Chapter 17: Mesopotamia

Edward Paice, *Tip and Run: The Great War in Africa* (London, 2007).

Chapter 18: East Africa

D. Jordan, *The Balkans, Italy and Africa* (London, 2012).

Chapter 19: Italy

? ? ?

Chapter 20: North Russia

? ? ?

Index